DIVINE
TRANSFORMATION

Other Books in the Soul Power Series

Tao I
Divine Soul Mind Body Healing and Transmission System
Divine Soul Songs
The Power of Soul
Soul Communication
Soul Wisdom

DIVINE TRANSFORMATION

The Divine Way to Self-clear Karma to Transform Your Health, Relationships, Finances, and More

Dr. and Master Zhi Gang Sha

ATRIA BOOKS

New York   London   Toronto   Sydney

Heaven's Library

Toronto

A Division of Simon & Schuster, Inc.   Toronto, ON
1230 Avenue of the Americas
New York, NY 10020

The information contained in this book is intended to be educational and not for diagnosis, prescription, or treatment of any health disorder whatsoever. This information should not replace consultation with a competent health-care professional. The content of the book is intended to be used as an adjunct to a rational and responsible health-care program prescribed by a health-care practitioner. The author and publisher are in no way liable for any misuse of the material.

First Atria Books hardcover edition September 2010

ATRIA BOOKS and colophon are trademarks of Simon & Schuster, Inc.

Heaven's Library is a trademark of Heaven's Library Publication Corp.

For information about special discounts for bulk purchases,
please contact Simon & Schuster Special Sales at 1-866-506-1949
or business@simonandschuster.com.

The Simon & Schuster Speakers Bureau can bring authors to your live event.
For more information or to book an event, contact the Simon & Schuster Speakers Bureau at 1-866-248-3049 or visit our website at www.simonspeakers.com.

Manufactured in the United States of America

10   9   8   7   6   5   4   3   2   1

Library of Congress Cataloging-in-Publication Data

Sha, Zhi Gang.
    Divine transformation : the divine way to self-clear karma to transform your health, relationships, finances, and more / Zhi Gang Sha.
        p.   cm.
    Includes index.
1. Self-help techniques.   2. Karma.   I. Title.
    BF632.S486 2010
    204'.4—dc22   2010026143

ISBN 978-1-4391-9968-8
ISBN 978-1-4391-9864-3 (ebook)

Contents

Soul Power Series   ix

How to Receive the Divine Soul Downloads Offered
    in the Books of the Soul Power Series   xxv

    • What to Expect After You Receive
    Divine Soul Downloads   xxvii

Foreword to the Soul Power Series by
    Dr. Michael Bernard Beckwith   xxix

How to Read This Book   xxxi

List of Divine Soul Downloads   xxxv

Introduction   xxxix

1   Important Wisdom of Divine Transformation   *1*

    • What Is Divine Transformation?   2

    • The Significance and Power of Divine Transformation   6

    • The Key to Divine Transformation Is Clearing
    Your Bad Karma   7

    • Apply Divine Treasures to Self-clear Your Bad Karma   14

    • Divine Karma Cleansing   21

2 Divine Transformation for Your Health   *23*

• Self-heal Your Physical Body, Including Self-clearing
  Your Karma (Soul Blockages), Mind Blockages,
  and Body Blockages   29
  o Pain   30
  o Inflammation and Infection   46
  o Growths, Including Cysts, Tumors, and Cancer   52

• Self-heal Your Emotional Body, Including Self-clearing
  Your Karma (Soul Blockages), Mind Blockages,
  and Body Blockages   68

• Self-heal Your Mental Body, Including Self-clearing
  Your Karma (Soul Blockages), Mind Blockages,
  and Body Blockages   79

• Self-heal Your Spiritual Body, Including
  Self-clearing Your Karma (Soul Blockages),
  Mind Blockages, and Body Blockages   88

• Golden Light   96

• Self-prevent Sickness in Your Spiritual, Mental,
  Emotional, and Physical Bodies   101

*3 Divine Transformation for Your Relationships
    and Beyond*   *111*

• Self-clear Your Karma (Soul Blockages),
  Mind Blockages, and Body Blockages
  for Relationships   118

• Self-balance Your Relationships with Life Partners   122

• Self-balance Your Relationships with
  Family Members   128

• Self-balance Your Relationships with Colleagues   131

- Balance the Relationships of Humanity   134
- Balance the Relationships of All Nations   137
- Balance the Relationships of All Planets
  (Including Mother Earth), All Stars,
  All Galaxies, and All Universes   140

4 *Divine Transformation for Your Finances
   and Business*   **147**
- Why Some People Have Wealth   150
- Financial Abundance Can Be Lost   151
- Types of Bad Karma   153
- Why Some People Have Financial Challenges   156
- Create Good Karma to Transform Your Finances   161
- Self-clear Your Karma (Soul Blockages),
  Mind Blockages, and Body Blockages
  for Finances and Business   171
- The Importance of the Name of a Business   177
- Follow the Tao of Business   178
- Soul Marketing and Its Significance   179
- Offer Unconditional Service to Receive Divine
  Blessings for Success in Finances and Business   185

5 *Divine Transformation for Your Spiritual Journey*   **187**
- Divine Service Law   188
- Shi Jia Mo Ni Fo's Enlightenment Story   188
- Divine Oneness   191
- Service Xiu Lian   194
- Ten Powers for Soul Enlightenment   221

6 *Divine Transformation to Help Humanity
   During Mother Earth's Transition*   225

   • Mother Earth's Transition—What and Why   225
   • Help Humanity and Mother Earth Pass
     Through This Difficult Time   227
        o Divine Soul Song *Love, Peace and Harmony*   228
        o Divine Soul Song *God Gives His Heart to Me* 230
        o Divine Chant *Tian Di Ren He Yi,
           Wan Ling Rong He*   232

   • Create Love, Peace, and Harmony for Humanity,
     Mother Earth, and All Universes   235

Conclusion   239
Acknowledgments   243
A Special Gift   247
Index   249
Other Books of the Soul Power Series   265

Soul Power Series

$\mathcal{T}$HE PURPOSE OF life is to serve. I have committed my life to this purpose. Service is my life mission.

My total life mission is to transform the consciousness of humanity and all souls in all universes, and enlighten them, in order to create love, peace, and harmony for humanity, Mother Earth, and all universes. This mission includes three empowerments.

My first empowerment is to teach *universal service* to empower people to be unconditional universal servants. The message of universal service is:

> *I serve humanity and all universes unconditionally.*
> *You serve humanity and all universes unconditionally.*
> *Together we serve humanity and all souls in all universes unconditionally.*

My second empowerment is to teach *healing* to empower people to heal themselves and heal others. The message of healing is:

I have the power to heal myself.
You have the power to heal yourself.
Together we have the power to heal the world.

My third empowerment is to teach *the power of soul*, which includes soul secrets, wisdom, knowledge, and practical soul techniques, and to transmit Divine Soul Power to empower people to transform every aspect of their lives and enlighten their souls, hearts, minds, and bodies.

The message of Soul Power is:

I have the Soul Power to transform my consciousness
  and every aspect of my life and enlighten my soul,
  heart, mind, and body.
You have the Soul Power to transform your conscious-
  ness and every aspect of your life and enlighten your
  soul, heart, mind, and body.
Together we have the Soul Power to transform con-
  sciousness and every aspect of all life and enlighten
  humanity and all souls.

To teach the power of soul is my most important empowerment. It is the key for my total life mission. The power of soul is the key for transforming physical life and spiritual life. It is the key for transforming and enlightening humanity and every soul in all universes.

The beginning of the twenty-first century is the transition period into a new era for humanity, Mother Earth, and all universes. This era is named the Soul Light Era. The Soul Light Era began on August 8, 2003. It will last fifteen thousand years. Natural disasters—including tsunamis, hurricanes, cyclones, earthquakes, floods, tornados, hail, blizzards, fires, drought, extreme temperatures, famine, and disease—political, religious, and ethnic wars, terrorism, proliferation of nuclear weapons, economic challenges, pollution, vanishing plant and animal species, and other such upheavals are part of this transition. In addition, millions of people are suffering from depression, anxiety, fear, anger, and worry. They suffer from pain, chronic conditions, and life-threatening illnesses. Humanity needs help. The consciousness of humanity needs to be transformed. The suffering of humanity needs to be removed.

The books of the Soul Power Series are brought to you by Atria Books and Heaven's Library. They reveal soul secrets and teach soul wisdom, soul knowledge, and practical soul techniques for your daily life. The power of soul can heal, prevent illness, rejuvenate, prolong life, and transform consciousness and every aspect of life, including relationships and finances. The power of soul is vital to serving humanity and Mother Earth during this transition period. The power of soul will awaken and transform the consciousness of humanity and all souls.

In the twentieth century and for centuries before, *mind over matter* played a vital role in healing, rejuvenation, and life transformation. In the Soul Light Era, *soul over matter*—Soul Power—will play *the* vital role to heal, rejuvenate, and transform all life.

There are countless souls on Mother Earth—souls of human beings, souls of animals, souls of other living things, and souls of inanimate things. *Everyone and everything has a soul.*

Every soul has its own frequency and power. Jesus had miraculous healing power. We have heard many heart-touching stories of lives saved by Guan Yin's[1] compassion. Mother Mary's love has created many heart-moving stories. All of these great souls were given Divine Soul Power to serve humanity. In all of the world's great religions and spiritual traditions, including Buddhism, Taoism, Christianity, Judaism, Hinduism, Islam, and more, there are similar accounts of great spiritual healing and blessing power.

I honor every religion and every spiritual tradition. However, I am not teaching religion. I am teaching Soul Power, which includes soul secrets, soul wisdom, soul knowledge, and practical soul techniques. Your soul has the power to heal, rejuvenate, and transform life. An animal's soul has the power to heal, rejuvenate, and transform life. The souls of the sun, the moon, an ocean, a tree, and a mountain have the power to heal, rejuvenate, and transform life. The souls of healing angels, ascended masters, holy saints, Taoist saints, Hindu saints, buddhas, and other high-level spiritual beings have great Soul Power to heal, rejuvenate, and transform life.

Every soul has its own standing. Spiritual standing, or soul standing, has countless layers. Soul Power also has layers. Not every soul can perform miracles like Jesus, Guan Yin, and Mother Mary. Soul Power depends on the soul's spiritual standing in Heaven. The higher a soul stands in Heaven, the more Soul Power that soul is given by the Divine. Jesus, Guan Yin, and Mother Mary all have a very high spiritual standing.

Who determines a soul's spiritual standing? Who gives the appropriate Soul Power to a soul? Who decides the direction for humanity, Mother Earth, and all universes? The top leader of the spiritual world is the decision maker. This top leader is

---

1. Guan Yin is known as the Bodhisattva of Compassion and, in the West, as the Goddess of Mercy.

the Divine. The Divine is the creator and manifestor of all universes.

In the Soul Light Era, all souls will join as one and align their consciousness with divine consciousness. At this historic time, the Divine has decided to transmit divine soul treasures to humanity and all souls to help humanity and all souls pass through Mother Earth's transition. Let me share two personal stories with you to explain how I reached this understanding.

First, in April 2003, I held a Power Healing workshop for about one hundred people at Land of Medicine Buddha, a retreat center in Soquel, California. As I was teaching, the Divine appeared. I told the students, "The Divine is here. Could you give me a moment?" I knelt and bowed down to the floor to honor the Divine. (At age six, I was taught to bow down to my tai chi masters. At age ten, I bowed down to my qi gong masters. At age twelve, I bowed down to my kung fu masters. Being Chinese, I learned this courtesy throughout my childhood.) I explained to the students, "Please understand that this is the way I honor the Divine, my spiritual fathers, and my spiritual mothers. Now I will have a conversation with the Divine."

I began by saying silently, "Dear Divine, I am very honored you are here."

The Divine, who was in front of me above my head, replied, "Zhi Gang, I come today to pass a spiritual law to you."

I said, "I am honored to receive this spiritual law."

The Divine continued, "This spiritual law is named the Universal Law of Universal Service. It is one of the highest spiritual laws in the universe. It applies to the spiritual world and the physical world."

The Divine pointed to the Divine. "I am a universal servant." The Divine pointed to me. "You are a universal servant." The

Divine swept a hand in front of the Divine. "Everyone and everything is a universal servant. A universal servant offers universal service unconditionally. Universal service includes universal love, forgiveness, peace, healing, blessing, harmony, and enlightenment. *If one offers a little service, one receives a little blessing from the universe and from me. If one offers more service, one receives more blessing. If one offers unconditional service, one receives unlimited blessing.*"

The Divine paused for a moment before continuing. "There is another kind of service, which is unpleasant service. Unpleasant service includes killing, harming, taking advantage of others, cheating, stealing, complaining, and more. *If one offers a little unpleasant service, one learns little lessons from the universe and from me. If one offers more unpleasant service, one learns more lessons. If one offers huge unpleasant service, one learns huge lessons.*"

I asked, "What kinds of lessons could one learn?"

The Divine replied, "The lessons include sickness, accidents, injuries, financial challenges, broken relationships, emotional imbalances, mental confusion, and any kind of disorder in one's life." The Divine emphasized, "This is how the universe operates. This is one of my most important spiritual laws for all souls in the universe to follow."

After the Divine delivered this universal law, I immediately made a silent vow to the Divine:

Dear Divine,

I am extremely honored to receive your Law of Universal Service. I make a vow to you, to all humanity, and to all souls in all universes that I will be an unconditional universal servant. I will give my total GOLD [gratitude, obedience, loyalty, devotion] *to you and to serving you. I am honored to be your servant and a servant of all humanity and all souls.*

Hearing this, the Divine smiled and left.

My second story happened three months later, in July 2003, while I was holding a Soul Study workshop near Toronto. The Divine came again. I again explained to my students that the Divine had appeared, and asked them to wait a moment while I bowed down 108 times and listened to the Divine's message. On this occasion, the Divine told me, "Zhi Gang, I come today to choose you as my direct servant, vehicle, and channel."

I was deeply moved and said to the Divine, "I am honored. What does it mean to be your direct servant, vehicle, and channel?"

The Divine replied, "When you offer healing and blessing to others, call me. I will come instantly to offer my healing and blessing to them."

I was deeply touched and replied, "Thank you so much for choosing me as your direct servant."

The Divine continued, "I can offer my healing and blessing by transmitting my permanent healing and blessing treasures."

I asked, "How do you do this?"

The Divine answered, "Select a person and I will give you a demonstration."

I asked for a volunteer with serious health challenges. A man named Walter raised his hand. He stood up and explained that he had liver cancer, with a two-by-three-centimeter malignant tumor that had just been diagnosed from a biopsy.

Then I asked the Divine, "Please bless Walter. Please show me how you transmit your permanent treasures." Immediately, I saw the Divine send a beam of light from the Divine's heart to Walter's liver. The beam shot into his liver, where it turned into a golden light ball that instantly started spinning. Walter's entire liver shone with beautiful golden light.

The Divine asked me, "Do you understand what software is?"

I was surprised by this question but replied, "I do not understand much about computers. I just know that software is a computer program. I have heard about accounting software, office software, and graphic design software."

"Yes," the Divine said. "Software is a program. Because you asked me to, I transmitted, or downloaded, my Soul Software for Liver to Walter. It is one of my permanent healing and blessing treasures. You asked me. I did the job. This is what it means for you to be my chosen direct servant and channel."

I was astonished. Excited, inspired, and humbled, I said to the Divine, "I am so honored to be your direct servant. How blessed I am to be chosen." Almost speechless, I asked the Divine, "Why did you choose me?"

"I chose you," said the Divine, "because you have served humanity for more than one thousand lifetimes. You have been very committed to serving my mission through all of your lifetimes. I am choosing you in this life to be my direct servant. You will transmit countless permanent healing and blessing treasures from me to humanity and all souls. This is the honor I give to you now."

I was moved to tears. I immediately bowed down 108 times again and made a silent vow:

Dear Divine,

I cannot bow down to you enough for the honor you have given to me. No words can express my greatest gratitude. How blessed I am to be your direct servant to download your permanent healing and blessing treasures to humanity and all souls! Humanity and all souls will receive your huge blessings through my service as your direct servant. I give my total life to you and to humanity. I will accomplish your tasks. I will be a pure servant to humanity and all souls.

I bowed again. Then I asked the Divine, "How should Walter use his Soul Software?"

"Walter must spend time to practice with my Soul Software," said the Divine. "Tell him that simply to receive my Soul Software does not mean he will recover. He must practice with this treasure every day to restore his health, step by step."

I asked, "How should he practice?"

The Divine gave me this guidance: "Tell Walter to chant repeatedly: *Divine Liver Soul Software heals me. Divine Liver Soul Software heals me. Divine Liver Soul Software heals me. Divine Liver Soul Software heals me.*"

I asked, "For how long should Walter chant?"

The Divine answered, "At least two hours a day. The longer

he practices, the better. If Walter does this, he could recover in three to six months."

I shared this information with Walter, who was excited and deeply moved. Walter said, "I will practice two hours or more each day."

Finally I asked the Divine, "How does the Soul Software work?"

The Divine replied, "My Soul Software is a golden healing ball that rotates and clears energy and spiritual blockages in Walter's liver."

I again bowed to the Divine 108 times. Then I stood up and offered three Soul Softwares to every participant in the workshop as divine gifts. Upon seeing this, the Divine smiled and left.

Walter immediately began to practice as directed for at least two hours every day. Two and a half months later, a CT scan and MRI showed that his liver cancer had completely disappeared. At the end of 2006 I met Walter again at a signing in Toronto for my book *Soul Mind Body Medicine*.[2] In May 2008 Walter attended one of my events at the Unity Church of Truth in Toronto. On both occasions Walter told me that there was still no sign of cancer in his liver. For nearly five years his Divine Soul Download healed his liver cancer. He was very grateful to the Divine.

This major event of being chosen as a direct divine servant happened in July 2003. As I mentioned, a new era for Mother Earth and all universes, the Soul Light Era, began on August 8, 2003. The timing may look like a coincidence but I believe there could be an underlying spiritual reason. Since July 2003 I have offered divine transmissions to humanity almost every day. I

---

2. *Soul Mind Body Medicine: A Complete Soul Healing System for Optimum Health and Vitality* (Novato, California: New World Library, 2006).

have offered more than ten divine transmissions to all souls in all universes.

I share this story with you to introduce the power of divine transmissions or Divine Soul Downloads. Now let me share the commitment that I made in *Soul Wisdom*,[3] the first book of my Soul Power Series, and that I have renewed in every one of my books since:

From now on, I will offer Divine Soul Downloads in every book I write.

Divine Soul Downloads are permanent divine healing and blessing treasures for transforming your life. There is an ancient saying: *If you want to know if a pear is sweet, taste it.* If you want to know the power of Divine Soul Downloads, experience it.

Divine Soul Downloads carry divine frequency with divine love, forgiveness, compassion, and light. Divine frequency transforms the frequency of all life. Divine love melts all blockages, including soul, mind, and body blockages, and transforms all life. Divine forgiveness brings inner peace and inner joy. Divine compassion boosts energy, stamina, vitality, and immunity. Divine light heals, prevents sickness, rejuvenates, and prolongs life.

A Divine Soul Download is a new soul created from the heart of the Divine. The Divine Soul Download transmitted to Walter was a Soul Software. Since then, I have transmitted several other types of Divine Soul Downloads, including Divine Soul Herbs, Divine Soul Acupuncture, Divine Soul Operation, Divine Soul Massage, and Divine Soul Mind Body Transplants.

---

3. *Soul Wisdom: Practical Soul Treasures to Transform Your Life* (New York/Toronto: Atria Books/Heaven's Library, 2008).

A Divine Soul Transplant is a new divine soul of an organ, a part of the body, a bodily system, cells, DNA, RNA, the tiny matter in cells, or the spaces between cells. When it is transmitted, it replaces the recipient's original soul of the organ, part of the body, system, cells, cell units, DNA, RNA, tiny matter in cells, or spaces between cells. A new divine soul can also replace the soul of a home or a business. A new divine soul can be transmitted to a pet, a mountain, a city, or a country to replace their original souls. A new divine soul can even replace the soul of Mother Earth.

A Divine Mind Transplant is also a light being created by the Divine. It carries divine consciousness to replace the original consciousness of the recipient's system, organ, part of the body, cells, cell units, DNA, RNA, tiny matter, or spaces.

A Divine Body Transplant is another light being created by the Divine. This light being carries divine energy and divine tiny matter to replace the original energy and tiny matter of the recipient's system, organ, part of the body, cells, cell units, DNA, RNA, tiny matter, or spaces.

Everyone and everything has a soul. The Divine can download any soul you can conceive of. These Divine Soul Downloads are permanent divine healing, blessing, and life-transformation treasures. They can transform the lives of anyone and anything. Because the Divine created these divine soul treasures, they carry Divine Soul Power, which is the greatest Soul Power among all souls. All souls in the highest layers of Heaven will support and assist Divine Soul Downloads. Divine Soul Downloads are the crown jewel of Soul Power.

Divine Soul Downloads are divine presence. The more Divine Soul Downloads you receive, the faster your soul, heart, mind, and body will be transformed. The more Divine Soul Downloads your home or business receives and the more Divine

Soul Downloads a city or country receives, the faster their souls, hearts, minds, and bodies will be transformed.

In the Soul Light Era, the evolution of humanity will be created by Divine Soul Power. Soul Power will transform humanity. Soul Power will transform animals. Soul Power will transform nature and the environment. Soul Power will assume the leading role in every field of human endeavor. Humanity will deeply understand that *the soul is the boss.*

Soul Power, including soul secrets, soul wisdom, soul knowledge, and practical soul techniques, will transform every aspect of human life. Soul Power will transform every aspect of organizations and societies. Soul Power will transform cities, countries, Mother Earth, all planets, stars, galaxies, and all universes. Divine Soul Power, including Divine Soul Downloads, will lead this transformation.

I am honored to have been chosen as a divine servant to offer Divine Soul Downloads to humanity, to relationships, to homes, to businesses, to pets, to cities, to countries, and more. In the last few years I have already transmitted countless divine souls to humanity and to all universes. I repeat to you now: *I will offer Divine Soul Downloads within each and every book of the Soul Power Series.* Clear instructions on how to receive these Divine Soul Downloads will be provided in the next section, "How to Receive the Divine Soul Downloads Offered in the Books of the Soul Power Series," as well as on the appropriate pages of each book.

I am a servant of humanity. I am a servant of the universe. I am a servant of the Divine. I am extremely honored to be a servant of all souls. I commit my total life and being as an unconditional universal servant.

I will continue to offer Divine Soul Downloads for my entire life. I will offer more and more Divine Soul Downloads to every soul. I will offer Divine Soul Downloads for every aspect of life for every soul.

I am honored to be a servant of Divine Soul Downloads.

Human beings, organizations, cities, and countries will receive more and more Divine Soul Downloads, which can transform every aspect of their lives and enlighten their souls, hearts, minds, and bodies. The Soul Light Era will shine Soul Power. The books in the Soul Power Series will spread Divine Soul Downloads, together with Soul Power—soul secrets, soul wisdom, soul knowledge, and practical soul techniques—to serve humanity, Mother Earth, and all universes. The Soul Power Series is a pure servant for humanity and all souls. The Soul Power Series is honored to be a Total GOLD[4] servant of the Divine, humanity, and all souls.

The final goal of the Soul Light Era is to join every soul as one in love, peace, and harmony. This means that the consciousness of every soul will be totally aligned with divine consciousness. There will be difficulties and challenges on the path to this final goal. Together we will overcome them. We call all souls of humanity and all souls in all universes to offer unconditional universal service, including universal love, forgiveness, peace, healing, blessing, harmony, and enlightenment. The more we offer unconditional universal service, the faster we will achieve this goal.

The Divine gives his heart to us. The Divine gives his love to us. The Divine gives Divine Soul Downloads to us. Our hearts meld with the Divine's heart. Our souls meld with the Divine's

---

4. Total GOLD means total gratitude, total obedience, total loyalty, and total devotion to the Divine.

soul. Our consciousnesses align with the Divine's consciousness. We will join hearts and souls together to create love, peace, and harmony for humanity, Mother Earth, and all universes.

> *I love my heart and soul*
> *I love all humanity*
> *Join hearts and souls together*
> *Love, peace and harmony*
> *Love, peace and harmony*

Love all humanity. Love all souls. Thank all humanity. Thank all souls.

Thank you. Thank you. Thank you.

Zhi Gang Sha

How to Receive the Divine Soul Downloads Offered in the Books of the Soul Power Series

*T*HE BOOKS OF the Soul Power Series are unique. For the first time in history, the Divine is downloading the Divine's soul treasures to readers as they read these books. Every book in the Soul Power Series will include Divine Soul Downloads that have been preprogrammed. When you read the appropriate paragraphs and pause for a minute, divine gifts will be transmitted to your soul.

In April 2005 the Divine told me to "leave Divine Soul Downloads to history." I thought, "A human being's life is limited. Even if I live a long, long life, I will go back to Heaven one day. How can I leave Divine Soul Downloads to history?"

In the beginning of 2008, as I was editing the paperback edition of *Soul Wisdom*, the Divine suddenly told me: "Zhi Gang, offer my downloads within this book." The Divine said, "I will preprogram my downloads in the book. Any reader can receive them as he or she reads the special pages." At the moment the

Divine gave me this direction, I understood how I could leave Divine Soul Downloads to history.

Preprogrammed Divine Soul Downloads are permanently stored within this book and every book in the Soul Power Series. If people read this book thousands of years from now, they will still receive the Divine Soul Downloads. As long as this book exists and is read, readers will receive the Divine Soul Downloads.

Allow me to explain further. The Divine has placed a permanent blessing within certain paragraphs in these books. These blessings allow you to receive Divine Soul Downloads as permanent gifts to your soul. Because these divine treasures reside with your soul, you can access them twenty-four hours a day—as often as you like, wherever you are—for healing, blessing, and life transformation.

It is very easy to receive the Divine Soul Downloads in these books. After you read the special paragraphs where they are preprogrammed, close your eyes. Receive the special download. It is also easy to apply these divine treasures. After you receive a Divine Soul Download, I will immediately show you how to apply it for healing, blessing, and life transformation.

You have free will. If you are not ready to receive a Divine Soul Download, simply say *I am not ready to receive this gift.* You can then continue to read the special download paragraphs, but you will not receive the gifts they contain. The Divine does not offer Divine Soul Downloads to those who are not ready or not willing to receive the Divine's treasures. However, the moment you are ready, you can simply go back to the relevant paragraphs and tell the Divine *I am ready.* You will then receive the stored special download when you reread the paragraphs.

The Divine has agreed to offer specific Divine Soul Downloads in these books to all readers who are willing to receive them.

The Divine has unlimited treasures. However, you can receive only the ones designated in these pages. Please do not ask for different or additional gifts. It will not work.

After receiving and practicing with the Divine Soul Downloads in these books, you could experience remarkable healing results in your spiritual, mental, emotional, and physical bodies. You could receive incredible blessings for your love relationships and other relationships. You could receive financial blessings and all kinds of other blessings.

Divine Soul Downloads are unlimited. There can be a Divine Soul Download for anything that exists in the physical world. The reason for this is very simple. *Everything has a soul.* A house has a soul. The Divine can download a soul to your house that can transform its energy. The Divine can download a soul to your business that can transform your business. If you are wearing a ring, that ring has a soul. If the Divine downloads a new divine soul to your ring, you can ask the divine soul in your ring to offer divine healing and blessing.

I am honored to have been chosen as a servant of humanity and the Divine to offer Divine Soul Downloads. For the rest of my life, I will continue to offer Divine Soul Downloads. I will offer more and more of them. I will offer Divine Soul Downloads for every aspect of every life.

I am honored to be a servant of Divine Soul Downloads.

What to Expect After You Receive Divine Soul Downloads

Divine Soul Downloads are new souls created from the heart of the Divine. When these souls are transmitted, you may feel a strong vibration. For example, you could feel warm or excited. Your body could shake a little. If you are not sensitive, you may not feel anything. Advanced spiritual beings with an open Third Eye can actually see a huge golden, rainbow, purple, or crystal light soul enter your body.

These divine souls are your yin companions[1] for life. They will stay with your soul forever. Even after your physical life ends, these divine treasures will continue to accompany your soul into your next life and all of your future lives. In these books, I will teach you how to invoke these divine souls anytime, anywhere to give you divine healing or blessing in this life. You also can invoke these souls to radiate out to offer divine healing or blessing to others. These divine souls have extraordinary abilities to heal, bless, and transform. If you develop advanced spiritual abilities in your next life, you will discover that you have these divine souls with you. Then you will be able to invoke these divine souls in the same way in your future lifetimes to heal, bless, and transform every aspect of your life.

It is a great honor to have a divine soul downloaded to your own soul. The divine soul is a pure soul without bad karma. The divine soul carries divine healing and blessing abilities. The download does not have any side effects. You are given love and light with divine frequency. You are given divine abilities to serve yourself and others. Therefore, humanity is extremely honored that the Divine is offering his downloads. I am extremely honored to be a servant of the Divine, of you, of all humanity, and of all souls to offer Divine Soul Downloads. I cannot thank the Divine enough. I cannot thank you, all humanity, and all souls enough for the opportunity to serve.

Thank you. Thank you. Thank you.

---

1. A yang companion is a physical being, such as a family member, friend, or pet. A yin companion is a soul companion without a physical form, such as your spiritual fathers and mothers in Heaven.

Foreword to the Soul Power Series

I HAVE ADMIRED DR. Zhi Gang Sha's work for some years now. In fact, I clearly remember the first time I heard him describe his soul healing system, Soul Mind Body Medicine. I knew immediately that I wanted to support this gifted healer and his mission, so I introduced him to my spiritual community at Agape. Ever since, it has been my joy to witness how those who apply his teachings and techniques experience increased energy, joy, harmony, and peace in their lives.

Dr. Sha's techniques awaken the healing power already present in all of us, empowering us to put our overall well-being in our own hands. His explanation of energy and message, and how they link consciousness, mind, body, and spirit, forms a dynamic information network in language that is easy to understand and, more important, easy to apply.

Dr. Sha's time-tested results have proven to thousands of students and readers that healing energies and messages exist within specific sounds, movements, and affirmative perceptions. Weaving in his own personal experiences, Dr. Sha's theories and practices of working directly with the life-force energy and spirit are practical, holistic, and profound. His recognition that Soul Power is most important for every aspect of life is vital to meeting the challenges of twenty-first-century living.

The worldwide representative of his renowned teacher, Dr. Zhi Chen Guo, one of the greatest qi gong masters and healers in the world, Dr. Sha is himself a master of ancient disciplines such as tai chi, qi gong, kung fu, the *I Ching*, and feng shui. He has blended the soul of his culture's natural healing methods with his training as a Western physician, and generously offers his wisdom to us through the books in his Soul Power Series. His contribution to those in the healing professions is undeniable, and the way in which he empowers his readers to understand themselves, their feelings, and the connection between their bodies, minds, and spirits is his gift to the world.

Through his Soul Power Series, Dr. Sha guides the reader into a consciousness of healing not only of body, mind, and spirit, but also of the heart. I consider his healing path to be a universal spiritual practice, a journey into genuine transformation. His professional integrity and compassionate heart are at the root of his being a servant of humankind, and my heartfelt wish for his readers is that they accept his invitation to awaken the power of the soul and realize the natural beauty of their existence.

Dr. Michael Bernard Beckwith
Founder, Agape International Spiritual Center

How to Read This Book

*I*N EVERY BOOK of my Soul Power Series, I reveal soul secrets and teach soul wisdom, soul knowledge, and practical soul techniques. Secret and sacred wisdom and knowledge are important. *Practice is even more important.* Since ancient times, serious Buddhist, Taoist, qi gong, and kung fu practitioners have spent hours and hours a day in practice. Their dedication empowers them to develop and transform their frequency, their consciousness, and their purification further and further. In the modern world, successful professionals in every field similarly spend hours a day for months and years in practice. Their commitment empowers them to develop and transform their power and abilities further and further.

Every book in my Soul Power Series offers new approaches to healing, rejuvenation, and life transformation. Along with the teachings of sacred wisdom and knowledge, I also offer Divine Soul Downloads as a servant, vehicle, and channel of the Divine. I am honored to serve you through these books. However, *the most important service offered in these books is the practices.* In this book I lead you in many practices. If you spend four or five minutes to do each practice, I fully understand that it will take you some time to finish all of them. Do a few practices today. Tomorrow do another few practices. Do a few more the day after tomorrow. The practices are vital. The practices in this book will help you to clear your bad karma. If you do not do them, how can you experience their power and benefits? If you do not experience their power and benefits, how can you fully understand and absorb the teaching?

This book, *Divine Transformation: The Divine Way to Self-clear Karma to Transform Your Health, Relationships, Finances, and More*, reveals even simpler, even more powerful, and even more profound soul secrets, wisdom, knowledge, and *practical techniques* than my previous books. The practices give you and every reader even more effective ways to heal, prevent sickness, rejuvenate, prolong life, and transform every aspect of life, including relationships and finances, to enlighten soul, heart, mind, and body, and, especially, to clear your bad karma. If you do not do the practices, this book will be only a theoretical exercise for you. You may find it interesting, even fascinating, but you will not receive the tremendous potential benefits for every aspect of your life.

The CD enclosed with this book offers you three Divine Soul Songs and one divine chant to lead and guide you in some of the basic practices. For those of you who seriously need or desire healing and transformation, and for the serious spiritual student and practitioner, *the audio version of this book* (available in a boxed set of CDs) *is an essential companion to this print version* that you have in your hands. In the audio version of this book, I lead you and guide you in all of the vital practices in depth and deliver additional blessings for your healing, prevention of sickness, rejuvenation, longevity, transformation, and enlightenment journeys.

My message to you is that as you read this book, make sure you do not miss the practices. Use the enclosed CD and the audio version of this book as essential practice guides and aids that could significantly boost and accelerate the results you obtain. I deliberately guide you in this book and lead you in the audio version of this book to do spiritual practices using the power of soul for healing, prevention of sickness, rejuvenation, prolonging life, and transforming every aspect of life, including relationships and finances and, especially, for self-clearing karma. Reading this book and, even more, practicing with the audio version of this book are like being at a workshop with me. When you go to a workshop and the teacher leads you in a meditation or practice, you do not run off to do something else, do you?

Do not rush through this book. Do every practice that I ask you to do. You will receive ten, fifty, a hundred times the benefit that you would receive if you simply read through the book quickly. To receive Divine Soul Downloads does not mean you automatically receive their benefits. Heavy karma takes time to self-clear. You must invoke the Divine Soul Downloads and practice to experience and receive divine healing and blessing. Remember also that going through this book just once is not enough. My advanced students go through my books many times. Every time they read and do the practices, they reach more and more "aha!" moments. They receive more and more remarkable healing, purification, and life transformation results.

These are important messages for you to remember as you read this book. I wish each of you will receive great healing, rejuvenation, purification, and life transformation by clearing your karma by applying the practices in this book, especially by doing them with me in the audio version. Receive the benefits of *soul over matter*, which is the power of soul. Receive the benefits of Divine Soul Power.

Practice. Practice. Practice.

Experience. Experience. Experience.

Benefit. Benefit. Benefit.

Hao! Hao! Hao!

Thank you. Thank you. Thank you.

List of Divine Soul Downloads

Chapter One

1. Divine Rainbow Light Ball and Divine Rainbow Liquid Spring of Divine Love Soul Transplant, 12
2. Divine Rainbow Light Ball and Divine Rainbow Liquid Spring of Divine Love Mind Transplant, 13
3. Divine Rainbow Light Ball and Divine Rainbow Liquid Spring of Divine Love Body Transplant, 13

Chapter Two

4. Divine Rainbow Light Ball and Divine Rainbow Liquid Spring of Divine Forgiveness Soul Transplant, 47
5. Divine Rainbow Light Ball and Divine Rainbow Liquid Spring of Divine Forgiveness Mind Transplant, 47
6. Divine Rainbow Light Ball and Divine Rainbow Liquid Spring of Divine Forgiveness Body Transplant, 47

7. Divine Rainbow Light Ball and Divine Rainbow Liquid Spring of Divine Compassion Soul Transplant, 53

8. Divine Rainbow Light Ball and Divine Rainbow Liquid Spring of Divine Compassion Mind Transplant, 53

9. Divine Rainbow Light Ball and Divine Rainbow Liquid Spring of Divine Compassion Body Transplant, 53

10. Divine Rainbow Light Ball and Divine Rainbow Liquid Spring of Divine Light Soul Transplant, 70

11. Divine Rainbow Light Ball and Divine Rainbow Liquid Spring of Divine Light Mind Transplant, 70

12. Divine Rainbow Light Ball and Divine Rainbow Liquid Spring of Divine Light Body Transplant, 70

13. Divine Rainbow Light Ball and Divine Rainbow Liquid Spring of Divine Sincerity Soul Transplant, 80

14. Divine Rainbow Light Ball and Divine Rainbow Liquid Spring of Divine Sincerity Mind Transplant, 80

15. Divine Rainbow Light Ball and Divine Rainbow Liquid Spring of Divine Sincerity Body Transplant, 81

16. Divine Rainbow Light Ball and Divine Rainbow Liquid Spring of Divine Blessing Soul Transplant, 89

17. Divine Rainbow Light Ball and Divine Rainbow Liquid Spring of Divine Blessing Mind Transplant, 89

18. Divine Rainbow Light Ball and Divine Rainbow Liquid Spring of Divine Blessing Body Transplant, 90

19. Divine Rainbow Light Ball and Divine Rainbow Liquid Spring of Divine Prevention of Sickness Soul Transplant, 101

20. Divine Rainbow Light Ball and Divine Rainbow Liquid Spring of Divine Prevention of Sickness Mind Transplant, 101

21. Divine Rainbow Light Ball and Divine Rainbow Liquid Spring of Divine Prevention of Sickness Body Transplant, 102

Chapter Three

22. Divine Rainbow Light Ball and Divine Rainbow Liquid Spring of Divine Harmony Soul Transplant, 124
23. Divine Rainbow Light Ball and Divine Rainbow Liquid Spring of Divine Harmony Mind Transplant, 124
24. Divine Rainbow Light Ball and Divine Rainbow Liquid Spring of Divine Harmony Body Transplant, 124
25. Divine Rainbow Light Ball and Divine Rainbow Liquid Spring of Divine Balance Soul Transplant, 134
26. Divine Rainbow Light Ball and Divine Rainbow Liquid Spring of Divine Balance Mind Transplant, 135
27. Divine Rainbow Light Ball and Divine Rainbow Liquid Spring of Divine Balance Body Transplant, 135
28. Divine Rainbow Light Ball and Divine Rainbow Liquid Spring of Divine Love Peace Harmony Soul Transplant, 140
29. Divine Rainbow Light Ball and Divine Rainbow Liquid Spring of Divine Love Peace Harmony Mind Transplant, 141
30. Divine Rainbow Light Ball and Divine Rainbow Liquid Spring of Divine Love Peace Harmony Body Transplant, 141

Introduction

EVERY HUMAN BEING, every family, every organization, every community, every city, every country, every planet—including Mother Earth—every star, every galaxy, and every universe wishes to transform its life. Everyone and every soul wishes to be happier, healthier, rejuvenated, and successful in every aspect of life, including relationships and finances.

There have been millions of writings and books about life transformation. They have offered incredible secrets, wisdom, knowledge, and techniques for transforming every aspect of life. I honor all books in history that help to transform any aspect of life.

This book reveals the *divine* way to transform all life, including health, relationships, finances, and every aspect of life for you, humanity, and all universes.

The books of my Soul Power Series teach that everyone and everything on Mother Earth and in countless universes consist of soul, mind, and body. Soul is spirit. Mind is consciousness. Body includes energy and matter.

My Soul Power Series emphasizes *soul over matter*, which means soul can make things happen in any aspect of your life. Soul has the power to:

- heal your spiritual, mental, emotional, and physical bodies
- prevent sickness in your spiritual, mental, emotional, and physical bodies
- purify your soul, heart, mind, and body
- rejuvenate your soul, heart, mind, and body
- transform your relationships
- transform your finances
- enlighten your soul, heart, mind, and body

If all souls were to join hearts and souls together, they could transform humanity, Mother Earth, and all universes beyond comprehension and imagination.

Soul is the boss. A human being's soul is the boss of the human being. An animal's soul is the boss of the animal. A family's soul is the boss of the family. An organization's soul is the boss of the organization. A city's soul is the boss of the city. A country's soul is the boss of the country. Mother Earth's soul is the boss of Mother Earth. A universe's soul is the boss of the universe.

In the Soul Power Series, I have shared with you and humanity that your soul is involved in your decision making process. Most of the time, your soul agrees with your mind's decision. When this happens, your soul and your mind are aligned. That decision could easily lead to success. In some cases, your soul does not agree with your mind's decision. Your mind insists on the mind's way. In these cases, the decision could very easily be blocked. Who blocks the decision? Mainly, your soul does. Because your soul is the boss of your life, when your soul decides to block a decision made by your mind, it is very hard for that decision to succeed.

Think about your life and the lives of your friends. You have all had successes. You have all also had failures. The vital soul wisdom I share with you and humanity is that if your soul and your mind are aligned, success is much easier to reach. If your mind does not listen to your soul, success is very difficult to reach. I have learned this very well from the Divine over many years. I am a servant and vessel for you, humanity, and the Divine. What I hear from the Divine, I deliver to you. I have *flowed* all of my books from the Divine's words. The Divine is above my head at this moment. What I hear is what I share. If it fits you, take it. Follow it. If it does not fit you, please make your choice to do whatever you wish.

There is an ancient teaching, "When the student is ready, the teacher appears. When the teacher appears, grab the teacher. When the teacher offers the teaching, grab the teaching and apply the teaching to transform your life."

I am a divine soul communicator. I "write" every one of my books through my Soul Communication Channel. The Divine gives me the flow for this whole book—every paragraph and every sentence. When I flow this book and all of my books, I am in a relaxed and sacred environment to receive the Divine's sacred words. What the Divine wants me to tell you now is, "The Divine can only teach the ready student. If you are ready to hear divine wisdom and learn the divine way to transform every aspect of your life, then you will grab the wisdom and apply it to transform your life. If you are not ready for these divine secrets, wisdom, knowledge, and practical techniques, then the Divine is patient and will wait for your readiness."

The Divine just told me at this moment to pay attention to the new divine soul secrets, wisdom, knowledge, and practical techniques that the Divine is sharing with you in this book. Now the Divine is saying, "Dear my daughters and my sons who are reading this book, remember Zhi Gang's previous book *Tao I,* which shared a one-sentence Tao secret:

Da Tao zhi jian

("Da" means *big.* "Tao" is *The Way.* "Zhi" means *extremely.* "Jian" means *simple.* Therefore, "Da Tao zhi jian," pronounced *dah dow jr jyen,* means *The Big Way is extremely simple.*) "You will witness Zhi Gang's teaching becoming simpler and simpler. This is my direction. Mother Earth is in a transition period. All kinds of natural disasters, conflicts, challenges, wars, sickness, and more will happen. Divine teaching must be simple, practical, and to the point. Divine secrets, wisdom, knowledge, and practical techniques will come directly to the point. Zhi Gang is a pure channel for me as your beloved Divine. He heals. He serves. He shares. He does not create these words from his own head. Zhi Gang is offering my teaching, healing, and life transformation on Mother Earth to serve humanity, Mother Earth, and all universes. This is how he writes every one of his books.

"Over the last eight years, Zhi Gang has trained more than one thousand Divine Soul Healers and Teachers worldwide. What are Divine Soul Healers and Teachers? I, as your beloved Divine, transmit my permanent healing treasures to these chosen ones when Zhi Gang Sha requests it. My Divine Soul Healers and Teachers also offer my teaching and healing worldwide.

"The books of the Soul Power Series and the Soul Power in Action Series will flow directly from me. Both of these book series share peoples' experiences of healing and life transformation from the teaching and practices, as well as soul communications from Zhi Gang Sha's trained teachers."

Thank you, Divine. I am honored to be your vehicle and channel in order to be your servant and a servant of humanity. I am honored to share your soul secrets, wisdom, knowledge, and practical techniques for every aspect of life.

This book is about divine transformation.

Divine transformation is the *divine* way to transform your health, relationships, finances, and every aspect of your life. This book also shares the divine way to transform humanity, Mother Earth, and all universes.

Divine transformation is the divine way to heal your spiritual, mental, emotional, and physical bodies.

Divine transformation is the divine way to prevent sickness in your spiritual, mental, emotional, and physical bodies.

Divine transformation is the divine way to transform all relationships.

Divine transformation is the divine way to transform your finances and business.

Divine transformation is the divine way to transform humanity.

Divine transformation is the divine way to transform Mother Earth.

Divine transformation is the divine way to transform all universes.

Learn divine transformation from this book.

Apply the secrets, wisdom, knowledge, and practical techniques of divine transformation to transform every aspect of life for you, humanity, Mother Earth, and all universes.

Create love, peace, and harmony for humanity, Mother Earth, and all universes.

I love my heart and soul
I love all humanity
Join hearts and souls together
Love, peace and harmony
Love, peace and harmony

DIVINE TRANSFORMATION

Important Wisdom of Divine Transformation

TRANSFORMATION MEANS CHANGE. Of course, we want to transform to a better condition. Human beings have many challenges, including challenges in health, relationships, and finances. Every human being wants to transform his or her health to a better condition. Many human beings want to rejuvenate their souls, hearts, minds, and bodies. Millions of people wish to transform their relationships to more love, peace, and harmony. Millions of people desire to transform their finances to abundance.

Millions of human beings are searching for soul secrets, wisdom, knowledge, and practical techniques to transform every aspect of life. Many books, radio and television programs, films, workshops, and seminars teach people how to transform their lives. Many great teachings in history have helped humanity and Mother Earth with their transformation.

I want you and humanity to know that this book teaches *di-*

vine transformation. You must know the what, why, and how of divine transformation. What *is* divine transformation? Why do you need to learn divine transformation? How can you apply divine transformation to transform your health, relationships, finances, and every aspect of your life?

What Is Divine Transformation?

Divine transformation is to apply divine secrets, wisdom, knowledge, and practical techniques to transform every aspect of your life, as well as the lives of humanity, Mother Earth, and all universes.

Divine secrets are secrets revealed by the Divine to transform every aspect of your life, as well as the lives of humanity, Mother Earth, and all universes.

Divine wisdom and knowledge are wisdom and knowledge revealed by the Divine to transform every aspect of your life, as well as the lives of humanity, Mother Earth, and all universes.

Divine practical techniques are vital to transform your life and the lives of humanity, Mother Earth, and all universes. They are also revealed by the Divine. They carry divine power and divine ability to transform every aspect of your life, as well as the lives of humanity, Mother Earth, and all universes.

Now is the first time in history that the Divine is formally transmitting divine power and abilities to humanity through books, CDs, DVDs, and other materials. This is done through Divine Soul Mind Body Transplants, which are permanent divine transmissions that the Divine creates and downloads to books, CDs, DVDs, and other materials. After receiving divine transmissions, these books, CDs, DVDs, and other materials are no longer the original books, CDs, DVDs, or materials. They become divine treasures for healing and life transformation. Every reader must be aware of this divine wisdom.

This is easy to understand. For example, if you see a blank sheet of paper, you treat this paper as paper. If a picture of Jesus, Mary, Guan Yin, or a saint is printed on this paper, you no longer treat this paper as an ordinary sheet of paper. You instantly have a respectful feeling for it. You cannot throw this sacred picture into the garbage. I have taught my students for many years that if a saint's picture has become worn, damaged, or torn, and you do not want to keep the picture, find a clean space in nature to burn it. When you burn the picture, say, "I love you. Go back to Heaven." Why should you do this? A saint's picture carries the soul, mind, and body of that saint. To respect the picture in this way is to respect the saint. To throw the picture into the garbage is to disrespect the saint.

Disrespecting the saint creates bad karma. When you disrespect a saint's picture, Heaven records it. All saints become aware of it. Later, when you have difficulties and challenges in your life, you may not get help from the saints when you call them. This is vital wisdom to remember. I offer this example and teaching to share with you that if the Divine has downloaded Divine Soul Mind Body Transplants to a book, CD, DVD, cup, blanket, or anything, do not treat the blessed items as ordinary materials. These materials become divine treasures. Show great respect to these treasures. The more you show your respect, the more divine blessings you will receive.

The divine transformation I share in this book is that the Divine can offer major Soul Mind Body Transplants to transform every aspect of life for you, humanity, Mother Earth, and all universes.

There are many kinds of divine transformation. The fastest kind of divine transformation is for the Divine to create treasures and transmit them to you as a reader of this book. These treasures are permanent. They will reside with your soul, mind, and body for the rest of your life. Even when you transition from this physical life, these treasures will follow your soul for all of your future lifetimes.

The Divine has not offered this kind of transformation before. In the first book of my Soul Power Series, *Soul Wisdom: Practical Soul Treasures to Transform Your Life*, the Divine started to offer Soul Mind Body Transplants to every reader. *Divine Transformation* is the seventh book in the Soul Power Series. In all seven books, the Divine has continued to offer divine treasures to every reader. Why is the Divine doing this? We are in Mother Earth's transition period. Mother Earth's transition is the purification process of Mother Earth. The root cause of Mother Earth's transition is the bad karma of humanity and Mother Earth. Chapter 2 of the authority book of my Soul Power Series, *The Power of Soul: The Way to Heal, Rejuvenate, Transform, and Enlighten All Life*,[1] is a major teaching on karma. The one-sentence secret of karma is:

Karma is the root cause of success and failure in every aspect of life.

Karma can be divided into good karma and bad karma. Your good karma is the record of your good services in your current life and all of your past lives. Good karma includes love, care, compassion, sincerity, honesty, generosity, kindness, purity, and other

---

1. *The Power of Soul: The Way to Heal, Rejuvenate, Transform, and Enlighten All Life* (New York/Toronto: Atria Books/Heaven's Library, 2009).

kinds of good service. Bad karma is the record of your unpleasant services, such as killing, harming, taking advantage, cheating, stealing, and all other kinds of unpleasant service, in all of your lifetimes.

Divine transformation emphasizes self-clearing of karma, which means self-clearing or cleansing bad karma. Karma cleansing is a "must" step for transforming every aspect of life. Millions of people want to transform their lives. They have studied many different teachings and learned many secrets. They have applied and practiced this or that kind of secret many times. They have participated in many workshops and seminars and read hundreds of books. But finally, many of these people have not seen the significant transformation that they desire in their lives.

Why? What is the key reason that people devote great effort but still do not receive the life transformation that they deeply wish to have? I offered the one-sentence explanation a few paragraphs above. The root reason is that their bad karma blocks their life transformation.

If you wish to study and apply the divine secrets, wisdom, knowledge, and practical techniques for life transformation in this book, you must seriously learn how to clear your karmic debt. If you can clear your own karmic debt, you will be able to receive divine transformation beyond words, comprehension, and imagination. In one sentence:

To clear your bad karma is to remove the root blockages to transforming every aspect of your life.

In this book, *Divine Transformation*, I will offer practical divine exercises to empower you to self-clear your bad karma. I will also offer many priceless divine treasures as gifts to you and humanity to transform your health, relationships, and finances, as well as every aspect of your life.

The Significance and Power of Divine Transformation

The Divine is the creator. The Divine is the boss of all souls in all universes. The Divine has unlimited power and abilities to transform every aspect of life beyond any comprehension. Therefore, divine transformation has the power and ability to:

- prevent sickness for you, your loved ones, humanity, Mother Earth, and all universes
- heal your spiritual, mental, emotional, and physical bodies
- heal your loved ones, humanity, Mother Earth, and all universes
- purify your soul, heart, mind, and body
- purify your loved ones, humanity, Mother Earth, and all universes
- rejuvenate your soul, heart, mind, and body
- rejuvenate your loved ones, humanity, Mother Earth, and all universes
- transform relationships for you, your loved ones, humanity, Mother Earth, and all universes
- transform finances for you, your loved ones, humanity, Mother Earth, and all universes
- transform business for you, your loved ones, humanity, Mother Earth, and all universes
- enlighten your soul, heart, mind, and body
- enlighten your loved ones, humanity, Mother Earth, and all universes

- transform and enlighten every aspect of life for you, your loved ones, humanity, Mother Earth, and all universes

The Key to Divine Transformation Is Clearing Your Bad Karma

Divine transformation is the divine way to transform every aspect of life. The key to transforming every aspect of your life is self-clearing your bad karma. If you have heavy bad karma, it would take great effort to self-clear it, but it definitely can be done.

I am delighted to share a divine way to self-clear bad karma. Bad karma comes from all of the mistakes you made in all of your previous lifetimes and in your present life,[2] as well as from some of the mistakes your ancestors made in all of their lifetimes.[3] As I shared in the one-sentence secret on page 4, bad karma is the root cause of failure in every aspect of life. Bad karma results in blockages in every aspect of life, including health, relationships, and finances. These blockages are the lessons we must learn to pay our spiritual debts.

To clear bad karma is to repay our spiritual debts to the souls we have hurt or harmed.

To clear bad karma is to cancel the lessons and disasters in health, relationships, and finances that we were supposed to learn because of the mistakes we have made.

To clear bad karma is to offer unconditional universal service

---

2. This is your *personal* karma.

3. This is your *ancestral* karma. It has two parts: ancestral karma on your fathers' side and ancestral karma on your mothers' side. It comes from some of your ancestors' mistakes in all of your lifetimes, so it comes from all of your fathers in all of your lifetimes (and their ancestors) and all of your mothers in all of your lifetimes (and their ancestors).

to all humanity and all souls. Service will accumulate good virtue to pay our spiritual debt. Then we are forgiven.

To clear bad karma is to receive forgiveness from the Divine and from all souls we and our ancestors harmed in this life and previous lives.

In the beginning of every book of my Soul Power Series, I share that the Divine gave me a universal law in April 2003. This universal law is named the Universal Law of Universal Service. It states:

> *I am a universal servant.*[4]
> *You are a universal servant.*
> *Everyone and everything is a universal servant.*
> *A universal servant offers universal service, including universal love, forgiveness, peace, healing, blessing, harmony, and enlightenment.*
> *If one offers a little universal service, one receives a little blessing from Heaven and me.*
> *If one offers more universal service, one receives more blessings from Heaven and me.*
> *If one offers unconditional universal service, one receives unlimited blessings from Heaven and me.*
> *If one offers a little unpleasant service, one learns little lessons. The lessons can include sickness, challenges in relationships and finances, and blockages in every aspect of life.*
> *If one offers more unpleasant service, one learns more lessons.*

---

4. These are the words of the Divine.

If one offers huge unpleasant service, one learns huge lessons.

The Universal Law of Universal Service is the law of karma. It explains how the universe operates. It explains how a human being's life is arranged.

A human being's life has two conditions. One is the *arranged condition*. How long a person will live, the condition of one's love relationships and family relationships, one's financial condition, and one's spiritual, mental, emotional, and physical health—all of these are arranged according to one's karma, good and bad.

The other condition of a human being's life is the *changeable condition*. This means that a person can transform his or her life. The karmic law explains this very clearly: If one offers universal service, all aspects of life, including health, relationships, finances, and more, can become better. One's life can become longer, healthier, and happier. If one offers unpleasant service, all aspects of life, including health, relationships, finances, and more, could become worse. One's life can become shorter, with more challenges and struggles in every aspect.

The Universal Law of Universal Service (or karmic law) can explain every aspect of everything and everyone's life. Therefore, how can one transform one's life? The answer can be summarized in one sentence:

**To transform life is to offer universal service;
the more universal service one offers, the
more transformation one can achieve.**

Karmic law explains clearly that life *can* be transformed. The key is to clear bad karma and to accumulate good karma or good virtue through good service.

Divine transformation is the *divine* way to transform every aspect of life. Divine transformation is the fastest way to transform every aspect of life. Divine transformation uses divine treasures to bless and accelerate the transformation process for any aspect of life. Divine transformation can be summarized in one sentence:

**Divine treasures offer divine transformation
for every aspect of life.**

Karma is the root cause of success and failure. Divine transformation applies divine treasures to assist you to clear your bad karma. These divine treasures are the key divine secrets, wisdom, knowledge, and practical techniques of divine transformation.

This is the seventh book in my Soul Power Series. The first six books are:

- *Soul Wisdom: Practical Soul Treasures to Transform Your Life*
- *Soul Communication: Opening Your Spiritual Channels for Success and Fulfillment*
- *The Power of Soul: The Way to Heal, Rejuvenate, Transform, and Enlighten All Life*
- *Divine Soul Songs: Sacred Practical Treasures to Heal, Rejuvenate, and Transform You, Humanity, Mother Earth, and All Universes*
- *Divine Soul Mind Body Healing and Transmission System: The Divine Way to Heal You, Humanity, Mother Earth, and All Universes*
- *Tao I: The Way of All Life*

Every book of my Soul Power Series offers Divine Soul Transplants, Divine Soul Mind Body Transplants, or Tao Transplants. The divine frequency and vibration of these permanent divine treasures offered as gifts in my books have increased step by step. Now, in this book, I will offer Divine Soul Mind Body Transplants with even higher-level divine frequency than in my previous books. In my future books, divine frequency and vibration and Tao frequency and vibration will increase further and further.

Prepare! I will now offer the first three Divine Soul Mind Body Transplants in this book:

Divine Rainbow Light Ball and Divine Rainbow Liquid Spring of Divine Love Soul Mind Body Transplants

A Divine Rainbow Light Ball is a divine yang treasure. A Divine Rainbow Liquid Spring is a divine yin treasure. These Divine Soul Mind Body Transplants carry divine yin yang treasures to help you self-clear bad karma and transform every aspect of life. The power and ability of these treasures are beyond any words. Applying these and other divine treasures to self-clear bad karma is the divine way to self-clear bad karma. I will show you how to do it.

The Divine Love Soul Transplant is a divine rainbow light being. The Divine Love Mind Transplant is another divine rainbow light being that carries divine consciousness. The Divine Love Body Transplant is a divine rainbow light being that carries divine energy and divine tiny matter.

Why do these Divine Love Soul Mind Body Transplants work? They work because they carry the divine soul, divine consciousness, divine energy, and divine tiny matter of divine love. In turn, all of these carry divine love, forgiveness, compassion, and light that can help you self-clear your bad karma and remove blockages in your consciousness (mind), as well as blockages in your energy and tiny matter (body). Divine love melts all blockages and transforms all life. Divine forgiveness brings inner peace and inner joy. Divine compassion boosts energy, stamina, vitality, and immunity. Divine light heals and blesses. Therefore, Divine Love Soul Mind Body Transplants can remove all kinds of blockages and transform all life.

Prepare now!

Sit up straight. Put the tip of your tongue as close as you can to the roof of your mouth, without touching. Put your left palm over your Message Center or heart chakra[5] and your right hand in the traditional prayer position, with fingers pointing upward. This is called the Soul Light Era Prayer Position. It is a special signal and connection with Heaven for the Soul Light Era.

Totally relax. Open your heart and soul to receive this great honor. It will take about one minute for you to receive these three priceless divine treasures.

Divine Order: Divine Rainbow Light Ball and Divine Rainbow Liquid Spring of Divine Love Soul Transplant

Transmission!

---

5. The Message Center is a fist-sized energy center located in the center of your chest, behind the sternum. The Message Center is very important for developing soul communication abilities and for healing. It is also the love center, forgiveness center, karma center, emotional center, life transformation center, soul enlightenment center, and more. Clearing blockages from your Message Center to open and develop your Message Center is key to your ability to communicate with your own soul and other souls.

**Divine Order: Divine Rainbow Light Ball
and Divine Rainbow Liquid Spring of
Divine Love Mind Transplant**

Transmission!

**Divine Order: Divine Rainbow Light Ball
and Divine Rainbow Liquid Spring of
Divine Love Body Transplant**

Transmission!

**Divine Order: Divine Rainbow Light Ball and
Divine Rainbow Liquid Spring of Divine Love
Soul Mind Body Transplants join as one.**

Hei Ya Ya Ya Ya Ya Ya You!

The last line is a Divine Order in Soul Language. It can be translated as follows:

*Divine Order to join Divine Rainbow Light Ball
and Divine Rainbow Liquid Spring of Divine Love
Soul Mind Body Transplants as one now.*

You are extremely blessed.

We cannot honor the Divine enough. Let us sing (or chant the words of) two Divine Soul Songs to express our greatest gratitude. The first Divine Soul Song is *God Gives His Heart to Me*.[6] The second Divine Soul Song is *Thank You, Divine:*

---

6. You can listen to this Divine Soul Song on the enclosed CD.

God gives his heart to me
God gives his love to me
My heart melds with his heart
My love melds with his love

Thank you, Divine
Thank you, Divine
Thank you, Divine
Thank you, Divine
Thank you, Divine

Apply Divine Treasures to Self-clear Your Bad Karma

Apply the Four Power Techniques, which are Body Power, Soul Power, Mind Power, and Sound Power. Let me summarize the key wisdom of the Four Power Techniques.

Body Power is special body positions and hand positions for healing and rejuvenation.

Soul Power is to say *hello* to the inner souls of your body, including the souls of your systems, organs, cells, cell units, DNA, and RNA, as well as to outer souls, including saints, healing angels, archangels, ascended masters, lamas, gurus, all kinds of spiritual fathers and mothers, the Divine, and Tao, to invoke their power for healing, rejuvenation, and life transformation.

Mind Power is creative visualization. The most important wisdom is to visualize golden or rainbow light to transform your health, relationships, and finances.

Sound Power is to chant or sing ancient healing mantras, Divine Soul Songs, and Tao songs for healing, rejuvenation, and life transformation for relationships, finances, and every aspect of life.

Now let us apply Divine Rainbow Light Ball and Divine Rainbow Liquid Spring of Divine Love Soul Mind Body Transplants to self-clear karma. I offered many Divine Golden Light Ball and Divine Golden Liquid Spring treasures in the first six books of my Soul Power Series. In this book I am offering Divine Rainbow Light Ball and Divine Rainbow Liquid Spring treasures. Divine Rainbow treasures have higher frequency than Divine Golden treasures. We are extremely blessed that the Divine is offering Divine Rainbow treasures to every reader of this book.

Body Power. Sit up straight. Put the tip of your tongue as close as you can to the roof of your mouth, without touching. Put your left palm over your Message Center. Put your right hand in the traditional prayer position, with fingers pointing upward. As explained earlier, this is the Soul Light Era Prayer Position.

Soul Power. Say *hello:*

> *Dear soul mind body of Divine Rainbow Light Ball*
>   *and Divine Rainbow Liquid Spring of Divine Love*
>   *Soul Mind Body Transplants,*
> *I love you, honor you, and appreciate you.*
> *You have the power to clear my soul mind body*
>   *blockages.*
> *You have the power to offer divine forgiveness for my*
>   *mistakes in past lives and this lifetime.*
> *You have the power to offer divine forgiveness for the*
>   *mistakes that my ancestors and I have made in past*
>   *lives and this lifetime.*
> *We are very grateful.*
> *We cannot thank you enough.*

Dear all souls whom my ancestors and I have hurt or
  harmed in all of our lifetimes,
We love you, honor you, and appreciate you.
Please forgive my ancestors and me for our mistakes of
  harming you.
We sincerely apologize.
My ancestors and I have learned from our mistakes.
We will serve humanity and all souls unconditionally.
Please forgive us again.
We are very honored and grateful that you can
  forgive us.
Dear all souls who have harmed me in any of my life-
  times,
I love you, honor you, and appreciate you.
I forgive you completely and unconditionally.
Please accept my forgiveness.
Thank you.

Mind Power. Visualize the Divine Rainbow Light Ball and Divine Rainbow Liquid Spring of Divine Love Soul Mind Body Transplants shining in your Message Center and whole body.

Sound Power. Chant silently or aloud:

Divine Rainbow Light Ball and Divine Rainbow Liq-
  uid Spring of Divine Love Soul Mind Body Trans-
  plants clear my soul mind body blockages.
All souls whom my ancestors and I have harmed,
  please forgive us.
We are extremely honored and appreciative.
Thank you, all.

Divine Rainbow Light Ball and Divine Rainbow Liquid Spring of Divine Love Soul Mind Body Transplants clear my soul mind body blockages.
All souls whom my ancestors and I have harmed,
please forgive us.
We are extremely honored and appreciative.
Thank you, all.

Divine Rainbow Light Ball and Divine Rainbow Liquid Spring of Divine Love Soul Mind Body Transplants clear my soul mind body blockages.
All souls whom my ancestors and I have harmed,
please forgive us.
We are extremely honored and appreciative.
Thank you, all.

Divine Rainbow Light Ball and Divine Rainbow Liquid Spring of Divine Love Soul Mind Body Transplants clear my soul mind body blockages.
All souls whom my ancestors and I have harmed,
please forgive us.
We are extremely honored and appreciative.
Thank you, all.

Continue by chanting repeatedly, silently or aloud:

Divine Love clears my soul mind body blockages.
Thank you.
Divine Love clears my soul mind body blockages.
Thank you.

Divine Love clears my soul mind body blockages.
   Thank you.
Divine Love clears my soul mind body blockages.
   Thank you.
Divine Love clears my soul mind body blockages.
   Thank you.
Divine Love clears my soul mind body blockages.
   Thank you.
Divine Love clears my soul mind body blockages.
   Thank you . . .

As I shared in the "How to Read This Book" section, please do not skip the practices in this book. Whenever I lead you in a practice, please stop reading. Chant for at least three to five minutes. The longer you chant, and the more times you chant, the better. There is no time limit. The more you chant with divine treasures, the faster your bad karma can be removed, and the more healing and blessing you will receive for the rest of this life and all your future lifetimes.

Close. After chanting and visualizing for at least three minutes, close the practice by saying:

Hao! Hao! Hao! (pronounced *how*)
Thank you. Thank you. Thank you.[7]

I would like to share one story about the importance of practice with you and every reader. In 2009, I met a successful Swiss businesswoman in Frankfurt, Germany. She had a very rare cen-

---

7. "Hao" means *good* or *perfect* in Chinese. The first *thank you* is to the Divine. The second *thank you* is to all the souls who came to assist you. The third *thank you* is to your own soul, heart, mind, and body.

tral nervous system illness, and suffered incredible pain in her head, neck, and back. Every year, the pain would become so severe that she had to be hospitalized several times. Each time, she would have to stay in the hospital for one to two weeks or even longer to control the pain. She took morphine every time she was hospitalized. There was no medical solution for her illness.

Shortly after this woman met me, she received Divine Karma Cleansing[8] of her personal karma and her ancestral karma on both fathers' and mothers' sides, including divine removal of curses[9] and negative memories.[10] She also received many Divine Soul Mind Body Transplants of bodily systems and organs. Afterward, she did not feel any improvement in her pain.

This story is a good example of my teaching: to receive Divine Karma Cleansing, Divine Soul Mind Body Transplants, and other divine blessings does not mean that you are healed. To receive Divine Karma Cleansing means you are forgiven for your mistakes in past lifetimes and in this lifetime. To receive Divine Soul Mind Body Transplants means you are given permanent divine treasures. You must invoke and apply (practice and chant with) these treasures to self-heal, rejuvenate, prolong life, and transform every aspect of life.

I just led you in a practice to apply your Divine Rainbow Light Ball and Divine Rainbow Liquid Spring of Divine Love Soul Mind Body Transplants to clear your soul mind body blockages. You may have suffered from a chronic condition for many

---

8. Divine Karma Cleansing is explained in the next section.

9. Curses can be extremely powerful blockages in one's life. Someone with a close connection with the Dark Side could put an unpleasant message on a person's soul, affecting any aspect of that one's life: health, relationships, finances, or business.

10. Negative memories are held in your soul and in the souls of your systems: organs, cells, DNA, and RNA. A very common type of negative memory is related to physical experiences you had in previous lifetimes.

years. Your systems, organs, and cells could already have been significantly damaged by that condition. In order to heal your systems, organs, and cells, you must apply divine treasures to restore your health step by step.

The Swiss woman understood my teaching. She believed my teaching. Although she did not feel any improvement after receiving Divine Karma Cleansing and many Divine Soul Mind Body Transplants, she remembered that I had said, "Everyone has to practice. There is no time limit. The more you practice, the better." She started to chant *Divine Soul Mind Body Transplants heal and rejuvenate me. Thank you, Divine.* This is exactly my teaching to everyone who receives Divine Karma Cleansing and Divine Soul Mind Body Transplants.

She practiced for a half-hour to one hour per time, two or three times a day. She made a commitment to practice for three to five, and sometimes six, hours per day on weekends. Because she had no solution for her chronic pain for many years, she really wanted to try my healing methods to restore her health. She chanted and chanted and chanted and chanted.

After about three months of dedicated practice, her pain suddenly stopped. Ever since—now more than one year later—the pain has not returned. Her doctor is extremely impressed by her improvement because her condition is very rare and, according to the doctor, has no conventional medical solution.

I have received thousands of heart-touching, moving, and amazing healing stories from people who have received Divine Karma Cleansing and Divine Soul Mind Body Transplants. This particular case is a little unique. After receiving divine blessings, the businesswoman experienced no apparent results at all, but she followed the teaching. She practiced persistently. She was committed to healing her condition.

This is proof of what the Divine told me: to receive divine treasures does not mean that you are healed. You must practice. This case is a good example for anyone who suffers from chronic or life-threatening conditions. Remember to practice. Be patient, confident, and persistent.

Divine Karma Cleansing

Since July 2003, I have offered Divine Karma Cleansing of personal, ancestral, relationship, and other karma for thousands of people worldwide. I do not clear people's karma. The Divine gave me the honor to offer Divine Karma Cleansing for humanity. People apply to have their karma cleared. The Divine approves. Then, the Divine does the job. Divine curse removal and divine removal of negative memories are also accomplished through a Divine Order.

When I offer Divine Karma Cleansing, I invoke the Divine, the leaders and workers of the Akashic Records, Heaven's generals, and Heaven's soldiers. I send a Divine Order to clear one's personal karma, ancestral karma, relationship karma, curses, or negative memories. When a person has bad karma, a dark soul or souls reside in the person's body to give the person karmic lessons. When I send a Divine Order for karma cleansing, Heaven's generals and soldiers will remove dark souls from a person's body and take them to the proper place. Dark souls related to the karma that has been cleared are no longer allowed to stay inside the person's body.

Karma cleansing is the Divine's special forgiveness. When the Divine Order is sent to clear your karma, your spiritual debt is forgiven. The Divine opens Heaven's virtue bank to give virtue to the souls you harmed in order to forgive you. The souls who were harmed receive major virtue from the Divine. This virtue blesses their future lives. Because they receive this virtue, they do not resent you anymore. They forgive you. Dark souls leave your body. The darkness in your book in the Akashic Records is replaced with golden and rainbow light.

I offered Divine Karma Cleansing service on a group basis in teleconferences and live webcasts through December 2009. Since then, I have been guided by the Divine to offer this major divine service only at my retreats and in private consultations. Starting in 2010, some of my Worldwide Representatives have also received the honor and authority to offer total Divine Karma Cleansing at retreats and in private consultations. Some of my Worldwide Representatives and I will continue to offer Divine Karma Cleansing for sickness karma, relationship karma between two people, financial karma, business karma, and residential karma at any time.

Thank you, Divine, for your karma cleansing. Divine Karma Cleansing is a unique divine service to heal and transform people's lives. I am honored to be a divine servant, vehicle, and channel to offer divine blessings to humanity. I am honored to be a servant of humanity.

Thank you. Thank you. Thank you.

Divine Transformation for Your Health

HUMANITY SUFFERS FROM all kinds of sicknesses. Humanity faces all kinds of challenges in relationships and finances. Humanity and Mother Earth struggle with wars, imbalances in nature, and more. There are many conflicts and all kinds of chaos on Mother Earth. What are the reasons? They can be summarized in one sentence:

All challenges in health, relationships, finances, and every aspect of life for humanity, Mother Earth, and all universes are due to soul mind body blockages.

Soul blockages are bad karma. For a human being, bad karma includes personal karma, ancestral karma, relationship karma, financial karma, emotional karma, curses, negative memories, and more. For an organization, bad karma includes karma of the business, relationship karma among employees, relationship karma between employees and the owner, karma of the business's building, karma of the business's site, karma of the business's name, and more. For a city and a country, bad karma includes unpleasant policies, taking advantage of its citizens, causing wars, and more. For Mother Earth, bad karma includes damaging natural resources and other aspects of the environment, and more.

Mind blockages are blockages of consciousness. They include negative mind-sets, negative attitudes, negative beliefs, ego, attachments, and more.

Body blockages are blockages in energy and matter.

The divine way to self-clear karma is to apply divine treasures. At the end of chapter 1, I led you in a practice to self-clear karma using Divine Love Soul Mind Body Transplants. Karma cleansing is to be forgiven. Divine treasures carry divine frequency and vibration with divine love, forgiveness, compassion, and light. They can offer divine forgiveness for your karmic debts.

It is very important to understand that everybody's karma is different because everybody's soul journey and lifetimes have been different. Some people have very light karma. In the last ten years, I have even met several people who were karma-free. Some people have light or moderate karma. Some people have heavy karma. Some people have very heavy karma.

The time and effort it takes to self-clear your karma depend on how heavy your karma is. If you have light karma, you could self-clear it very quickly by applying divine treasures. If you have heavy or very heavy karma, it could take you a long time to self-clear it, even by applying divine treasures a lot.

Applying divine treasures to self-clear karma is a revolutionary way to clear karma because it is a divine way. For the first time in history, the Divine is willing to download permanent divine treasures to readers of a book. You can then apply these divine treasures to self-clear your karma. This divine way is much, much quicker than the normal way. The normal way is to accumulate good karma by offering unconditional service for thirty years, fifty years, or even for many lifetimes in order to pay your karmic debt. Applying divine treasures to self-clear karma is a divine way. But you *must* be aware that it still takes a lot of practice to clear karma. Remember, I have shared in many of my books that divine treasures are like lightbulbs. To switch them on, you must invoke them and practice. (I showed you how in the practice near the end of chapter 1.) Otherwise, the divine treasures are switched off and resting.

In summary, do not think that karma can be self-cleared easily. If you carry heavy karma, it can take a long time to self-clear it even by applying divine treasures, but you can be sure that this divine way is tremendously faster than the normal way.

Heavy karma is due to very serious mistakes in previous lifetimes and in this lifetime, including killing, harming, taking advantage, cheating, stealing, and more. It takes much time and serious effort to completely self-clear heavy karma. Even with the assistance of divine treasures, we must practice dedicatedly. Realize that with these divine treasures, the Divine is offering us divine forgiveness. The more we practice, the more divine forgiveness we will receive. Until our karma is completely cleared, we must still learn some karmic lessons. We need to apologize sincerely for our mistakes. We need to commit to not making the same mistakes again. We need to ask for forgiveness from the souls we have hurt or harmed. We need to serve others unconditionally by making them healthier and happier. Divine treasures carry divine love, forgiveness, compassion, and light to forgive us quickly, but it does take time and personal effort. Be patient, persistent, and confident.

Offering service to others is also important for self-clearing karma. Serve others with love, care, compassion, generosity, kindness, sincerity, integrity, grace, humility, purity, and more. Heaven records every service. When you serve, virtue is given in the form of Heaven's flowers to your soul and your book in the Akashic Records. Virtue is spiritual currency. Virtue will pay your karmic debts. When your karmic debts are paid, the lessons you were to learn are canceled. Disasters that were arranged for your life are removed on the spot. These disasters could include life-threatening sickness, extremely challenging relationships and finances, and major blockages in any aspect of life. This explains some of the significance and benefits of karma cleansing.

The divine way to self-clear karma means that the Divine downloads permanent divine treasures to readers of this book. These divine treasures carry huge amounts of virtue, which I just explained is Heaven's flowers and spiritual currency. This divine virtue can pay your spiritual debts. Your karmic lessons will then be canceled.

As I shared earlier, divine treasures are like divine lightbulbs. If you apply these divine treasures by practicing with them to self-clear karma, you have turned these divine lightbulbs on. If you do not practice, the divine lightbulbs stay turned off. Divine lightbulbs radiate divine frequency and vibration with divine love, forgiveness, compassion, and light to you, Mother Earth, and all universes. These qualities can transform the frequency and vibration of humanity, Mother Earth, and all universes.

Therefore, when you turn on divine treasures to self-clear karma, you are not only receiving karma cleansing from divine virtue (Heaven's flowers or spiritual currency), you also are serving humanity, Mother Earth, and all universes. This will give you even more virtue!

If you understand this, you will know that there are no limitations for applying divine treasures to self-clear karma. Even after your bad karma is completely cleared, you should continue to practice with your divine treasures because you will continue to gain more virtue to transform every aspect of your life further. In other words, to continue to practice with divine treasures even after you have self-cleared your karma is to receive more virtue to bless the rest of your current life and all of your future lifetimes.

In physical life, people save money. They save money to buy something they want. They save money for a "rainy day." They save money for retirement. When your physical life ends, you cannot bring one cent to Heaven, even if you have millions and billions of dollars. The important divine wisdom I have just shared with you is to turn on your divine treasures as much as you can. Practice for a longer time and practice more times every day. There is no time limit. The more you apply divine treasures to self-clear karma and to transform every aspect of your life, the more virtue you will receive. Virtue is spiritual money. Virtue blesses you far more than physical money. The more virtue you can receive, the more blessings you will receive in every aspect of your current life and all of your future lives.

To apply divine treasures to self-clear karma and transform every aspect of life is to deposit virtue in Heaven. The Akashic Records is the place in Heaven where all of one's lives are recorded, including one's activities, behaviors, and thoughts. All of your good services and unpleasant services are recorded. Good service is virtue. The more virtue you can deposit, the more blessed your future lives will be. Virtue blesses every aspect of life. Virtue follows you for all of your lives.

Physical money cannot do this. If you have money, you are blessed, but make sure you use your money wisely. To use money wisely is to use money to serve others. To serve others is to make others happier and healthier. To serve others is to create love, peace, and harmony for humanity, Mother Earth, and all universes.

If one has a lot of physical money, it is because this person has served well in previous lives and in this life. If this person uses money wisely, he or she will continue to gain virtue. Future lives and the rest of this life will receive many more blessings. If this person uses money to harm others, he or she will create bad karma. Lessons will be given in future lives and in the rest of this life.

Some people make money by gambling, cheating, taking advantage of others, or from businesses that create unhealthy products and services. Bad karma is created. There is no way to avoid karmic law. Sooner or later, karmic lessons will be given. This is how a human being's life is arranged and managed by the Akashic Records. The Akashic Records not only records one's lives, it also gives the rewards or lessons appropriate to one's life.

In the rest of this book, I will lead you in many practices to apply divine treasures to self-clear karma. These practices are the divine way to self-clear karma. They are powerful beyond words. If you practice, many of you could receive instant life transformation. Many others could receive significant life transformation with a little practice. Some of you will need more time to see significant life transformation. Why are everyone's results different? I explained the reason very clearly above: results depend on the degree of bad karma.

Persist. Practice. Self-clear your bad karma as quickly as possible. In one sentence:

The sooner one self-clears karma by applying divine treasures, the sooner one can receive life transformation.

You are blessed.

Humanity is blessed.

We are all blessed to have the opportunity to receive divine treasures to self-clear karma.

Self-heal Your Physical Body,
Including Self-clearing Your Karma (Soul Blockages),
Mind Blockages, and Body Blockages

If one is sick, karma is the root cause. In my 2006 book, *Soul Mind Body Medicine: A Complete Soul Healing System for Optimum Health and Vitality*, and in all of the books of my Soul Power Series, I have shared with humanity that any sickness is due to soul mind body blockages.

Soul blockages are bad karma. They include personal karma, ancestral karma, relationship karma, curses, and negative memories.

Mind blockages are blockages of consciousness. They include negative mind-sets, negative attitudes, negative beliefs, ego, and attachments.

Body blockages are blockages of energy and matter.

In the fifth book of my Soul Power Series, *Divine Soul Mind Body Healing and Transmission System: The Divine Way to Heal You, Humanity, Mother Earth, and All Universes*,[1] I explained soul mind body blockages in much more detail. Please study more divine secrets, wisdom, knowledge, and practical techniques in that book.

In this book, I am teaching the divine way to self-clear

---

1. *Divine Soul Mind Body Healing and Transmission System: The Divine Way to Heal You, Humanity, Mother Earth, and All Universes* (New York/Toronto: Atria Books/Heaven's Library, 2009).

soul blockages, which are bad karma; mind blockages, which are blockages of consciousness; and body blockages, which are blockages of energy and tiny matter. In the next three sections, I will lead you in practices to self-clear soul mind body blockages for any kind of pain, any kind of inflammation, any kind of infection, and any kind of growths, including cysts, tumors, and cancer. Practice a lot with divine treasures to clear soul mind body blockages. You could receive remarkable healing beyond imagination.

PAIN

Any kind of pain could be related to soul mind body blockages. Divine transformation is to apply divine treasures to self-clear soul mind body blockages in order to transform your health and any aspect of life.

Near the end of chapter 1, you received the first three permanent divine treasures offered in this book: Divine Rainbow Light Ball and Divine Rainbow Liquid Spring of Divine Love Soul Mind Body Transplants. Now let me lead you to apply these three incredible divine treasures to clear the soul mind body blockages that are the root cause of any pain that you may be suffering.

Apply the Four Power Techniques, which are Body Power, Soul Power, Mind Power, and Sound Power. Let me summarize the essence of the Four Power Techniques. I explain them in greater detail in my books *Power Healing: The Four Keys to Energizing Your Body, Mind, and Spirit*[2] and *Soul Mind Body*

---

2. *Power Healing: The Four Keys to Energizing Your Body, Mind, and Spirit* (San Francisco: HarperSanFrancisco, 2002).

Medicine: A Complete Soul Healing System for Optimum Health and Vitality.

Body Power. Use special body and hand positions to heal, boost energy, stamina, vitality, and immunity, rejuvenate, prolong life, and transform relationships, finances, and any aspect of life.

There are various techniques of Body Power, including the One Hand Near, One Hand Far Body Power Technique, the One Hand Healing Technique, the Yin Yang Palm, the Universal Connection Body Power Technique, the Divine Soul Song of Yin Yang Body Power Technique, and many more. All Body Power techniques can be summarized in one sentence:

> **Where you put your hands is where you receive healing and rejuvenation.**

Now let me share another secret for Body Power. Make a fist. The point where your middle finger touches your palm is an acupuncture point named Lao Gong (pronounced *lao* [rhymes with *now*] *gawng*), also known as Pericardium Meridian 8. The area around the Lao Gong point is the important energy area where the body connects with nature. It radiates healing energy. When you put your palm over an area of your body where you are sick, energy will radiate out from the Lao Gong area to promote energy flow and healing in the area of sickness.

Soul Power. Invoke the power of inner souls and outer souls to self-heal, heal others, boost energy, stamina, vitality, and immunity, rejuvenate, prolong life, and transform relationships, finances, and any aspect of life.

Inner souls include one's own soul, which I call the body

soul, and the souls of bodily systems, organs, cells, cell units, DNA, RNA, spaces between the cells, and tiny matter inside the cells.

Outer souls are all other souls in the physical world and the spiritual world. They include the souls of healing angels, archangels, ascended masters, Christian saints, Taoist saints, other saints, buddhas, bodhisattvas, lamas, gurus, and all other spiritual fathers and mothers on Mother Earth and in Heaven. Outer souls also include the souls of the sun, moon, planets, stars, galaxies, and all universes. Outer souls also include the souls of humanity, as well as the souls of nature on Mother Earth, including the souls of oceans, mountains, trees, and more.

Every soul carries power to heal, rejuvenate, and transform life. Every soul has its own frequency and power to heal, rejuvenate, and transform life. Different saints have different frequencies and powers to heal, rejuvenate, and transform life.

You can invoke any soul for healing, rejuvenation, and life transformation, including the soul of the Divine. The Divine is our father and mother. The Divine is always delighted to bless your request as appropriate.

Soul Power is extremely powerful. Divine transformation is simply divine soul transformation. *Transform the soul first; then transformation of the mind, body, and every aspect of life will follow.*

Mind Power. Apply creative visualization to heal, boost energy, stamina, vitality, and immunity, rejuvenate, prolong life, and transform relationships, finances, and any aspect of life.

To visualize golden light is vital wisdom. The ancient spiritual healing secret is: *Golden light shines; all sickness disappears.*

In this book, the Divine offers you and every reader many

Divine Rainbow Light Ball and Divine Rainbow Liquid Spring Divine Soul Mind Body Transplants. Divine rainbow light carries an even higher divine frequency and vibration than divine golden light. We are extremely grateful.

Sound Power. Chant healing mantras, sacred mantras, Soul Songs, Divine Soul Songs, Tao Songs, and special vibrational healing sounds to heal, boost energy, stamina, vitality, and immunity, rejuvenate, prolong life, and transform relationships, finances, and any aspect of life.

People have chanted healing mantras since ancient times. The Divine has given me many new mantras for the Soul Power Series. These new mantras are unique. For healing, rejuvenation, and life transformation, you can simply chant, for example:

> *Divine Soul Mind Body Transplants heal and rejuvenate me.*
> *Thank you, Divine.*

or

> *Divine treasures transform my relationships and finances.*
> *Thank you, Divine.*

or

> *Tao Soul Herbs heal, prevent sickness, and rejuvenate me.*
> *Thank you, Tao.*

or

> *Divine and Tao treasures heal, prevent sickness, rejuve-*
> *nate, prolong life, purify my soul, heart, mind, and*
> *body, and transform every aspect of my life.*
> *Thank you, Divine and Tao.*

Divine Soul Mind Body Transplants are divine treasures. They carry divine frequency and vibration with divine love, forgiveness, compassion, and light. The power of Divine Soul Mind Body Transplants is beyond words and comprehension. They can transform all life.

What you, as the recipient of Divine Soul Mind Body Transplants, must do is turn them on and practice with them. To chant new divine mantras like those in the four examples above is to turn on your Divine Soul Mind Body Transplants. To chant more is to practice more. As I have said many times, there is no time limit to this practice. The longer, the better. If you have a serious, chronic, or life-threatening condition; if you have heavy bad karma; if you want to receive healing and life transformation in any aspect of life as quickly as possible, it is vital to practice for a total of at least two hours per day.

The Divine Soul Mind Body Transplants offered to you and all readers through my Soul Power Series represent the first time in history that the Divine has offered Soul Mind Body Transplants in this way. This is the first time all humanity has been given an opportunity to receive priceless permanent divine treasures. The Divine gave me the great honor to be a servant of humanity and the Divine to offer these treasures to you and every reader of my Soul Power Series books. You can instantly apply the divine treasures you receive to transform every aspect of your life.

The new divine mantras I have received for the Soul Power Series are extremely simple: directly chant the divine treasures to heal, bless, and transform any aspect of your life. *Da Tao zhi jian.* "The Big Way is extremely simple."

We are extremely honored and blessed that the Divine transmits priceless permanent treasures to every reader that we can apply to transform every aspect of our lives.

I have explained the essence of the Four Power Techniques. In every practice, we will use the Four Power Techniques to offer divine transformation for every aspect of life.

Practice Using Divine Treasures to Heal Pain

Now I would like to lead you in a practice for healing pain.

Body Power. Sit up straight. Put the tip of your tongue as close as you can to the roof of your mouth, without touching. Put one palm on your lower abdomen, below the navel. Put your other palm on the painful area for which you wish to receive healing.

Soul Power. Say *hello:*

> *Dear soul mind body of Divine Rainbow Light Ball*
> *and Divine Rainbow Liquid Spring of Divine Love*
> *Soul Mind Body Transplants,*
> *I love you, honor you, and appreciate you.*
> *You have the power to clear the soul mind body block-*
> *ages causing my pain.*
> *You have the power to offer divine forgiveness for my*
> *mistakes in past lives and this lifetime.*
> *You have the power to heal my pain.*

I am very grateful.
I cannot thank you enough.
Dear all souls whom my ancestors and I have hurt or
*   harmed in all of our lifetimes,*
We love you, honor you, and appreciate you.
Please forgive my ancestors and me for our mistakes of
*   harming you.*
We sincerely apologize.
We cannot honor you enough.
Dear all souls who have harmed me in any of my life-
*   times,*
I love you, honor you, and appreciate you.
I forgive you completely and unconditionally.
Please accept my forgiveness.
Thank you.

Mind Power. Visualize rainbow light and rainbow liquid shining in your painful area.

Sound Power. Chant silently or aloud:

Divine Rainbow Light Ball and Divine Rainbow Liq-
*   uid Spring of Divine Love Soul Mind Body Trans-*
*   plants clear the soul mind body blockages causing*
*   my pain and heal my pain.*
All souls whom my ancestors and I have harmed,
*   please forgive us.*
Thank you, all.

Divine Rainbow Light Ball and Divine Rainbow Liq-
*   uid Spring of Divine Love Soul Mind Body Trans-*

plants clear the soul mind body blockages causing
  my pain and heal my pain.
All souls whom my ancestors and I have harmed,
  please forgive us.
Thank you, all.

Divine Rainbow Light Ball and Divine Rainbow Liq-
  uid Spring of Divine Love Soul Mind Body Trans-
  plants clear the soul mind body blockages causing
  my pain and heal my pain.
All souls whom my ancestors and I have harmed,
  please forgive us.
Thank you, all.

Divine Rainbow Light Ball and Divine Rainbow Liq-
  uid Spring of Divine Love Soul Mind Body Trans-
  plants clear the soul mind body blockages causing
  my pain and heal my pain.
All souls whom my ancestors and I have harmed,
  please forgive us.
Thank you, all.

Continue by chanting repeatedly, silently or aloud:

Divine Love clears the soul mind body blockages caus-
  ing my pain. Thank you.
Divine Love clears the soul mind body blockages caus-
  ing my pain. Thank you.
Divine Love clears the soul mind body blockages caus-
  ing my pain. Thank you.
Divine Love clears the soul mind body blockages caus-
  ing my pain. Thank you.

Divine Love clears the soul mind body blockages causing
   my pain. Thank you.
Divine Love clears the soul mind body blockages causing
   my pain. Thank you.
Divine Love clears the soul mind body blockages causing
   my pain. Thank you . . .

I really want you to do this and the other practices in this book. Please stop reading and put this book down now. Close your eyes. Chant for three to five minutes. The longer you chant and the more often you chant, the better. There is no time limit. The more you chant, the faster you will heal and the more blessings you will receive for the rest of this life and all of your future lifetimes.

For chronic and life-threatening conditions, the Divine Guidance given to me since July 2003 has been to chant for two hours or more each day. Add all of your practice time together to total at least two hours.

Close. After chanting and visualizing for at least three minutes, close the practice by saying:

> *Hao! Hao! Hao!*
> *Thank you. Thank you. Thank you.*

I first shared the Four Power Techniques in my 2002 book, *Power Healing: The Four Keys to Energizing Your Body, Mind, and Spirit*. The Four Power Techniques are treasures for self-healing and for healing others. I have just led you in a practice that applies the Four Power Techniques together with Divine Soul Mind

Body Transplants of Divine Love. The more you apply the techniques to practice, the better the results you could receive. Practice as much as you can each day to restore your health as soon as possible.

Now, I am delighted to offer the key sacred wisdom and knowledge about singing or chanting Divine Soul Songs and other divine mantras.

In my teaching, chanting is Sound Power. In ancient spiritual teaching, chanting was called *mouth secrets*. Ancient spiritual teaching also recognized *body secrets* (Body Power in my teaching) and *thinking secrets* (Mind Power in my teaching).

Ancient spiritual teaching emphasized joining mouth secrets, body secrets, and thinking secrets together as one. In my teaching, I add one more secret or "power technique": Soul Power. I emphasize that each one of the Four Power Techniques is powerful, but they are much more powerful when used together. Soul secrets, or Soul Power, is the most important secret because soul is the boss of a human being. Soul is the boss of an organization. Soul is the boss of a city. Soul is the boss of a country. Finally, the Divine is the boss for all souls in all universes.

Let me explain the secret of chanting. To chant is to repeat a special healing mantra. There are many ancient sacred mantras that have been practiced throughout history. One example is Guan Yin's six-word enlightenment mantra:

Weng Ma Ni Ba Ma Hong

Pronounced *wung mah nee bah mah hawhng*, this mantra has served millions of people throughout history by blessing their healing and life transformation for relationships, finances, and every aspect of life.

Mantras carry a special frequency and vibration of love and light to remove all kinds of blockages for healing and life transformation. The one-sentence secret of chanting mantras is:

What you chant is what you become.

Let me explain in more detail. Everyone and everything has a soul. Every word has a soul. *Weng* has a soul. *Ma* has a soul. *Ni* has a soul. *Ba* has a soul. *Ma* has a soul. *Hong* has a soul. The entire mantra, *Weng Ma Ni Ba Ma Hong*, also has a soul. When you chant *Weng Ma Ni Ba Ma Hong*, you receive blessings from all of these souls and more. Millions of people throughout history have chanted *Weng Ma Ni Ba Ma Hong*. Millions of people continue to chant this mantra. This mantra has gathered all of the love, light, compassion, peace, purity, and more of those who have chanted it. When you chant *Weng Ma Ni Ba Ma Hong*, you receive blessings from all of this. If your Third Eye is open, you can see that the soul of this mantra is huge.

To chant a mantra is to heal.

At the same time, to chant a mantra is to make a spiritual calling. When you chant *Weng Ma Ni Ba Ma Hong*, Guan Yin hears you and comes instantly to you. Countless buddhas and bodhisattvas also hear you. They too will come instantly to you. The millions and billions of souls who have chanted this mantra throughout history will come to you also. Therefore, to chant a mantra is to call and gather souls. When these great spiritual fathers and mothers come to you, they know exactly what you need, and they will help you instantly.

How much help you can receive depends upon your karma:

- If you have no bad karma, you could receive the biggest blessing right away.
- If you have a little bad karma, the souls who have gathered will help you to clear this karma and bless you quickly.
- If you have heavy bad karma, the souls who have gathered will still help you, but the benefits could be small or slow to come.
- If you have extremely heavy karma, you may not notice any benefits at all. In fact, you do receive some benefits. The blessings from the souls who have gathered will definitely clear at least part of your karma, but because your karma is extremely heavy, this may not be enough for you to feel or notice the benefits right away.

Karma is the root cause of success and failure in every aspect of life. To transform every aspect of life, you must clear bad karma first. Remember to chant from the bottom of your heart. Especially, ask sincerely for forgiveness from the people and the souls you and your ancestors have harmed in past lifetimes and in this lifetime.

Here is how to practice:

Forgiveness Practice to Self-clear Karma for Healing and Life Transformation

Body Power. Sit up straight. Put your left palm over your Message Center, also known as the heart chakra, in the middle of your chest. Hold your right hand in the traditional prayer position, with fingers pointing upward.

Soul Power. Say *hello:*

> *Dear soul mind body of Weng Ma Ni Ba Ma Hong,*
> *I love you, honor you, and appreciate you.*
> *Please heal* _____ (make your requests).
> *Please transform my relationship with* _____ (name
>   a person or persons).
> *Dear all the people, animals, and nature that my an-*
>   *cestors and I have harmed in this life and past lives,*
> *I sincerely ask for your forgiveness.*
> *Please forgive my ancestors and me.*
> *Dear anyone who has harmed me in this life and in*
>   *my previous lives,*
> *I offer you my total forgiveness.*
> *Dear Weng Ma Ni Ba Ma Hong,*
> *Please bless me.*
> *I am very grateful.*
> *Thank you. Thank you. Thank you.*

Mind Power. Visualize rainbow light radiating in all of the souls you have called, as well as in your own soul, heart, mind, and body, from head to toe and skin to bone.

Sound Power. Chant repeatedly, silently or aloud:

> *Weng Ma Ni Ba Ma Hong*
> *Weng Ma Ni Ba Ma Hong*
> *Weng Ma Ni Ba Ma Hong*
> *Weng Ma Ni Ba Ma Hong*
> *Weng Ma Ni Ba Ma Hong*

Weng Ma Ni Ba Ma Hong
Weng Ma Ni Ba Ma Hong . . .

Stop reading now. Put this book down and continue to chant *Weng Ma Ni Ba Ma Hong* nonstop for three to five minutes. Chant from the bottom of your heart with sincere apologies for all of the mistakes that you and your ancestors have made to hurt or harm any soul.

Sincerity and honesty move Heaven.

Sincerity and honesty can bring you remarkable forgiveness.

Sincerity and honesty can transform all life.

Continue to chant:

Weng Ma Ni Ba Ma Hong
Weng Ma Ni Ba Ma Hong
Weng Ma Ni Ba Ma Hong
Weng Ma Ni Ba Ma Hong
Weng Ma Ni Ba Ma Hong
Weng Ma Ni Ba Ma Hong
Weng Ma Ni Ba Ma Hong . . .

Close. After chanting for at least three minutes, close:

Hao! Hao! Hao!
Thank you. Thank you. Thank you.

While you chant, if your Third Eye is open, you could see images of your ancestors or yourself harming others in this life or in previous lives. You may see dark souls leaving your body. You may see dark energy dissipating from your body like clouds. If you have advanced spiritual abilities, you could see Guan Yin or countless buddhas and bodhisattvas sharing their virtue (spiritual flowers) with you. You may also be able to see Heaven's virtue bank open to give you and your ancestors flowers.

If you do not apologize sincerely for your mistakes, you and your ancestors could receive much less virtue. Therefore, it is extremely important to apologize sincerely before you chant. This is a very important teaching that you can use for all of the practices in this book and for your entire life. Grab these important secrets and wisdom to benefit every aspect of your life.

Chanting Benefits Every Aspect of Life

A human being could have issues in many aspects of life, including:

- physical blockages
- emotional imbalances
- mental imbalances
- spiritual blockages
- relationship challenges
- financial challenges

Chanting mantras can greatly benefit all of these issues. As I have explained, to chant is to gather spiritual fathers and mothers and, especially, the Divine to help transform any issues.

Mantras carry soul frequency and vibration with love, forgiveness, compassion, and light. Soul frequency and vibration can transform the frequency and vibration of all life.

Love melts all blockages and transforms all life.
Forgiveness brings inner joy and inner peace.

Compassion boosts energy, stamina, vitality, and
immunity.
Light heals, prevents sickness, rejuvenates, prolongs life,
and transforms relationships and finances, as well as
every aspect of life.

Spiritual beings must face spiritual testing. Why? A spiritual being desires and intends to reach enlightenment. Bad karma will block the enlightenment journey. Therefore, a spiritual being who is on the enlightenment journey must face serious karma cleansing. The spiritual journey begins with the karma cleansing journey. When facing karmic issues, the purification process could be very challenging. The spiritual testing could be very heavy. Purification leads to spiritual testing. Spiritual testing leads to more purification—when the tests are passed.

On the spiritual journey, testing can come in many forms. For example:

- You have physical health challenges.
- Your life partner does not support you, and even challenges you.
- You have other relationship challenges, financial challenges, and more.
- Your trust, confidence, persistence, determination, faith, and more are directly tested by the spiritual world.
- Your emotional balance is tested.
- Your love, care, compassion, forgiveness, patience, kindness, sincerity, honesty, integrity, and more are tested.

- You may have difficulties in any other aspect of your life when you are on the spiritual journey.

The spiritual journey is not a smooth and peaceful journey. A spiritual being could face huge challenges in many aspects of life. The key wisdom is to understand why a spiritual being who is committed to the spiritual journey could have many challenges. The root cause, as always, is bad karma. All of these challenges are part of the purification process for karma cleansing.

Bad karma goes against your spiritual journey. Bad karma blocks your spiritual journey. Bad karma can pull you back from the spiritual journey. To pass spiritual testing, chanting is one of the most important practices and methods for a spiritual being who wishes to move further on the spiritual journey and reach soul enlightenment and advanced soul enlightenment.

INFLAMMATION AND INFECTION

Inflammation and infection are common issues for humanity. They can be serious, chronic, and even life threatening.

Now I am delighted to offer the next three permanent divine treasures to you and every reader to assist in healing and transforming inflammation, infection, and more:

Divine Rainbow Light Ball and Divine Rainbow Liquid Spring of Divine Forgiveness Soul Mind Body Transplants

Prepare. Sit up straight. Put the tip of your tongue as close as you can to the roof of your mouth, without touching. Put your left palm over your Message Center or heart chakra and your right hand in the traditional prayer position, with fingers pointing upward. Totally relax. Open your heart and soul to receive this great honor. It will take about one minute for you to receive these three priceless treasures.

**Divine Order: Divine Rainbow Light Ball
and Divine Rainbow Liquid Spring of
Divine Forgiveness Soul Transplant**

Transmission!

**Divine Order: Divine Rainbow Light Ball
and Divine Rainbow Liquid Spring of
Divine Forgiveness Mind Transplant**

Transmission!

**Divine Order: Divine Rainbow Light Ball
and Divine Rainbow Liquid Spring of
Divine Forgiveness Body Transplant**

Transmission!

**Divine Order: Divine Rainbow
Light Ball and Divine Rainbow Liquid
Spring of Divine Forgiveness Soul Mind
Body Transplants join as one.**

Hei Ya Ya Ya Ya Ya Ya You!

The last line is a Divine Order in Soul Language. It can be translated as follows:

Divine Order to join Divine Rainbow Light Ball and
Divine Rainbow Liquid Spring of Divine Forgiveness
Soul Mind Body Transplants as one now.

You are extremely blessed. We cannot honor the Divine enough. Let us chant or sing *God Gives His Heart to Me* and *Thank You, Divine*:

God gives his heart to me
God gives his love to me
My heart melds with his heart
My love melds with his love

Thank you, Divine
Thank you, Divine
Thank you, Divine
Thank you, Divine
Thank you, Divine

Practice Using Divine Treasures to Heal Inflammation and Infection

Now let us apply the Four Power Techniques together with Divine Forgiveness Soul Mind Body Transplants to heal all inflammation and infection:

Body Power. Sit up straight. Put the tip of your tongue as close as you can to the roof of your mouth, without touching. Put one palm over your lower abdomen, below the navel. Put your other palm over the area of inflammation or infection.

Soul Power. Say *hello:*

> *Dear soul mind body of Divine Rainbow Light Ball*
> *and Divine Rainbow Liquid Spring of Divine For-*
> *giveness Soul Mind Body Transplants,*
> *I love you, honor you, and appreciate you.*
> *You have the power to clear the soul mind body block-*
> *ages causing my inflammation* (or *infection*).
> *You have the power to offer divine forgiveness for my*
> *mistakes in past lives and this lifetime.*
> *You have the power to heal my inflammation* (or
> *infection*).
> *I am very grateful.*
> *I cannot thank you enough.*
> *Dear all souls whom my ancestors and I have hurt or*
> *harmed in all of our lifetimes,*
> *I love you, honor you, and appreciate you.*
> *Please forgive my ancestors and me for our mistakes of*
> *harming you.*
> *I sincerely apologize.*
> *I cannot honor you enough.*
> *Dear all souls who have harmed me in any of my*
> *lifetimes,*
> *I love you, honor you, and appreciate you.*
> *I forgive you completely and unconditionally.*
> *Please accept my forgiveness.*
> *Thank you.*

This is a divine forgiveness practice. Ask the souls whom your ancestors and you have harmed in all lifetimes to forgive you. At the same time, forgive all of the souls who have harmed you in all lifetimes.

Mind Power. Visualize rainbow light and rainbow liquid shining in your area of inflammation or infection.

Sound Power. Chant silently or aloud:

> *Divine Rainbow Light Ball and Divine Rainbow Liquid Spring of Divine Forgiveness Soul Mind Body Transplants clear the soul mind body blockages causing my inflammation* (or *infection*) *and heal my inflammation* (or *infection*).
> *All souls whom my ancestors and I have harmed, please forgive us.*
> *Thank you, all.*

> *Divine Rainbow Light Ball and Divine Rainbow Liquid Spring of Divine Forgiveness Soul Mind Body Transplants clear the soul mind body blockages causing my inflammation* (or *infection*) *and heal my inflammation* (or *infection*).
> *All souls whom my ancestors and I have harmed, please forgive us.*
> *Thank you, all.*

> *Divine Rainbow Light Ball and Divine Rainbow Liquid Spring of Divine Forgiveness Soul Mind Body Transplants clear the soul mind body blockages caus-*

ing my inflammation (or *infection*) *and heal my in-*
flammation (or *infection*).
All souls whom my ancestors and I have harmed,
    please forgive us.
Thank you, all.

Divine Rainbow Light Ball and Divine Rainbow Liq-
    uid Spring of Divine Forgiveness Soul Mind Body
    Transplants clear the soul mind body blockages caus-
    ing my inflammation (or *infection*) *and heal my in-*
    flammation (or *infection*).
All souls whom my ancestors and I have harmed,
    please forgive us.
Thank you, all.

Continue by chanting repeatedly, silently or aloud:

Divine Forgiveness clears the soul mind body blockages
    causing my inflammation (or *infection*). *Thank you.*
Divine Forgiveness clears the soul mind body blockages
    causing my inflammation (or *infection*). *Thank you.*
Divine Forgiveness clears the soul mind body blockages
    causing my inflammation (or *infection*). *Thank you.*
Divine Forgiveness clears the soul mind body blockages
    causing my inflammation (or *infection*). *Thank you.*
Divine Forgiveness clears the soul mind body blockages
    causing my inflammation (or *infection*). *Thank you.*
Divine Forgiveness clears the soul mind body blockages
    causing my inflammation (or *infection*). *Thank you.*
Divine Forgiveness clears the soul mind body blockages
    causing my inflammation (or *infection*). *Thank*
    you . . .

Please stop reading and put this book down now. Close your eyes. Chant for three to five minutes.

Close. After chanting for at least three minutes, close:

> *Hao! Hao! Hao!*
> *Thank you. Thank you. Thank you.*

The longer you chant and the more often you chant, the better. There is no time limit. The more you chant, the faster you will heal and the more blessings you will receive for the rest of this life and all of your future lifetimes.

For chronic and life-threatening conditions, chant for a total of at least two hours a day. The more you do this practice, the better the results you could receive. Practice as much as you can to restore your health as soon as possible.

GROWTHS, INCLUDING CYSTS, TUMORS, AND CANCER

Cancer is frequently a life-threatening illness. Everyone knows a family member, loved one, friend, or colleague who has suffered from cancer.

Now I am delighted to offer the seventh, eighth, and ninth permanent divine treasures in this book to you and every reader to offer divine transformation of cancer, tumors, and cysts by clearing bad karma that is their root cause:

Divine Rainbow Light Ball and Divine Rainbow Liquid Spring of Divine Compassion Soul Mind Body Transplants

Prepare. Sit up straight. Put the tip of your tongue as close as you can to the roof of your mouth, without touching. Put your hands in the Soul Light Era Prayer Position, with your left palm over your Message Center or heart chakra and your right hand in the traditional prayer position, with fingers pointing upward. Totally relax. Open your heart and soul to receive this great honor. It will take about one minute for you to receive these three priceless treasures.

**Divine Order: Divine Rainbow Light Ball
and Divine Rainbow Liquid Spring of
Divine Compassion Soul Transplant**

Transmission!

**Divine Order: Divine Rainbow Light Ball
and Divine Rainbow Liquid Spring of
Divine Compassion Mind Transplant**

Transmission!

**Divine Order: Divine Rainbow Light Ball
and Divine Rainbow Liquid Spring of
Divine Compassion Body Transplant**

Transmission!

**Divine Order: Divine Rainbow Light Ball
and Divine Rainbow Liquid Spring of
Divine Compassion Soul Mind Body
Transplants join as one.**

Hei Ya Ya Ya Ya Ya Ya You!

The last line is a Divine Order in Soul Language. It can be translated as follows:

Divine Order to join Divine Rainbow Light Ball and
Divine Rainbow Liquid Spring of Divine Compassion
Soul Mind Body Transplants as one now.

You are extremely blessed. We cannot honor the Divine enough. Let us chant or sing *God Gives His Heart to Me*:

God gives his heart to me
God gives his love to me
My heart melds with his heart
My love melds with his love

Practice Using Divine Treasures to Heal Growths,
Including Cysts, Tumors, and Cancer

Now let us apply the Four Power Techniques together with Divine Compassion Soul Mind Body Transplants to heal growths of any kind, including cysts, benign and malignant tumors, and cancer:

Body Power. Sit up straight. Put the tip of your tongue as close as you can to the roof of your mouth, without touching. Put one palm over your lower abdomen, below the navel. Put your other palm over the cyst, tumor, or cancerous area.

Soul Power. Say *hello*:

Dear soul mind body of Divine Rainbow Light Ball
and Divine Rainbow Liquid Spring of Divine
Compassion Soul Mind Body Transplants,

I love you, honor you, and appreciate you.
You have the power to clear the soul mind body block-
   ages causing my growth(s) (specify the details of
   your cyst[s], tumor[s], or cancer).
You have the power to offer divine forgiveness for my
   mistakes in past lives and this lifetime.
You have the power to heal my growth(s) (specify the
   details).
I am very grateful.
I cannot thank you enough.
Dear all souls whom my ancestors and I have hurt or
   harmed in all of our lifetimes,
I love you, honor you, and appreciate you.
Please forgive my ancestors and me for our mistakes of
   harming you.
I sincerely apologize.
I cannot honor you enough.
Dear all souls who have harmed me in any of my
   lifetimes,
I love you, honor you, and appreciate you.
I forgive you completely and unconditionally.
Please accept my forgiveness.
Thank you.

Mind Power. Visualize rainbow light and rainbow liquid shining in and around your growth(s).

Sound Power. Chant repeatedly, silently or aloud:

Divine Rainbow Light Ball and Divine Rainbow Liquid Spring of Divine Compassion Soul Mind Body

Transplants clear the soul mind body blockages caus-
ing my growth(s) and heal my growth(s).
All souls whom my ancestors and I have harmed,
please forgive us.
Thank you, all.

Divine Rainbow Light Ball and Divine Rainbow
Liquid Spring of Divine Compassion Soul Mind
Body Transplants clear the soul mind body
blockages causing my growth(s) and heal my
growth(s).
All souls whom my ancestors and I have harmed,
please forgive us.
Thank you, all.

Divine Rainbow Light Ball and Divine Rainbow
Liquid Spring of Divine Compassion Soul Mind
Body Transplants clear the soul mind body
blockages causing my growth(s) and heal my
growth(s).
All souls whom my ancestors and I have harmed,
please forgive us.
Thank you, all.

Divine Rainbow Light Ball and Divine Rainbow Liq-
uid Spring of Divine Compassion Soul Mind Body
Transplants clear the soul mind body blockages caus-
ing my growth(s) and heal my growth(s).
All souls whom my ancestors and I have harmed,
please forgive us.
Thank you, all.

Continue by chanting repeatedly, silently or aloud:

> *Divine Compassion clears the soul mind body block-*
> *ages causing my growth(s). Thank you.*
> *Divine Compassion clears the soul mind body block-*
> *ages causing my growth(s). Thank you.*
> *Divine Compassion clears the soul mind body block-*
> *ages causing my growth(s). Thank you.*
> *Divine Compassion clears the soul mind body block-*
> *ages causing my growth(s). Thank you.*
> *Divine Compassion clears the soul mind body block-*
> *ages causing my growth(s). Thank you.*
> *Divine Compassion clears the soul mind body block-*
> *ages causing my growth(s). Thank you.*
> *Divine Compassion clears the soul mind body block-*
> *ages causing my growth(s). Thank you . . .*

Please stop reading and put this book down now. Close your eyes. Chant for three to five minutes.

Close. After chanting for at least three minutes, close:

> *Hao! Hao! Hao!*
> *Thank you. Thank you. Thank you.*

The longer you chant and the more often you chant, the better. There is no time limit. The more you chant, the faster you will heal and the more blessings you will receive for the rest of this life and all of your future lifetimes.

For chronic and life-threatening conditions such as cancer, chant for a total of at least two hours a day. The more you do this practice, the better the results you could receive. Practice as much as you can to restore your health as soon as possible.

We have received hundreds of stories of transformation of chronic and life-threatening conditions from receiving Divine Karma Cleansing and from applying divine and Tao treasures and chanting. Remember my teaching: one must practice a lot to receive the greatest benefit.

I am delighted to share the following two heart-touching stories with you.

THE GREATEST CHALLENGE I HAVE FACED IN THIS LIFETIME

On October 2, 2009, I was diagnosed by ultrasound with two tumors in my bladder, each 3.5 cm in size. These were later confirmed by CT scan.

On November 30, 2009, I had surgery to remove the tumors. I went home right after the surgery, even though one normally spends two days in recovery because of bleeding. So that I would not be alarmed, the doctor warned me that I was going to bleed. After just two hours at home, I started to bleed heavily. Suddenly I couldn't even lift my head to get out of bed. In desperation, I started praying and doing soul healing on myself. Nothing worked. I started thinking if I don't do something soon, I am going to die. I looked around for some guidance and I saw Master Sha's book Divine Soul Mind Body Healing and Transmission System *by my bed. Master Sha had taught me to place the book on my Message Center (heart chakra) for healing, so I grabbed the book, but I was so weak, I couldn't lift it. I touched Master Sha's picture on the back of the book and said,*

"*Master Sha, please stop the bleeding, or I am going to die.*" *I lost consciousness completely.*

I awoke three and one half hours later, totally rested and without any bleeding whatsoever. It was around five o'clock in the morning and I decided to go to the hospital to tell my doctor what had happened. He couldn't believe I was walking around without any bleeding at all.

On January 23, 2010, I had a second operation to clear any trace of tumor left from the first operation. One week later, on January 30, 2010, I was given terrible news. My doctor said, "I am so sorry, but your cancer is not aggressive; it is super *aggressive, and you have developed a third tumor in less than two months." The doctor told me that the bladder must be removed as soon as possible, otherwise I might lose my sexual organs and my life. I was speechless, disoriented, and totally shocked. I asked for alternatives. He said there was one, which was to place a weak bacteria in the bladder to trigger my immune system to attack the cancer cells. When I asked what the statistics were for this option, he said that there were none at this time. Complications of this procedure are that the bacteria could spread to the rest of the body, causing death. I couldn't believe what I was hearing. I told the doctor that I had to think about it because at that point I couldn't make a decision about treatment. He warned me that there was very little time to wait for the operation to remove the bladder to be successful.*

In despair, I called Master Sha for help. I was driving, feeling very happy because I had just served someone in great need of healing (and with wonderful results) when Master Sha returned my call. Master Sha told me that I had very high-level karma, and that he couldn't help me right away. Hearing this, my heart almost stopped at that moment. I asked Master Sha for a blessing for my immune sys-

tem, which he did immediately. I felt the rush of light going through my entire body, especially in my bladder. I knew this would help me a lot. Master Sha told me to attend the upcoming Soul Healing Week in Toronto, Canada, and that he would help me. The Divine uplifted Master Sha's soul standing before the Soul Healing Week, and he offered me high-level Divine Karma Cleansing during his Sunday Divine Blessings teleconference on March 14, 2010. I was looking for a miracle.

This high-level Divine Karma Cleansing was amazing and mind-blowing. With my Third Eye, I saw lots of dark souls leave my bladder and body. Then Master Sha offered me a Tao Soul Transplant for Bladder to replace the old soul of my bladder, which was extremely tired. In addition, Master Sha offered me Tao Cell Package to replace all the old cell souls of my bladder. This was the most delightful experience to see and feel this incredible light coming to me. My body was like a Christmas tree—full of light.

The next day I found myself running for the first time in six months. I hadn't dared to do any exercise. I felt like a child, so happy and free. My beloved teacher and spiritual father, Master Sha, offered me additional healing and blessing for three straight days during the Soul Healing Week. I was so grateful and honored for his generosity and love.

I went home and continued eating properly. I also started listening to Master Sha's CDs twenty-four hours a day, seven days a week, and drinking lots of water. I used a natural product applied directly to my bladder because I received this message by Divine Guidance directly. By the end of March, the cancer started coming out of me through my urine. I was shocked to see what was coming out of me every day for several days.

Then I received a direct soul communication from the cancer itself. The cancer told me, "I am ready to leave." I was in tears. I was full of gratitude and love. Our beloved teacher, Master Sha, has taught us that love melts all blockages. I asked the cancer, "How can I help you to leave faster?" It answered, "Don't rush me; I will go at my own pace. Just relax." Full of gratitude and love, I thanked the cancer for all the teaching and awakening it brought to my life.

Five days later, there was no more matter in my urine so I requested my doctor do an ultrasound to check for any tumors. On April 15, 2010, I got the incredible news that there were no tumors, no thickening, nor any trace of the two operations. The doctor said that my bladder looked like a baby's bladder—totally perfect. The doctor started shouting on the phone, "This is a miracle! This is a miracle!" I knew it was.

The miracle's name is Divine Karma Cleansing. I cannot thank enough my most beloved spiritual teacher and master, Master Sha, for his unconditional love. He is a true example of what it is to be a Total GOLD (gratitude, obedience, loyalty, and devotion to the Divine) servant. Without Master Sha's assistance and teachings, I would not be here to share this story with you today so you also can benefit from my beloved Master Sha's incredible blessings and teachings based on love, gratitude, forgiveness, and so much more.

I am committing my life to serve, to teach, and to assist all those in need, with all my heart and soul, until my last breath.

With love and gratitude,

Marcelo Celis
Los Angeles, California

HEALING MY STAGE IV CANCER

My name is Marsha Valutis. In the beginning of August 2009, I was introduced to Patricia Smith, a Worldwide Representative of Master Zhi Gang Sha. At that time, I was depressed and needed help. I had been on a spiritual path for several years and had previously healed from devastating circumstances, including deep depression and severe illness, but this time I was in a very low vibration and felt I did not have the inner strength to do it again. I was far removed from my spiritual practices, deeply depressed, and unmotivated to do anything but find a way out. I was completely focused on suicide.

At the end of August, at Patricia's suggestion, I went to the hospital for my depression. I only got worse news: I had lymphoma in my stomach. I got this diagnosis on September 9, 2009. A little later it was confirmed to be at stage IV by bone marrow biopsy.

While in the hospital, I tapped on Master Sha's book, The Power of Soul, *as Patricia guided me to do. I was in a very depressed state and wondered how I would deal with these circumstances. I had no income and no health insurance. I had hoped the cancer would be terminal, but it was treatable with chemotherapy. I continued to call Patricia, and she continued to encourage me to chant.*

I postponed chemotherapy and began chanting. I joined many of the daily chanting practice teleconferences offered by the Institute of Soul Healing and Enlightenment and Master Sha. As quickly as possible, I received a Divine Soul Mind Body Healing and Transmission System for Cancer and Depression from Master Sha in his Sunday Divine Blessings teleconference. I followed the instructions to chant for many hours a day. In addition to my divine treasures, I chanted the Divine Soul Songs Love, Peace and Harmony, God Gives His Heart to Me, Divine Soul Song of Yin Yang, *and* Divine Soul

Song of Five Elements, *as they were a part of each group practice session I joined.*

Upon doing this regular practice, my mood improved significantly. Within weeks, life was beautiful again, despite my health and financial issues. I chanted everywhere: on my walks, in the store, and in the doctors' offices and hospitals. I also practiced forgiveness almost every day, and at specific times when I knew it was needed. I experienced some extremely heartfelt moments of great healing while doing forgiveness practices.

In November 2009, I participated via webcast in Master Sha's Soul Healing and Enlightenment Retreat and Divine Rejuvenation Retreat from the Big Island of Hawaii. I received many blessings, including a Divine Order for Soul Enlightenment, personal karma cleansing, and other gifts and Divine Soul Downloads offered at these retreats, including higher-level Divine Soul Mind Body Healing and Transmission Systems for both cancer and depression. It was an incredible experience. I knew I was transforming at very deep levels.

Immediately after the retreats, life became somewhat bumpy and challenging. I had many practical and spiritual issues to deal with, and strong mind-sets. I continued to work with Patricia Smith, who compassionately introduced my case to Master Sha in mid-December. Master Sha generously blessed me and my condition again, cleansing my ancestral karma and giving very high-level Divine Soul Mind Body Transplants for all major Five Element yin organs (liver, heart, spleen, lungs, and kidneys) and my immune system. The honor fee for these priceless blessings was incredibly modest. I was extremely blessed!

I continued my practices. The pain actually became worse, to the point of being intolerable. As the spiritual and mental blockages were being removed quickly, it seemed that the energy and matter block-ages were really pushing hard. Like a powerful, rushing river hitting a dam, energy was moving up against the tumor site, creating great pain. At the beginning of 2010, I was hospitalized for pain man-agement. I continued to chant and do the practices I learned from Master Sha and his teachers and, once again, Master Sha blessed me, boosting my Lower Dan Tian and downloading a Divine Light Wall to protect me from dark souls. I believe he also gave a Divine Order to remove my negative mind-sets. I felt deeply blessed.

While in the hospital, a doctor recommended that I take a "non-toxic" drug therapy to assist with reducing the pain and tumor size, and to "keep the cancer at bay." I felt good about this choice and, after consulting with Patricia, I began this hospital treatment on January 3, 2010. I returned weekly for an infusion until February 22, 2010. Meanwhile, I learned and practiced creative ways to use my Divine Soul Downloads to heal and bless others while I was there, and to promote the highest healing and harmony with my own treat-ments by invoking and blessing all the souls involved. For example, one day the nurse had a hard time starting my intravenous. I prayed and did a soul conference with her, the needles, tubing, medicine, and my veins, asking them to work in harmony for my healing. Fi-nally, after several attempts, she apologized and a well of emotion within me opened. I had been through this process so often in my life, with no conscious regard given to my body or my beloved veins. It was a beautiful opportunity. We took a break, and then together we spoke to my veins. The needle slid right in.

I became very grateful to the infusions. They participated in my healing by reducing the tumor size and the pain, allowing me to practice more. After my last infusion, I continued to practice. I found alternating between sitting and moving practice to be pow-

erful. Singing the Divine Soul Songs of Yin Yang and Five Ele-
ments while sitting, followed by either freestyle Soul Song or singing
Love, Peace and Harmony *while doing Soul Movement was quite*
effective. Blockages were removed continuously. I am very sensitive
to this feeling, and found it very inspiring. Sometimes I could not
stop the Soul Song singing and Soul Movement because the releases
felt so good, and I would continue way past my bedtime! Soon, I
set my sights on completing the Soul Song and Soul Dance Healer
Certification Program, and wanted to join Master Sha in person in
Toronto in March for his Soul Song Soul Dance Healer Certification
Retreat.

One day after practicing, I noticed discomfort in my stomach and
spleen. I sat up, paying very close attention to this area and began
talking to it and all the souls there. I sensed a knot involving more
than the cancerous growth, including scar tissue from previous surger-
ies, adhesions, and blockages. I spoke to all of them, giving them my
deepest love and affection, and turned on my divine treasures, asking
them to give their greatest love, light, compassion, and forgiveness to
these souls. While I was deeply connected with them, I told them it
was okay to be well, and asked them to unravel themselves and to be
free. A clear feeling of willingness and surrender came over me, and
I witnessed within my being the literal and figurative unraveling of
this blockage. In gratitude, I continued my connection to these souls.
There was great relief and joy as the healing occurred. There was a
space inside that I hadn't felt in a very long time; maybe never. The
blockage was gone!

This was about a week before my trip to Toronto for the Soul
Song Soul Dance Healer Certification Retreat. The day before I left,
I had a CT scan. While in Toronto, Master Sha gave me more huge
blessings, including high-level Divine Karma Cleansing and a new

level of healing for cancer. Upon my return home, I learned that the CT scan results were completely normal.

I had healed from serious circumstances in the past by using spiritual practices and disciplines but with Master Sha, I healed from life-threatening cancer and depression more easily and much more enjoyably. I was spending my days joyfully singing Soul Song and doing Soul Dance!

Yes, there were tough times. It took effort, commitment, and willingness to open myself to love—divine love. Master Sha's methods create this openness to love, whether one is conscious of it or not. This is a significant point: Master Sha's techniques bypass the ego and transform it at the same time! Truly, the ego is not in charge when one chooses to receive and invoke divine treasures and sing Soul Songs much of the day to heal and bless. And when our karma is cleansed through Master Sha, the way is made much easier. The Divine has forgiven and paid our debt. Our job is to honor the Divine and serve unconditionally. A brilliant aspect of this healing approach is that we are given so many wonderful ways to serve and to maintain and elevate our frequency and vibration so that we can see and make new and better choices. If we don't do this, we can easily fall back into the same karmic patterns. We still have the responsibility to learn our lessons.

Here is a summary of the practices I did to heal stage IV lymphoma:

- in-depth daily morning invocation (soul conference) with all realms of the Divine, Master Sha, my Heaven's Team, my body soul, all the souls, minds, and bodies in my being, all divine treasures downloaded on my soul, all Divine Soul Songs and mantras, all divine treasures downloaded to anyone and anything on Mother Earth, the soul of my cancer, and more, followed by singing

Soul Song for five minutes to honor my prayer and my requests

- *two to five one-hour teleconference practice (chanting) sessions a day, five days a week*
- *regular forgiveness practice, and spontaneous forgiveness practices as needed*
- *sing Divine Soul Song* Love, Peace and Harmony *for one to three hours at a time*
- *alternate sitting practices with moving practices*
- *sing Divine Soul Songs and my own Soul Song while doing Soul Movement*
- *regularly communicate with my inner souls and the soul of my cancer*
- *Soul Orders*
- *regular sessions with teacher and healer Patricia Smith, a Worldwide Representative of Master Sha*
- *participate in all Institute of Soul Healing and Enlightenment offerings, including Saturday Free Soul Healing Blessings for Humanity and Sunday Divine Blessings*
- *evening prayer and invocation before bedtime*
- *invoke Master Sha's books to heal and bless me as I slept*

On my knees, I thank you Tao, Divine, and Master Sha for these services, practices, blessings, and treasures. I can never thank you enough. I can never bow down enough.

Marsha Valutis, PhD
Melbourne, Florida

Self-heal Your Emotional Body, Including Self-clearing Your Karma (Soul Blockages), Mind Blockages, and Body Blockages

Five Elements theory has guided the practice of traditional Chinese medicine for five thousand years. The five elements are Wood, Fire, Earth, Metal, and Water.

The Wood element includes the liver, gallbladder, eyes, and tendons, and anger in the emotional body.

The Fire element includes the heart, small intestine, tongue, and blood vessels, and depression and anxiety in the emotional body.

The Earth element includes the spleen, stomach, mouth and lips, gums and teeth, and muscles, and worry in the emotional body.

The Metal element includes the lungs, large intestine, nose, and skin, and grief and sadness in the emotional body.

The Water element includes the kidneys, urinary bladder, ears, and bones, and fear in the emotional body.

Anger, depression, anxiety, worry, grief, sadness, and fear have been addressed by traditional Chinese medicine for five thousand years. They are major emotional imbalances for humanity. The connection between the emotional body and the physical body has always been understood and used in diagnosis and treatment by traditional Chinese medicine. This connection is shown clearly by the various organs, tissues, and unbalanced emotions belonging to each of the Five Elements.

For soul healing of emotions, I have shared this divine wisdom in my previous books:

In order to balance all emotions, the Message Center is the key area of the body.

The Message Center is one of the most important spiritual centers in a human being. It is the center for soul communication, soul healing, emotions, karma, life transformation, and soul enlightenment.

Because the Message Center is the soul communication center, it carries the messages of the whole body, including the messages of the emotions. To balance the Message Center is to balance the emotions.

Next I will offer another three major permanent divine treasures:

Divine Rainbow Light Ball and Divine Rainbow Liquid Spring of Divine Light Soul Mind Body Transplants

Divine light can heal, prevent sickness, purify and rejuvenate the soul, heart, mind, and body, prolong life, and transform every aspect of life, including relationships and finances. The power of these three divine treasures cannot be explained enough. I wish you and humanity would really pay attention to these and all other priceless divine treasures. I am extremely honored to be a servant of humanity and the Divine to offer these extremely powerful treasures to humanity. I cannot honor the Divine enough for divine love, forgiveness, compassion, light, generosity, and kindness.

I would like to remind you and everyone who has received these divine treasures to always be grateful. We are so blessed. These Divine Soul Mind Body Transplants can heal, protect, and transform every aspect of life. They can literally save life.

Now prepare to receive the tenth, eleventh, and twelfth permanent divine treasures offered to you and every reader of this book. Sit up straight. Put the tip of your tongue as close as you can to the roof of your mouth, without touching. Put your left palm over your Message Center and your right hand in the traditional prayer position. Totally relax. Open your heart and soul to receive this great honor. It will take about one minute for you to receive these three priceless treasures.

**Divine Order: Divine Rainbow Light Ball
and Divine Rainbow Liquid Spring of
Divine Light Soul Transplant**

Transmission!

**Divine Order: Divine Rainbow Light Ball
and Divine Rainbow Liquid Spring of
Divine Light Mind Transplant**

Transmission!

**Divine Order: Divine Rainbow Light Ball
and Divine Rainbow Liquid Spring of
Divine Light Body Transplant**

Transmission!

**Divine Order: Divine Rainbow Light Ball and
Divine Rainbow Liquid Spring of Divine Light
Soul Mind Body Transplants join as one.**

Hei Ya Ya Ya Ya Ya You!

The last words in Soul Language can be translated as follows:

> *Divine Order to join Divine Rainbow Light Ball*
> *and Divine Rainbow Liquid Spring of Divine Light*
> *Soul Mind Body Transplants as one now.*

You are extremely blessed. We cannot honor the Divine enough. Let us chant or sing *Thank You, Divine* to express our greatest gratitude:

> *Thank you, Divine*
> *Thank you, Divine*
> *Thank you, Divine*
> *Thank you, Divine*
> *Thank you, Divine*

Practice Using Divine Treasures to Heal the Emotional Body

Now let us apply the Four Power Techniques together with Divine Light Soul Mind Body Transplants to balance and heal the unbalanced emotions of anger, depression, anxiety, worry, grief, sadness, fear, and more:

Body Power. Sit up straight. Put one palm over your Message Center. Put your other palm over the major yin organ (liver, heart, spleen, lung, or kidney) associated with the emotion you wish to balance.

Soul Power. Say *hello:*

> *Dear soul mind body of Divine Rainbow Light Ball*
> *and Divine Rainbow Liquid Spring of Divine Light*
> *Soul Mind Body Transplants,*

I love you, honor you, and appreciate you.
You have the power to clear the soul mind body block-
　　ages causing my unbalanced emotion of _____
　　(name the emotion you want to balance).
You have the power to offer divine forgiveness for my
　　mistakes in past lives and this lifetime.
You have the power to balance and heal my _____
　　(name the emotion again).
I am very grateful.
I cannot thank you enough.
Dear all souls whom my ancestors and I have hurt or
　　harmed in all of our lifetimes,
I love you, honor you, and appreciate you.
Please forgive my ancestors and me for our mistakes of
　　harming you.
I sincerely apologize.
I cannot honor you enough.
Dear all souls who have harmed me in any of my
　　lifetimes,
I love you, honor you, and appreciate you.
I forgive you completely and unconditionally.
Please accept my forgiveness.
Thank you.

Mind Power. Visualize rainbow light and rainbow liquid shining in your Message Center.

Sound Power. Chant silently or aloud:

　　Divine Rainbow Light Ball and Divine Rainbow Liq-
　　uid Spring of Divine Light Soul Mind Body Trans-

plants clear the soul mind body blockages causing
  my unbalanced emotion of _____ and balance
  and heal my _____ (repeat the name of the
  emotion).
All souls whom my ancestors and I have harmed,
  please forgive us.
Thank you, all.

Divine Rainbow Light Ball and Divine Rainbow Liq-
  uid Spring of Divine Light Soul Mind Body Trans-
  plants clear the soul mind body blockages causing
  my unbalanced emotion of _____ and balance
  and heal my _____.
All souls whom my ancestors and I have harmed,
  please forgive us.
Thank you, all.

Divine Rainbow Light Ball and Divine Rainbow Liq-
  uid Spring of Divine Light Soul Mind Body Trans-
  plants clear the soul mind body blockages causing
  my unbalanced emotion of _____ and balance
  and heal my _____.
All souls whom my ancestors and I have harmed,
  please forgive us.
Thank you, all.

Divine Rainbow Light Ball and Divine Rainbow Liq-
  uid Spring of Divine Light Soul Mind Body Trans-
  plants clear the soul mind body blockages causing
  my unbalanced emotion of _____ and balance
  and heal my _____.

All souls whom my ancestors and I have harmed,
*   please forgive us.*
Thank you, all.

Continue by chanting repeatedly, silently or aloud:

Divine Light clears the soul mind body blockages
*   causing my _____ (name the emotion again).*
Thank you.
Divine Light clears the soul mind body blockages caus-
*   ing my _____. Thank you.*
Divine Light clears the soul mind body blockages caus-
*   ing my _____. Thank you.*
Divine Light clears the soul mind body blockages caus-
*   ing my _____. Thank you.*
Divine Light clears the soul mind body blockages caus-
*   ing my _____. Thank you.*
Divine Light clears the soul mind body blockages caus-
*   ing my _____. Thank you.*
Divine Light clears the soul mind body blockages caus-
*   ing my _____. Thank you . . .*

Please stop reading and put this book down now. Close your eyes. Chant for three to five minutes.

Close. After chanting for at least three minutes, close:

Hao! Hao! Hao!
Thank you. Thank you. Thank you.

The longer you chant and the more often you chant, the better. There is no time limit. The more you chant, the faster you will heal and the more blessings you will receive for the rest of this life and all of your future lifetimes.

For serious and chronic emotional imbalances such as severe depression, chant for a total of at least two hours a day. The more you do this practice, the better the results you could receive. Practice as much as you can to restore your health as soon as possible.

In fact, you can apply divine treasures to balance and heal all of your unbalanced emotions in one practice. Here is how:

Body Power. Sit up straight. Put your hands in the Soul Light Era Prayer Position.

Soul Power. Say *hello:*

> *Dear soul mind body of Divine Rainbow Light Ball*
> *and Divine Rainbow Liquid Spring of Divine Love,*
> *Divine Forgiveness, Divine Compassion, and Di-*
> *vine Light Soul Mind Body Transplants,*
> *I love you, honor you, and appreciate you.*
> *You have the power to clear the soul mind body block-*
> *ages causing all of my unbalanced emotions, includ-*
> *ing anger, depression, anxiety, worry, grief, sadness,*
> *fear, guilt, and more.*
> *You have the power to offer divine forgiveness for my*
> *mistakes in past lives and this lifetime.*
> *You have the power to balance and heal all of my emo-*
> *tions.*

I am very grateful.
I cannot thank you enough.
Dear all souls whom my ancestors and I have hurt or
*   harmed in all of our lifetimes,*
I love you, honor you, and appreciate you.
Please forgive my ancestors and me for our mistakes of
*   harming you.*
I sincerely apologize.
I cannot honor you enough.
Dear all souls who have harmed me in any of my life-
*   times,*
I love you, honor you, and appreciate you.
I forgive you completely and unconditionally.
Please accept my forgiveness.
Thank you.

Mind Power. Visualize rainbow light and rainbow liquid shining in you from head to toe, skin to bone, including your emotional body.

Sound Power. Chant silently or aloud:

Divine Rainbow Light Ball and Divine Rainbow Liq-
*   uid Spring of Divine Love, Divine Forgiveness, Di-*
*   vine Compassion, and Divine Light Soul Mind*
*   Body Transplants clear the soul mind body blockages*
*   causing my unbalanced emotions and balance and*
*   heal all of my emotions.*
All souls whom my ancestors and I have harmed,
*   please forgive us.*
Thank you, all.

Divine Rainbow Light Ball and Divine Rainbow Liquid Spring of Divine Love, Divine Forgiveness, Divine Compassion, and Divine Light Soul Mind Body Transplants clear the soul mind body blockages causing my unbalanced emotions and balance and heal all of my emotions.
All souls whom my ancestors and I have harmed, please forgive us.
Thank you, all.

Divine Rainbow Light Ball and Divine Rainbow Liquid Spring of Divine Love, Divine Forgiveness, Divine Compassion, and Divine Light Soul Mind Body Transplants clear the soul mind body blockages causing my unbalanced emotions and balance and heal all of my emotions.
All souls whom my ancestors and I have harmed, please forgive us.
Thank you, all.

Divine Rainbow Light Ball and Divine Rainbow Liquid Spring of Divine Love, Divine Forgiveness, Divine Compassion, and Divine Light Soul Mind Body Transplants clear the soul mind body blockages causing my unbalanced emotions and balance and heal all of my emotions.
All souls whom my ancestors and I have harmed, please forgive us.
Thank you, all.

Continue by chanting repeatedly, silently or aloud:

*Divine Love, Forgiveness, Compassion, and Light clear
the soul mind body blockages causing my unbalanced emotions. Thank you.*

*Divine Love, Forgiveness, Compassion, and Light clear
the soul mind body blockages causing my unbalanced emotions. Thank you.*

*Divine Love, Forgiveness, Compassion, and Light clear
the soul mind body blockages causing my unbalanced emotions. Thank you.*

*Divine Love, Forgiveness, Compassion, and Light clear
the soul mind body blockages causing my unbalanced emotions. Thank you.*

*Divine Love, Forgiveness, Compassion, and Light clear
the soul mind body blockages causing my unbalanced emotions. Thank you.*

*Divine Love, Forgiveness, Compassion, and Light clear
the soul mind body blockages causing my unbalanced emotions. Thank you.*

*Divine Love, Forgiveness, Compassion, and Light clear
the soul mind body blockages causing my unbalanced emotions. Thank you . . .*

Please stop reading and put this book down now. Close your
eyes. Chant for three to five minutes.

Close. After chanting for at least three minutes, close:

Hao! Hao! Hao!
Thank you. Thank you. Thank you.

The longer you chant and the more often you chant, the better. There is no time limit. The more you chant, the faster you

will heal and the more blessings you will receive for the rest of this life and all of your future lifetimes.

For serious and chronic emotional imbalances such as paralyzing phobias, chant for a total of at least two hours a day. The more you do this practice, the better the results you could receive. Practice as much as you can to restore health in your emotional body as soon as possible.

Self-heal Your Mental Body,
Including Self-clearing Your Karma (Soul Blockages),
Mind Blockages, and Body Blockages

Mental conditions include mental confusion, poor concentration, loss of memory, obsessive-compulsive disorder, Alzheimer's disease, bipolar disorder, other serious mental disorders, and more.

If you killed, harmed, took advantage of others, cheated, or stole in your past or present lifetimes, any of these actions and behaviors could be the cause of mental conditions in this lifetime. It doesn't matter what the action or behavior was. The vital wisdom is that bad karma is the root blockage causing mental conditions.

To self-heal mental conditions, you must first self-clear bad karma to remove the root blockage causing your mental condition. As you have already learned and experienced, in this book I offer you divine treasures and practical techniques to self-clear karma.

Remember that you have the power to self-clear karma without any other assistance. However, divine treasures can give you great help to self-clear karma. The forgiveness practice that I have included in most of the practices in this book (specifically, asking the souls that your ancestors and you have harmed in your past and present lifetimes to forgive your mistakes) can also greatly help you self-clear karma. The divine way to self-clear bad karma is to apply divine treasures together with the forgiveness practice.

It is vital to ask for forgiveness *sincerely.* Apologize to the souls you have hurt or harmed sincerely. Sincerity moves Heaven. Sincerity moves the souls you are asking. You can receive remarkable results if you apologize sincerely.

Now prepare to receive the thirteenth, fourteenth, and fifteenth permanent divine treasures offered to you and every reader of this book:

Divine Rainbow Light Ball and Rainbow Liquid Spring of Divine Sincerity Soul Mind Body Transplants

Sit up straight. Put the tip of your tongue as close as you can to the roof of your mouth, without touching. Put your left palm over your Message Center and your right hand in the traditional prayer position. Totally relax. Open your heart and soul to receive this great honor. It will take about one minute for you to receive these three priceless treasures.

Divine Order: Divine Rainbow Light Ball and Divine Rainbow Liquid Spring of Divine Sincerity Soul Transplant

Transmission!

Divine Order: Divine Rainbow Light Ball and Divine Rainbow Liquid Spring of Divine Sincerity Mind Transplant

Transmission!

**Divine Order: Divine Rainbow Light Ball
and Divine Rainbow Liquid Spring of
Divine Sincerity Body Transplant**

Transmission!

**Divine Order: Divine Rainbow Light Ball and
Divine Rainbow Liquid Spring of Divine Sincerity
Soul Mind Body Transplants join as one.**

Hei Ya Ya Ya Ya Ya Ya You!

The Soul Language in the last Divine Order can be translated as follows:

*Divine Order to join Divine Rainbow Light Ball and
Divine Rainbow Liquid Spring of Divine Sincerity
Soul Mind Body Transplants as one now.*

You are extremely blessed. We cannot honor the Divine enough. Let us chant or sing *God Gives His Heart to Me* to express our greatest gratitude:

*God gives his heart to me
God gives his love to me
My heart melds with his heart
My love melds with his love*

Practice Using Divine Treasures to Heal the Mental Body

Now let us apply the Four Power Techniques together with Divine Sincerity Soul Mind Body Transplants to heal the mental body:

Body Power. Sit up straight. Put one palm over your Message Center. Put your other palm over your forehead.

Soul Power. Say *hello:*

> *Dear soul mind body of Divine Rainbow Light Ball*
>   *and Divine Rainbow Liquid Spring of Divine Sin-*
>   *cerity Soul Mind Body Transplants,*
> *I love you, honor you, and appreciate you.*
> *You have the power to clear the soul mind body block-*
>   *ages in my mental body, including* _____ (you may
>   name and request divine soul healing blessings
>   for specific mental conditions).
> *You have the power to offer divine forgiveness for my*
>   *mistakes in past lives and this lifetime.*
> *You have the power to heal my mental body,*
>   *including* _____.
> *I am very grateful.*
> *I cannot thank you enough.*
> *Dear all souls whom my ancestors and I have hurt or*
>   *harmed in all of our lifetimes,*
> *I love you, honor you, and appreciate you.*
> *Please forgive my ancestors and me for our mistakes of*
>   *harming you.*
> *I sincerely apologize.*

I cannot honor you enough.
Dear all souls who have harmed me in any of my
  lifetimes,
I love you, honor you, and appreciate you.
I forgive you completely and unconditionally.
Please accept my forgiveness.
Thank you.

Mind Power. Visualize rainbow light and rainbow liquid shining in your Message Center, heart, brain, and entire mental body.

Sound Power. Chant silently or aloud:

Divine Rainbow Light Ball and Divine Rainbow Liq-
  uid Spring of Divine Sincerity Soul Mind Body
  Transplants clear the soul mind body blockages in
  my mental body and heal my mental body.
All souls whom my ancestors and I have harmed,
  please forgive us.
Thank you, all.

Divine Rainbow Light Ball and Divine Rainbow Liq-
  uid Spring of Divine Sincerity Soul Mind Body
  Transplants clear the soul mind body blockages in
  my mental body and heal my mental body.
All souls whom my ancestors and I have harmed,
  please forgive us.
Thank you, all.

Divine Rainbow Light Ball and Divine Rainbow Liquid Spring of Divine Sincerity Soul Mind Body Transplants clear the soul mind body blockages in my mental body and heal my mental body.
All souls whom my ancestors and I have harmed, please forgive us.
Thank you, all.

Divine Rainbow Light Ball and Divine Rainbow Liquid Spring of Divine Sincerity Soul Mind Body Transplants clear the soul mind body blockages in my mental body and heal my mental body.
All souls whom my ancestors and I have harmed, please forgive us.
Thank you, all.

Continue by chanting repeatedly, silently or aloud:

Divine Sincerity clears the soul mind body blockages in my mental body. Thank you.
Divine Sincerity clears the soul mind body blockages in my mental body. Thank you.
Divine Sincerity clears the soul mind body blockages in my mental body. Thank you.
Divine Sincerity clears the soul mind body blockages in my mental body. Thank you.
Divine Sincerity clears the soul mind body blockages in my mental body. Thank you.
Divine Sincerity clears the soul mind body blockages in my mental body. Thank you.

Divine Sincerity clears the soul mind body blockages in
my mental body. Thank you . . .

Please do this practice now. Stop reading and put this book
down. Chant for three to five minutes. Close your eyes.

Close. After chanting for at least three minutes, close:

> *Hao! Hao! Hao!*
> *Thank you. Thank you. Thank you.*

The longer you chant and the more often you chant, the better. There is no time limit. The more you chant, the faster you
will self-heal your mental body.

For serious and chronic mental disorders, chant for a total of
at least two hours a day. Practice as much as you can to restore
your health as soon as possible.

So far, I have offered fifteen priceless Divine Soul Mind Body
Transplants in this book:

- Divine Rainbow Light Ball and Divine Rainbow
  Liquid Spring of Divine Love Soul Mind Body
  Transplants
- Divine Rainbow Light Ball and Divine Rainbow
  Liquid Spring of Divine Forgiveness Soul Mind Body
  Transplants
- Divine Rainbow Light Ball and Divine Rainbow
  Liquid Spring of Divine Compassion Soul Mind
  Body Transplants

- Divine Rainbow Light Ball and Divine Rainbow Liquid Spring of Divine Light Soul Mind Body Transplants
- Divine Rainbow Light Ball and Divine Rainbow Liquid Spring of Divine Sincerity Soul Mind Body Transplants

The Divine and I will offer you many more treasures in the rest of this book. These divine treasures carry divine virtue to pay your karmic debt. When you invoke and practice with them, you are given this virtue. Heaven and these divine treasures are literally paying down your karmic debt for you.

Another key wisdom is that when you spend the time to practice with these divine treasures and chant, you are literally offering divine love, forgiveness, compassion, light, and sincerity to humanity, to all souls in the world, and to all souls in all universes.

These divine treasures carry divine frequency and vibration, which can transform the frequency and vibration of you, your loved ones, humanity, organizations, communities, cities, countries, Mother Earth, and all universes.

These divine treasures are like lightbulbs. The moment you begin to chant, these lightbulbs are turned on to shine on Mother Earth as a service to transform all darkness. Imagine one bulb in a large hall. Its light is limited. If one hundred bulbs were to shine together in the same hall, it would be much brighter. Imagine further if thousands, even millions, of lightbulbs were to shine in the same hall.

Now imagine millions of people chanting divine treasures on Mother Earth. Millions of lightbulbs would shine together on Mother Earth. The divine frequency and vibration from divine treasures would transform the frequency and vibration of all humanity, Mother Earth, and all universes.

When you practice and chant with the divine treasures:

- You are serving.
- You are receiving virtue that pays down your spiritual debt and clears blockages from your soul, heart, mind, and body.
- You are transforming the frequency and vibration of your soul, heart, mind, and body to divine frequency and vibration. This will greatly assist and accelerate your healing, prevention of sickness, rejuvenation, prolonging of life, transformation of relationships and finances, and enlightenment of your soul, heart, mind, and body.
- You are transforming the frequency and vibration of the souls, hearts, minds, and bodies of your loved ones to divine frequency and vibration.
- You are transforming the frequency and vibration of your organizations to divine frequency and vibration.
- You are transforming the frequency and vibration of your city to divine frequency and vibration.
- You are transforming the frequency and vibration of your country to divine frequency and vibration.
- You are transforming the frequency and vibration of humanity to divine frequency and vibration.
- You are transforming the frequency and vibration of Mother Earth to divine frequency and vibration.
- You are transforming the frequency and vibration of all universes to divine frequency and vibration.

- You are creating love, peace, and harmony for you, your loved ones, humanity, Mother Earth, and all universes.

You can clearly see the incredible benefits of chanting with divine treasures. These benefits are immeasurable and unpredictable.

Self-heal Your Spiritual Body, Including Self-clearing Your Karma (Soul Blockages), Mind Blockages, and Body Blockages

A human being has a soul. There are layers of souls in a human being. A bodily system has a soul. An organ has a soul. A cell has a soul. DNA and RNA have souls. Tiny matter inside a cell has a soul. Even a space between cells has a soul. In addition, energy has a soul. An acupuncture point has a soul. A meridian[3] has a soul. Each energy center and spiritual center in the body has a soul.

In one sentence:

Every part of the body has a soul.

To self-clear karma, you must understand this wisdom that there are layers of souls in a human being. You need to clear the karma of *all* of them. You may desire and think to clear your soul's karma, but you may be thinking only of your body soul. That is not enough! There is also the karma of your organs' souls, systems' souls, cells' souls, and more. Therefore, when you prac-

---

3. In traditional Chinese medicine, meridians are the pathways of qi (vital energy or life force). Acupuncture points lie on the meridians.

tice self-clearing karma, you need to address all of these layers of karma.

It is my honor to show you how to self-clear karma for all layers of souls in your body. In this section, I will offer huge divine treasures to help you and humanity self-clear all layers of karma in the body. These sixteenth, seventeenth, and eighteenth divine treasures offered in this book are:

Divine Rainbow Light Ball and Divine Rainbow Liquid Spring of Divine Blessing Soul Mind Body Transplants

Prepare. Sit up straight. Put the tip of your tongue as close as you can to the roof of your mouth, without touching. Put your left palm over your Message Center (heart chakra) and your right hand in the traditional prayer position, with fingers pointing upward. Totally relax. Open your heart and soul to receive this great honor. It will take about one minute for you to receive these three priceless treasures.

Divine Order: Divine Rainbow Light Ball and Divine Rainbow Liquid Spring of Divine Blessing Soul Transplant

Transmission!

Divine Order: Divine Rainbow Light Ball and Divine Rainbow Liquid Spring of Divine Blessing Mind Transplant

Transmission!

**Divine Order: Divine Rainbow Light Ball
and Divine Rainbow Liquid Spring of
Divine Blessing Body Transplant**

Transmission!

**Divine Order: Divine Rainbow Light Ball and
Divine Rainbow Liquid Spring of Divine Blessing
Soul Mind Body Transplants join as one.**

Hei Ya Ya Ya Ya Ya Ya You!

The Soul Language to deliver the last Divine Order can be translated as follows:

*Divine Order to join Divine Rainbow Light Ball and
Divine Rainbow Liquid Spring of Divine Blessing
Soul Mind Body Transplants as one now.*

You are extremely blessed. We cannot honor the Divine enough. Let us chant or sing *Thank You, Divine,* to express our greatest gratitude:

Thank you, Divine
Thank you, Divine
Thank you, Divine
Thank you, Divine
Thank you, Divine

Every time we receive priceless divine treasures, we must immediately offer our gratitude by chanting or singing *God Gives*

His Heart to Me or *Thank You, Divine.* We cannot appreciate and honor the Divine and divine treasures enough. These permanent divine treasures can literally save your life and the lives of your loved ones.

We have received thousands and thousands of heart-touching and moving stories about the benefits of divine treasures since July 2003, when I started to offer Divine Soul Transplants. I have offered countless Divine Soul Mind Body Transplants to humanity and countless souls. I cannot honor the Divine enough for the Divine's love, forgiveness, compassion, light, kindness, and generosity.

I emphasize again that these divine treasures are permanent gifts. The Divine just created these last three divine treasures in the Divine's heart for every reader on the spot. For the first time in history, the Divine has committed to offer Divine Soul Mind Body Transplants to every reader of this book and, in fact, to every reader of any book in the Soul Power Series. These Divine Soul Mind Body Transplants will stay with your soul and the soul of every recipient. These treasures will follow your soul forever—even after your physical life ends. These rainbow light and rainbow liquid souls will be with your soul in all of your future lifetimes. They will bless your life forever. How blessed we are! Therefore, gratitude to the Divine is very important. We truly cannot thank the Divine enough for divine love, forgiveness, compassion, light, kindness, and generosity.

Practice Using Divine Treasures to Heal the Spiritual Body

Now let us apply the Four Power Techniques together with Divine Blessing Soul Mind Body Transplants to heal the spiritual body:

Body Power. Sit up straight. Put your left palm over your Message Center. Put your right hand in the traditional prayer position, with fingers pointing upward.

Soul Power. Say *hello:*

> *Dear soul mind body of Divine Rainbow Light Ball*
> *and Divine Rainbow Liquid Spring of Divine*
> *Blessing Soul Mind Body Transplants,*
> *I love you, honor you, and appreciate you.*
> *You have the power to clear the soul mind body block-*
> *ages in my spiritual body, including the soul of my*
> *body and the souls of all of my systems, organs, cells,*
> *cell units, DNA, RNA, spaces between cells, and*
> *tiny matter inside cells.*
> *You have the power to offer divine forgiveness for my*
> *mistakes in past lives and this lifetime.*
> *Please forgive my mistakes at all of my soul levels, in-*
> *cluding the soul of my body and the souls of all of*
> *my systems, organs, cells, cell units, DNA, RNA,*
> *spaces between cells, and tiny matter inside cells.*
> *You have the power to heal my spiritual body, includ-*
> *ing all of my soul levels.*
> *I am very grateful.*
> *I cannot thank you enough.*
> *Dear all souls whom my ancestors and I have hurt or*
> *harmed in all of our lifetimes,*
> *I love you, honor you, and appreciate you.*
> *Please forgive my ancestors and me for our mistakes of*
> *harming you.*

I sincerely apologize.
I cannot honor you enough.
Dear all souls who have harmed me in any of my
    lifetimes,
I love you, honor you, and appreciate you.
I forgive you completely and unconditionally.
Please accept my forgiveness.
Thank you.

Mind Power. Visualize rainbow light and rainbow liquid shining in all levels of your entire spiritual body, from head to toe and skin to bone.

Sound Power. Chant silently or aloud:

Divine Rainbow Light Ball and Divine Rainbow Liquid Spring of Divine Blessing Soul Mind Body Transplants clear the soul mind body blockages in my spiritual body, including the soul of my body and the souls of all of my systems, organs, cells, cell units, DNA, RNA, spaces between cells, and tiny matter inside cells, and heal my spiritual body.
All souls whom my ancestors and I have harmed,
    please forgive us.
Thank you, all.

Divine Rainbow Light Ball and Divine Rainbow Liquid Spring of Divine Blessing Soul Mind Body Transplants clear the soul mind body blockages in

my spiritual body, including the soul of my body
and the souls of all of my systems, organs, cells, cell
units, DNA, RNA, spaces between cells, and tiny
matter inside cells, and heal my spiritual body.
All souls whom my ancestors and I have harmed,
    please forgive us.
Thank you, all.

Divine Rainbow Light Ball and Divine Rainbow Liq-
    uid Spring of Divine Blessing Soul Mind Body
    Transplants clear the soul mind body blockages in
    my spiritual body, including the soul of my body
    and the souls of all of my systems, organs, cells, cell
    units, DNA, RNA, spaces between cells, and tiny
    matter inside cells, and heal my spiritual body.
All souls whom my ancestors and I have harmed,
    please forgive us.
Thank you, all.

Divine Rainbow Light Ball and Divine Rainbow Liq-
    uid Spring of Divine Blessing Soul Mind Body
    Transplants clear the soul mind body blockages in
    my spiritual body, including the soul of my body
    and the souls of all of my systems, organs, cells, cell
    units, DNA, RNA, spaces between cells, and tiny
    matter inside cells, and heal my spiritual body.
All souls whom my ancestors and I have harmed,
    please forgive us.
Thank you, all.

Continue by chanting repeatedly, silently or aloud:

*Divine Blessing clears the soul mind body blockages in
my spiritual body. Thank you.*
*Divine Blessing clears the soul mind body blockages in
my spiritual body. Thank you.*
*Divine Blessing clears the soul mind body blockages in
my spiritual body. Thank you.*
*Divine Blessing clears the soul mind body blockages in
my spiritual body. Thank you.*
*Divine Blessing clears the soul mind body blockages in
my spiritual body. Thank you.*
*Divine Blessing clears the soul mind body blockages in
my spiritual body. Thank you.*
*Divine Blessing clears the soul mind body blockages in
my spiritual body. Thank you.*
*Divine Blessing clears the soul mind body blockages in
my spiritual body. Thank you . . .*

Please do it with me now. Chant for three to five minutes.
Close your eyes.

Close. After chanting for at least three minutes, close:

Hao! Hao! Hao!
Thank you. Thank you. Thank you.

The longer you chant and the more often you chant, the better. There is no time limit. The more you chant, the faster you
will self-heal your spiritual body.

For serious and chronic blockages in any aspect of your life,
chant for a total of at least two hours a day. Practice as much
as you can to heal every level of your spiritual body as soon as
possible.

I have shared the one-sentence secret of soul healing many times:

Heal the soul first; then healing of the mind and body will follow.

Soul is the boss. Therefore, the most important healing is to heal the soul. If the souls are not healed, it is very difficult to heal the mind and body completely. I wish you will do the practice for self-healing every level of the spiritual body as much as possible.

Golden Light

This is the seventh book of my Soul Power Series. In the first six books, the Divine transmits Golden Light Ball and Golden Liquid Spring Divine Soul Mind Body Transplants as permanent divine gifts to readers.

Golden light absolutely carries sacred and secret healing and blessing power. I have shared a sacred one-sentence healing secret in several of my previous books:

Jin guang zhao ti, bai bing xiao chu

"Jin" (pronounced *jeen*) means *gold*. "Guang" (pronounced *gwahng*) means *light*. "Zhao" (pronounced *jow,* rhymes with *now*) means *shines*. "Ti" (pronounced *tee*) means *body*. "Bai" (pronounced *bye*) means *one hundred*. In Chinese, "bai" represents *all* or *every*. "Bing" means *sicknesses*. "Xiao chu"(pronounced *shee-yow choo*) means *remove*.

Therefore, "Jin guang zhao ti, bai bing xiao chu" means:

Golden light shines; all sicknesses are removed.

Golden Light Self-healing Practice

Now let me share a simple practice to apply the healing secret of golden light.

As usual, apply the Four Power Techniques:

Body Power. Sit up straight. Put the tip of your tongue as close as you can to the roof of your mouth, without touching. Put one of your palms over your lower abdomen, below the navel. Put the other palm over the area of your body where you wish to receive healing.

Soul Power. Say *hello:*

> *Dear soul mind body of golden light,*
> *I love you, honor you, and appreciate you.*
> *You have the power to forgive my mistakes in past lives*
>   *and this lifetime.*
> *Please forgive my mistakes.*
> *I am very grateful.*
> *I cannot thank you enough.*
> *Dear all souls whom my ancestors and I have hurt or*
>   *harmed in all of our lifetimes,*
> *I love you, honor you, and appreciate you.*
> *Please forgive my ancestors and me for our mistakes of*
>   *harming you.*
> *I sincerely apologize.*
> *I cannot honor you enough.*
> *Dear all souls who have harmed me in any of my*
>   *lifetimes,*
> *I love you, honor you, and appreciate you.*

I forgive you completely and unconditionally.
Please accept my forgiveness.
Thank you.

Mind Power. Visualize golden light from Heaven, Earth, and all universes in all directions pouring into and through your body, from head to toe and skin to bone.

Sound Power. Chant repeatedly, silently or aloud:

> *Jin guang zhao ti, bai bing xiao chu*
> *Jin guang zhao ti, bai bing xiao chu*
> *Jin guang zhao ti, bai bing xiao chu*
> *Jin guang zhao ti, bai bing xiao chu*
> *Jin guang zhao ti, bai bing xiao chu*
> *Jin guang zhao ti, bai bing xiao chu*
> *Jin guang zhao ti, bai bing xiao chu . . .*

Alternatively, you may chant in English:

> *Golden light shines; all sicknesses are removed.*
> *Golden light shines; all sicknesses are removed.*
> *Golden light shines; all sicknesses are removed.*
> *Golden light shines; all sicknesses are removed.*
> *Golden light shines; all sicknesses are removed.*
> *Golden light shines; all sicknesses are removed.*
> *Golden light shines; all sicknesses are removed . . .*

Please do this practice now. I really want you to chant for three to five minutes per time. The longer you chant, and the more often you chant, the better. For chronic and life-threatening conditions, chant for a total of at least two hours per day. There is no time limit for this practice.

This golden light meditation and chanting practice is extremely powerful for self-healing. It is an ancient secret I am honored to share with you and humanity. You can do this practice anytime, anywhere. You can receive remarkable healing and blessing to transform every aspect of your life.

In most of the other practices in this book, we apply rainbow light and rainbow liquid divine treasures. This is also a sacred and secret practice. Rainbow light is the next layer of light above golden light. When you meditate and chant with rainbow light, you could receive even better results than with golden light. This can be summarized in a one-sentence secret:

Rainbow light shines; all sicknesses are removed faster.

Divine Golden Light is not ordinary golden light. It is the highest golden light in all universes. Divine Golden Light Ball is a divine yang treasure. Divine Golden Liquid Spring is a divine yin treasure. Divine Golden Light Ball and Divine Golden Liquid Spring are divine yin yang treasures together.

To receive *one* Divine Golden Light Ball and Divine Golden Liquid Spring is beyond words. The more Divine Golden Light Balls and Divine Golden Liquid Springs one receives, the more divine power one becomes a vehicle and vessel for.

As a servant of humanity and the Divine, in this book I offer Divine Rainbow Light Ball and Divine Rainbow Liquid Spring Divine Soul Mind Body Transplants. Divine Rainbow Light Ball is a divine yang treasure. Divine Rainbow Liquid Spring is a divine yin treasure. Divine Rainbow Light Ball and Divine Rainbow Liquid Spring are divine yin yang treasures together.

Divine Rainbow Light Ball and Divine Rainbow Liquid Spring is the next higher layer after Divine Golden Light Ball and Divine Golden Liquid Spring. Divine Golden Light Ball and Divine Golden Liquid Spring Divine Soul Mind Body Transplants are already beyond comprehension, so even more are the power and abilities of Divine Rainbow Light Ball and Divine Rainbow Liquid Spring Divine Soul Mind Body Transplants beyond comprehension.

Readers of the first six books of my Soul Power Series received Divine Golden Light Ball and Divine Golden Liquid Spring Divine Soul Mind Body Transplants in those books. As in this book, the seventh of my Soul Power Series, after you received divine treasures, I guided you to apply them for healing, rejuvenation, and transformation of every aspect of life, including relationships and finances.

After you read this book to receive Divine Rainbow Light Ball and Divine Rainbow Liquid Spring Divine Soul Mind Body Transplants and practice and chant with them, you can experience for yourself and realize that Divine Rainbow Light Ball and Divine Rainbow Liquid Spring Divine Soul Mind Body Transplants are the next step of divine treasures. Divine power is getting higher. We are the beneficiaries. We are extremely honored. We are extremely blessed. Divine generosity and divine commitment to help humanity to pass through this difficult time leave us speechless.

Self-prevent Sickness in Your Spiritual, Mental, Emotional, and Physical Bodies

Preventing sickness is vital for one's life. If one can prevent sickness, one does not need to get sick. How blessed this one would be!

I am delighted to offer major, priceless Divine Soul Mind Body Transplants to assist you to prevent sickness:

Divine Rainbow Light Ball and Divine Rainbow Liquid Spring of Divine Prevention of Sickness Soul Mind Body Transplants

These are the nineteenth, twentieth, and twenty-first permanent divine treasures offered as divine gifts to you and every reader of this book.

Prepare. Sit up straight. Put the tip of your tongue as close as you can to the roof of your mouth, without touching. Put your left palm over your Message Center and your right hand in the traditional prayer position. Totally relax. Open your heart and soul to receive this great honor. It will take about one minute for you to receive these three priceless treasures.

Divine Order: Divine Rainbow Light Ball and Divine Rainbow Liquid Spring of Divine Prevention of Sickness Soul Transplant

Transmission!

Divine Order: Divine Rainbow Light Ball and Divine Rainbow Liquid Spring of Divine Prevention of Sickness Mind Transplant

Transmission!

**Divine Order: Divine Rainbow Light Ball
and Divine Rainbow Liquid Spring of Divine
Prevention of Sickness Body Transplant**

Transmission!

**Divine Order: Divine Rainbow Light Ball and Divine
Rainbow Liquid Spring of Divine Prevention of
Sickness Soul Mind Body Transplants join as one.**

Hei Ya Ya Ya Ya Ya Ya You!

The last line is a Divine Order in Soul Language. It can be translated as follows:

*Divine Order to join Divine Rainbow Light Ball and
Divine Rainbow Liquid Spring of Divine Prevention of
Sickness Soul Mind Body Transplants as one now.*

You are extremely blessed. We cannot honor the Divine enough. Let us chant or sing *God Gives His Heart to Me* to express our greatest gratitude:

*God gives his heart to me
God gives his love to me
My heart melds with his heart
My love melds with his love*

These Divine Prevention of Sickness treasures are extremely powerful. They have never been offered to humanity before. I am honored to be a servant of humanity and the Divine to offer these priceless treasures to you.

Apply them to prevent sickness. The benefits are beyond comprehension. Let us do it now.

Practice with Divine Treasures to Prevent Sickness

We will apply the Four Power Techniques together with Divine Prevention of Sickness Divine Soul Mind Body Transplants to prevent sickness in our spiritual, mental, emotional, and physical bodies:

Body Power. Sit up straight. Put the tip of your tongue as close as you can to the roof of your mouth, without touching. Put one palm over your Message Center. Put the other palm over your lower abdomen, below the navel.

Soul Power. Say *hello:*

> *Dear soul mind body of Divine Rainbow Light*
> *Ball and Divine Rainbow Liquid Spring of*
> *Divine Prevention of Sickness Soul Mind Body*
> *Transplants,*
> *I love you, honor you, and appreciate you.*
> *You have the power to clear my soul mind body block-*
> *ages to preventing sickness in my spiritual, mental,*
> *emotional, and physical bodies.*
> *You have the power to offer divine forgiveness for my*
> *mistakes in past lives and this lifetime.*
> *I am very grateful.*
> *I cannot thank you enough.*

Dear all souls whom my ancestors and I have hurt or
harmed in all of our lifetimes,
I love you, honor you, and appreciate you.
Please forgive my ancestors and me for our mistakes of
harming you.
I sincerely apologize.
I cannot honor you enough.
Dear all souls who have harmed me in any of my life-
times,
I love you, honor you, and appreciate you.
I forgive you completely and unconditionally.
Please accept my forgiveness.
Thank you.

Mind Power. Visualize rainbow light and rainbow liquid shining in your spiritual, mental, emotional, and physical bodies, from head to toe and skin to bone.

Sound Power. Chant silently or aloud:

Divine Rainbow Light Ball and Divine Rainbow Liq-
uid Spring of Divine Prevention of Sickness Soul
Mind Body Transplants clear my soul mind body
blockages to preventing sickness in my spiritual,
mental, emotional, and physical bodies.
All souls whom my ancestors and I have harmed,
please forgive us again.
Thank you, all.

Divine Rainbow Light Ball and Divine Rainbow Liq-
uid Spring of Divine Prevention of Sickness Soul

Mind Body Transplants clear my soul mind body
blockages to preventing sickness in my spiritual,
mental, emotional, and physical bodies.
All souls whom my ancestors and I have harmed,
please forgive us again.
Thank you, all.

Divine Rainbow Light Ball and Divine Rainbow Liq-
uid Spring of Divine Prevention of Sickness Soul
Mind Body Transplants clear my soul mind body
blockages to preventing sickness in my spiritual,
mental, emotional, and physical bodies.
All souls whom my ancestors and I have harmed,
please forgive us again.
Thank you, all.

Divine Rainbow Light Ball and Divine Rainbow Liq-
uid Spring of Divine Prevention of Sickness Soul
Mind Body Transplants clear my soul mind body
blockages to preventing sickness in my spiritual,
mental, emotional, and physical bodies.
All souls whom my ancestors and I have harmed,
please forgive us again.
Thank you, all.

Now chant repeatedly, silently or aloud:

Divine Prevention of Sickness clears my soul mind
body blockages to preventing sickness. Thank you.
Divine Prevention of Sickness clears my soul mind
body blockages to preventing sickness. Thank you.

Divine Prevention of Sickness clears my soul mind
  body blockages to preventing sickness. Thank you.
Divine Prevention of Sickness clears my soul mind
  body blockages to preventing sickness. Thank you.
Divine Prevention of Sickness clears my soul mind
  body blockages to preventing sickness. Thank you.
Divine Prevention of Sickness clears my soul mind
  body blockages to preventing sickness. Thank you.
Divine Prevention of Sickness clears my soul mind
  body blockages to preventing sickness. Thank you . . .

Alternatively, you can chant the following simple sentences repeatedly:

Divine Prevention of Sickness prevents all sickness.
  Thank you, Divine.
Divine Prevention of Sickness prevents all sickness.
  Thank you, Divine.
Divine Prevention of Sickness prevents all sickness.
  Thank you, Divine.
Divine Prevention of Sickness prevents all sickness.
  Thank you, Divine.
Divine Prevention of Sickness prevents all sickness.
  Thank you, Divine.
Divine Prevention of Sickness prevents all sickness.
  Thank you, Divine.
Divine Prevention of Sickness prevents all sickness.
  Thank you, Divine . . .

Please stop reading and do this practice. I really want you to take every opportunity to practice. If you do not practice, you will not receive benefits from your divine treasures. Close your eyes and chant for at least three minutes now.

Close. After chanting for at least three minutes, close:

> *Hao! Hao! Hao!*
> *Thank you. Thank you. Thank you.*

The longer you chant and the more often you chant, the better. There is no time limit. The more you chant, the faster you will be able to prevent sickness in your spiritual, mental, emotional, and physical bodies.

The Third Way to Chant

As I have taught for years, there are two ways to chant or sing. One way is out loud. The other way is silently, which is to chant quietly in your heart. A human being has large and small cells. To vibrate both kinds of cells is important. To chant out loud is to vibrate the bigger cells. To chant silently is to vibrate the smaller cells.

Now let me teach you the third way to chant, which is named "thinking chanting."

"Thinking chanting" is chanting from your mind. For example, to "thinking chant" *Divine Prevention of Sickness prevents all sickness. Thank you, Divine,* you literally are just *thinking* these two sentences. Thinking chanting also carries incredible power.

You can apply thinking chanting when you practice and chant with your divine treasures. The Divine Rainbow Light Ball and Divine Rainbow Liquid Spring Divine Soul Mind Body Transplants already carry divine frequency and vibration with divine love, forgiveness, compassion, and light.

I emphasize again—and I cannot emphasize enough—five important, fundamental one-sentence teachings. I wish that you and every reader will imprint them on your soul, heart, mind, and body. The five sentences are:

- Divine frequency and vibration transform the frequency and vibration of your soul, heart, mind, and body.
- Divine love melts all blockages and transforms all life.
- Divine forgiveness brings inner joy and inner peace.
- Divine compassion boosts energy, stamina, vitality, and immunity.
- Divine light heals, prevents sickness, rejuvenates, and prolongs life, as well as transforms relationships, finances, and every aspect of life.

Because Divine Rainbow Light Ball and Divine Rainbow Liquid Spring Soul Mind Body Transplants carry divine frequency and vibration with divine love, forgiveness, compassion, and light, when you think about them, you are literally turning them on. What I am sharing is that just to think about your divine treasures is to turn them on. They are just like a lightbulb. You turn on the light switch and the lightbulb is on.

When you turn your divine treasures on, they start to vibrate to remove soul mind body blockages for healing, prevention of sickness, rejuvenation, prolonging of life, and life transformation at the same time.

Thinking chanting is very powerful because it automatically turns on the divine treasures. In addition, everyone has his or her own thinking power (mind power). Highly developed spiritual beings have much more thinking power than ordinary beings because of their spiritual and energy practices and development.

How can you develop your thinking power? One powerful way is to apply your thinking power repeatedly to one thing. For example, you have just applied Divine Rainbow Light Ball and Divine Rainbow Liquid Spring of Divine Prevention of Sickness Soul Mind Body Transplants to prevent sickness in your spiritual, mental, emotional, and physical bodies.

Apply your thinking power in this simple way:

Think *Divine Prevention treasures prevent all sickness in me. Thank you, Divine.* Think this repeatedly. Think in your mind that all sickness is prevented for you.

This is another extremely powerful way to chant, which I gave the name *thinking chanting.* Do thinking chanting again and again. You could receive remarkable results for prevention of all sickness.

In one sentence:

Preventing sickness is extremely important.

Apply thinking chanting more. Continue your yang chanting, which is to chant out loud, and your yin chanting, which is to silently chant in your heart. Add thinking chanting. I wish you will prevent all sickness as quickly as possible.

Divine Transformation for Your Relationships and Beyond

MILLIONS OF PEOPLE have good relationships. At the same time, millions of people have challenging relationships. Most people have some good relationships and some challenging relationships.

Let me ask you a few questions:

- Do you have a true love?
- Do you have a good relationship with your spouse or life partner?
- Do you have a good relationship with your boyfriend or girlfriend?
- Do you have good relationships with your children?
- Do you have good relationships with your parents?
- Do you have good relationships with your colleagues?
- Do you have good relationships with your boss?

I believe you have at least one or two relationships that you need to improve. Some of you may have serious challenges with relationships. Many books about transformation of relationships have been written in almost all languages on Mother Earth. Many workshops, seminars, retreats, and training programs worldwide teach about transformation of relationships. I honor each book, each teaching, and each training.

Let me ask you one more question.

Do your soul, heart, mind, and body have good relationships with each other?

This is a very important question. If your soul, heart, mind, and body do not have harmonized relationships, you could have major challenges in health, relationships, finances, and more.

In this book, I am honored to teach divine transformation for all life. Divine transformation is to apply permanent divine treasures, including Divine Soul Mind Body Transplants, to transform every aspect of life. Relationships are a very important aspect of life. Everyone wants a true love. No one wants to struggle with a challenging relationship. In this chapter, I share with you divine transformation of relationships.

In my previous book, *Tao I: The Way of All Life*,[1] I shared a one-sentence secret for all teaching, all training, all methods, all techniques, and all life:

Da Tao zhi jian

"Da" means *big*. "Tao" means *The Way*. "Zhi" means *extremely*. "Jian" means *simple*. "Da Tao zhi jian" means *The Big Way is extremely simple*.

1. *Tao I: The Way of All Life* (New York/Toronto: Atria Books/Heaven's Library, 2010).

Many people on Mother Earth have received complicated training and use complicated methods and techniques. They may think that good solutions could be complicated, or that a complicated solution must be good.

In my teaching, that is not true. The truth for everything is extremely simple. Why do I say this? If you have read all of my Soul Power Series books, you would realize that I always teach the Four Power Techniques: Body Power, Soul Power, Mind Power, and Sound Power. I always offer Divine Soul Mind Body Transplants. I always give many practices. Reading my books is just like being in my workshop, seminar, or retreat. I always emphasize that the most important thing is not to skip the practices and chanting. You may read only one line of a practice, see the chanting, and say, "I know this already." You may skip doing the practice and chanting. This is the biggest loss for you.

If you are in a workshop and the teacher leads you to chant for a few minutes, you keep chanting if the teacher continues to lead you and does not say "Stop." You are practicing. In the same way, when I write in my books for you to chant for three to five minutes, please stop reading the book and chant for three to five minutes. It is just as though you are in a workshop with me. The practices are the most important parts of my books.

To practice is to heal.

To practice is to prevent sickness.

To practice is to rejuvenate your soul, heart, mind, and body.

To practice is to prolong your life.

To practice is to transform your relationships.

To practice is to transform your finances and business.

To practice is to transform every aspect of your life.

To practice is to enlighten your soul, heart, mind, and body.

To practice is to transform your family.

To practice is to increase your intelligence, wisdom, knowledge, and practical techniques.

To practice is to transform organizations and society.

To practice is to transform cities and countries.

To practice is to transform Mother Earth.

To practice is to transform all universes.

Recall my teaching in every book. Practice is the key. Explaining and discussing are important.

Explaining is not enough.

Discussing is not enough.

Action is the key.

Practice is action.

Action is experience.

Experience transforms all life.

In one sentence:

If you want to know if a pear is sweet, taste it; if you want to know if a practice works, experience it.

Apply the Four Power Techniques together with divine treasures to transform every aspect of life. The practices in all of my books are extremely simple. Sooner or later you will have an "aha!" moment. You will suddenly realize that healing is not difficult. It is simple. It is extremely simple. Transformation of any aspect of life is not difficult. It is simple.

The difficulty in spreading my teaching worldwide is overcoming people's thoughts. Some people think that healing and transformation cannot be so simple. They think the practical techniques of the Soul Power Series are too simple to believe. Mind blockages block them from even trying these simplest practices.

In order to help you and every reader to really master the simplicity for self-healing and self-transformation of your relationships, finances, and more, I am sending a Divine Order to humanity in Soul Language:

> *Hei Ya*
> *Hei Ya You Yi*
> *Hei Ya You Yi*
> *Ya Hei Ya Hei*
> *Ya Yi Hei*
> *Hei Ya*
> *Ya Hei Yi Ya*
> *Ya Hei Yi Ya*
> *Yi Ya You Hei*
> *Ya Hei*
> *Yi Ya You Hei*
> *Ya Yi You Hei*
> *Yi Ya Hei You*
> *Ya Yi Ya Hei*
> *Ya Hei*
> *Ya Hei*
> *Ya Hei*

Let me translate this Divine Order for you:

> *Dear soul mind body of all humanity,*
> *Dear all souls in countless planets, stars, galaxies, and*
>   *universes,*
> *Master Sha offers divine transformation in the simplest way.*
> *This way is to use permanent divine treasures to trans-*

> *form all life, including health, relationships, and*
> *finances.*
> *The teaching and practices are extremely simple.*
> *Trust the simplicity.*
> *Do the practices.*
> *Receive the benefits quickly.*
> *You are blessed.*
> *Your beloved Divine*

Thank you. Thank you. Thank you.

I am honored to be a servant of humanity and the Divine to send this Divine Order and divine calling to serve you, all humanity, and all souls.

One day you will have a "wow!" moment. You will suddenly say, "Wow, I got it! I know how to heal myself. I know how to transform my relationships, finances, and every aspect of my life. I know how to help my loved ones. I know how to transform my family, community, and organizations. I know how to help humanity and Mother Earth pass through this difficult time."

To summarize the practical techniques of this book, of all the books of my Soul Power Series, and of all of my teaching in one sentence:

The Four Power Techniques and divine treasures transform all life.

Practice Using Divine Treasures to Transform All Life

Let us do one of the simplest and most powerful practices for three minutes. This is one-sentence chanting to transform every aspect of your life.

Body Power. Sit up straight. Put the tip of your tongue near the roof of your mouth without touching. Put your left palm over your Message Center and put your right palm in the traditional prayer position.

Soul Power. Say *hello:*

> *Dear soul mind body of the Four Power Techniques*
>   *and all my divine treasures,*
> *I love you, honor you, and appreciate you.*
> *You have the power to transform every aspect of my*
>   *life.*
> *I am very grateful.*
> *I cannot thank you enough.*

Mind Power.
Visualize rainbow light shining in your body from head to toe, skin to bone.
Visualize rainbow light shining in your loved ones.
Visualize rainbow light shining in your family.
Visualize rainbow light shining in your finances and business.
Visualize rainbow light shining in every aspect of your life.

Sound Power. Chant repeatedly, silently or aloud:

> *Four Power Techniques and divine treasures transform*
>   *all my life. Thank you.*
> *Four Power Techniques and divine treasures transform*
>   *all my life. Thank you.*
> *Four Power Techniques and divine treasures transform*
>   *all my life. Thank you.*

*Four Power Techniques and divine treasures transform
    all my life. Thank you.*
*Four Power Techniques and divine treasures transform
    all my life. Thank you.*
*Four Power Techniques and divine treasures transform
    all my life. Thank you.*
*Four Power Techniques and divine treasures transform
    all my life. Thank you . . .*

Please stop reading now. Really chant for at least three minutes.

Close. After chanting for at least three minutes, close:

Hao! Hao! Hao!
Thank you. Thank you. Thank you.

The longer you chant and the more times you chant, the better. There is no time limit.

To chant this simplest mantra is one of the most powerful practices. *Da Tao zhi jian.* The benefits for all life cannot be explained enough.

I began this chapter with an important teaching about divine simplicity. Please do not skip the practices and chanting. Chanting is vital to transform your relationships and every aspect of your life.

Self-clear Your Karma (Soul Blockages), Mind Blockages, and Body Blockages for Relationships

The root blockage for any relationship is karma. Therefore, to transform any relationship, self-clearing karma is a "must."

Killing, harming, taking advantage of others, stealing, cheating, abusing others, and more in past lifetimes and in this life all create bad karma, which is the root blockage for all kinds of relationships.

If you are a highly developed spiritual being who can communicate with the Divine and the Akashic Records (the place in Heaven that records every person's lives, including one's activities, behaviors, and even thoughts), you can receive messages from the Akashic Records and the Divine about what kind of bad karma you or anyone has.

The key to transforming all relationships is to self-clear all bad karma for all relationships.

How can you do it? Use divine transformation. Apply the priceless divine treasures that you have received in this book to do major self-clearing of all kinds of relationship karma.

Let us do it now.

Apply the Four Power Techniques:

Body Power. Sit up straight. Put the tip of your tongue near the roof of your mouth without touching. Put your hands in the Soul Light Era Prayer Position.

Soul Power. Say *hello:*

> *Dear soul mind body of Divine Rainbow Light Ball*
> *and Divine Rainbow Liquid Spring of Divine Love*
> *Soul Mind Body Transplants,*
> *Dear soul mind body of Divine Rainbow Light Ball*
> *and Divine Rainbow Liquid Spring of Divine*
> *Forgiveness Soul Mind Body Transplants,*

*Dear soul mind body of Divine Rainbow Light Ball
   and Divine Rainbow Liquid Spring of Divine
   Compassion Soul Mind Body Transplants,*
*Dear soul mind body of Divine Rainbow Light Ball
   and Divine Rainbow Liquid Spring of Divine Light
   Soul Mind Body Transplants,*
I love you, honor you, and appreciate you.
*You have the power to clear the soul mind body block-
   ages in all of my relationships in past lives and in
   this life, including forgiving my mistakes in past
   lives and in this life, and to heal all my
   relationships.*
I am very grateful.
I cannot thank you enough.
*Dear all souls whom my ancestors and I have hurt in
   all of our lives,*
We love you, honor you, and appreciate you.
*Please forgive my mistakes and my ancestors' mistakes
   of harming you.*
We sincerely apologize.
We cannot honor you enough.
*Dear all souls who have harmed me in all
   lifetimes,*
I love you, honor you, and appreciate you.
I completely forgive you.
Please accept my forgiveness.
Thank you.
*All souls whom my ancestors and I have harmed,
   please forgive us again.*
Thank you, all.

Mind Power.

Visualize divine rainbow light shining within you and all of your loved ones.

Visualize divine rainbow light shining within you and all of your family members.

Visualize divine rainbow light shining within you and all of your colleagues.

Visualize divine rainbow light shining within you and all of your bosses.

Visualize divine rainbow light shining within you and all persons and souls with whom you have or have had a relationship.

Sound Power. Chant repeatedly, silently or aloud:

> *Divine Love, Forgiveness, Compassion, and Light treasures clear all of my relationship karma. Thank you.*
> *Divine Love, Forgiveness, Compassion, and Light treasures clear all of my relationship karma. Thank you.*
> *Divine Love, Forgiveness, Compassion, and Light treasures clear all of my relationship karma. Thank you.*
> *Divine Love, Forgiveness, Compassion, and Light treasures clear all of my relationship karma. Thank you.*
> *Divine Love, Forgiveness, Compassion, and Light treasures clear all of my relationship karma. Thank you.*
> *Divine Love, Forgiveness, Compassion, and Light treasures clear all of my relationship karma. Thank you.*
> *Divine Love, Forgiveness, Compassion, and Light treasures clear all of my relationship karma. Thank you*
> *. . .*

Please stop reading. Do this practice now. Chant for at least three minutes.

Close. After chanting for at least three minutes, close:

> *Hao! Hao! Hao!*
> *Thank you. Thank you. Thank you.*

The longer you chant and the more times you chant, the better. There is no time limit.

Applying these twelve major divine treasures together is so powerful that no words can explain it enough and no thoughts can comprehend it enough.

Always remember gratitude. I emphasize my teaching again. I teach total GOLD. G is *gratitude*. O is *obedience*. L is *loyalty*. D is *devotion*. Total GOLD is to the Divine.

Self-balance Your Relationships with Life Partners

Many people have major challenges with their loved ones. Some people have married and divorced a few times. Some people have many boyfriends or girlfriends and still do not feel happy. Many people have searched without success for their "soul mate."

Why do people have relationship challenges? I have offered the teaching for many years: relationship challenges are due to bad karma.

When I was in Japan in September 2007, one lady consulted with me. She told me, "I am very upset. My husband has six girlfriends. I caught him with a few of them. I am so angry. I am so sick because of this." I asked her, "Could you close your eyes and give me a moment?" I then connected with the Akashic Records and asked to be shown the past lives between her husband and her. Almost immediately, the Akashic Records showed me that in a past life, the woman was the husband, while her husband was the wife in that lifetime. They were married and the husband in that lifetime had twelve girlfriends. These twelve girlfriends stood in front of me in soul form. I counted them one by one.

I asked this woman to open her eyes and said, "Your husband has six girlfriends now. There are spiritual reasons for this from past lifetimes. Do you believe in past lives?" She answered, "Yes, I do." I then shared with her what the Akashic Records had shown me: "In a past life, you were the husband. You married your current husband, who became your wife in that lifetime. You had twelve girlfriends. Because you did this to him in that past lifetime, in this lifetime he is doing the same thing to you. This is how karma works."

The woman suddenly became very quiet. She completely accepted what I had just told her. She asked me what she should do. I told her, "Forgive your husband. Continue to give him love and forgiveness and he could transform." The woman was extremely grateful.

This story is an example of how karma works for relationships: If you have challenges with your loved ones, there is a spiritual reason from previous lifetimes.

If you have not opened your Third Eye or other spiritual channels, you cannot get information about past lifetimes directly from the Akashic Records or the Divine. That is all right. What is important is to know the spiritual wisdom. If you have challenges with your loved ones, bad karma could be the root cause.

In the beginning of this chapter, you learned how to self-clear karma for all kinds of relationships. That practice will be applied to every kind of relationship in this chapter. I suggest you go back now and do that practice to self-clear the karma of your relationships again.

Now, let me lead you further to transform your relationships with your loved ones. I will offer three more major divine treasures:

Divine Rainbow Light Ball and Divine Rainbow Liquid Spring of Divine Harmony Soul Mind Body Transplants

Prepare. Sit up straight. Put the tip of your tongue as close as you can to the roof of your mouth, without touching. Put your hands in the Soul Light Era Prayer Position. Totally relax. Open your heart and soul to receive this great honor. It will take about one minute for you to receive the twenty-second, twenty-third, and twenty-fourth priceless divine treasures offered to you in this book.

Divine Order: Divine Rainbow Light Ball and Divine Rainbow Liquid Spring of Divine Harmony Soul Transplant

Transmission!

Divine Order: Divine Rainbow Light Ball and Divine Rainbow Liquid Spring of Divine Harmony Mind Transplant

Transmission!

Divine Order: Divine Rainbow Light Ball and Divine Rainbow Liquid Spring of Divine Harmony Body Transplant

Transmission!

**Divine Order: Divine Rainbow Light Ball and
Divine Rainbow Liquid Spring of Divine Harmony
Soul Mind Body Transplants join as one.**

Hei Ya Ya Ya Ya Ya Ya You!

The last Divine Order can be translated as follows:

*Divine Order to join Divine Rainbow Light Ball and
Divine Rainbow Liquid Spring of Divine Harmony
Soul Mind Body Transplants as one now.*

You are extremely blessed. We cannot honor the Divine
enough. Let us sing *God Gives His Heart to Me* to express our
greatest gratitude:

God gives his heart to me
God gives his love to me
My heart melds with his heart
My love melds with his love

*Practice Using Divine Treasures to Balance Your
Relationships with Life Partners*

Now apply the Four Power Techniques together with Divine
Harmony Soul Mind Body Transplants to balance your relationships with your life partners:

Body Power. Sit up straight. Put the tip of your tongue as close as you can to the roof of your mouth, without touching. Put your left palm over your Message Center and your right palm in the traditional prayer position.

Soul Power. Say *hello:*

> *Dear soul mind body of Divine Rainbow Light Ball*
>   *and Divine Rainbow Liquid Spring of Divine*
>   *Harmony Soul Mind Body Transplants,*
> *I love you, honor you, and appreciate you.*
> *You have the power to clear the soul mind body block-*
>   *ages in my relationships with my life partners in*
>   *past lives and in this life.*
> *You have the power to offer divine forgiveness for my*
>   *mistakes to my life partners in past lives and in this*
>   *life.*
> *You have the power to heal my relationships with my*
>   *life partners.*
> *I am very grateful.*
> *I cannot thank you enough.*
> *Dear souls of my life partners in past lives and in this*
>   *life,*
> *I love you, honor you, and appreciate you.*
> *Please forgive my ancestors and me for our mistakes of*
>   *harming you in any way.*
> *We sincerely apologize.*
> *We cannot honor you enough.*
> *I also completely forgive you for any hurt or harm you*
>   *have done to me in any of our lifetimes.*
> *Please accept my forgiveness.*

Thank you.
Souls of all of my life partners, please forgive us
   again.
Thank you, all.

Mind Power. Visualize rainbow light shining within you and your life partners.

Sound Power. Chant repeatedly, silently or aloud:

Divine Harmony treasures clear all of my relationship
   karma with my life partners and heal us. Thank you.
Divine Harmony treasures clear all of my relationship
   karma with my life partners and heal us. Thank you.
Divine Harmony treasures clear all of my relationship
   karma with my life partners and heal us. Thank you.
Divine Harmony treasures clear all of my relationship
   karma with my life partners and heal us. Thank you.
Divine Harmony treasures clear all of my relationship
   karma with my life partners and heal us. Thank you.
Divine Harmony treasures clear all of my relationship
   karma with my life partners and heal us. Thank you.
Divine Harmony treasures clear all of my relationship
   karma with my life partners and heal us. Thank you
   . . .

Please stop reading and do this practice now. Chant with your heart and soul for at least three minutes. The longer you chant and the more often you chant, the better. There is no time limit.

Close. After chanting and visualizing for at least three minutes, close the practice by saying:

> *Hao! Hao! Hao!*
> *Thank you. Thank you. Thank you.*

Self-balance Your Relationships with Family Members

Many people have relationship challenges with their children, grandchildren, parents, stepparents, grandparents, and more.

The root cause of these challenges is karma. For example, if your child does not respect you, very often this is because in a previous life you were the child, your child was your parent, and you did not respect him or her.

There are many karmic relationship issues like this between family members. If you have relationship challenges with one or more of your family members, ask a highly developed spiritual being to do a spiritual reading with the Akashic Records and the Divine. I cannot say 100 percent of the time, but almost always there is a past life reason for your current relationship challenges. The root cause, bad karma in your relationship, could have occurred in several past lifetimes.

It is vital to understand this wisdom. After you understand this wisdom, you will be more forgiving of your family members' mistakes toward you. You will ask for forgiveness for your mistakes toward them. You will learn and sincerely practice self-clearing your relationship karma in order to transform relationship challenges with your family members.

Let us apply the Four Power Techniques and your Divine Blessing Soul Mind Body Transplants to do it now:

Body Power. Sit up straight. Put the tip of your tongue as close as you can to the roof of your mouth, without touching. Put your hands in the Soul Light Era Prayer Position.

Soul Power. Say *hello*:

> *Dear soul mind body of Divine Rainbow Light Ball*
>   *and Divine Rainbow Liquid Spring of Divine*
>   *Blessing Soul Mind Body Transplants,*
> *I love you, honor you, and appreciate you.*
> *You have the power to clear the soul mind body block-*
>   *ages in my relationships with all of my family*
>   *members, including my children, stepchildren,*
>   *grandchildren, parents, stepparents, grandparents,*
>   *and more, in past lives and in this life.*
> *You have the power to offer divine forgiveness for my*
>   *mistakes toward my family members in past lives*
>   *and in this life.*
> *You have the power to heal my relationships with all of*
>   *my family members.*
> *I am very grateful.*
> *I cannot thank you enough.*
> *Dear souls of my family members in all my lifetimes,*
> *I love you, honor you, and appreciate you.*
> *Please forgive my ancestors and me for our mistakes of*
>   *harming you in any way.*
> *We sincerely apologize.*
> *We cannot honor you enough.*
> *At the same time, I completely forgive you for your*
>   *mistakes of harming me in any of my lifetimes.*

Please accept my forgiveness.
Thank you.
All souls of my family members, please forgive my
    ancestors and me again.
Thank you, all.

Mind Power. Visualize rainbow light shining within you and your family members.

Sound Power. Chant repeatedly, silently or aloud:

Divine Blessing treasures clear all of my relationship
    karma with my family members and heal us.
Thank you.
Divine Blessing treasures clear all of my relationship
    karma with my family members and heal us.
Thank you.
Divine Blessing treasures clear all of my relationship
    karma with my family members and heal us.
Thank you.
Divine Blessing treasures clear all of my relationship
    karma with my family members and heal us.
Thank you.
Divine Blessing treasures clear all of my relationship
    karma with my family members and heal us.
Thank you.
Divine Blessing treasures clear all of my relationship
    karma with my family members and heal us.
Thank you.

> *Divine Blessing treasures clear all of my relationship*
> *karma with my family members and heal us.*
> *Thank you . . .*

Please stop reading. Do this practice now. Chant for at least three minutes.

Close. After chanting and visualizing for at least three minutes, close the practice:

> *Hao! Hao! Hao!*
> *Thank you. Thank you. Thank you.*

The longer you chant and the more times you chant, the better. There is no time limit.

Self-balance Your Relationships with Colleagues

Many people have relationship challenges with some of their colleagues. They could dislike each other, say disrespectful and unkind words to each other, complain and even lie about each other, damage each other's relationships with other colleagues, be jealous, be competitive, and more.

The root cause of relationship challenges between you and your colleagues is bad karma.

Self-clear the karma between you and your colleagues and do divine transformation between you and your colleagues.

Let me lead you to practice with the Four Power Techniques and divine treasures:

Body Power. Sit up straight. Put the tip of your tongue as close as you can to the roof of your mouth, without touching. Put your hands in the Soul Light Era Prayer Position.

Soul Power. Say *hello:*

> *Dear soul mind body of Divine Rainbow Light Ball*
>   *and Divine Rainbow Liquid Spring of Divine*
>   *Blessing Soul Mind Body Transplants,*
> *I love you, honor you, and appreciate you.*
> *You have the power to clear the soul mind body block-*
>   *ages in all of my relationships with all of my col-*
>   *leagues, including all of my coworkers and bosses*
>   *in past lives and in this life.*
> *You have the power to offer divine forgiveness for my*
>   *mistakes in my relationships with all of my col-*
>   *leagues in all lifetimes.*
> *You have the power to heal all relationships with all of*
>   *my colleagues in all lifetimes.*
> *I am extremely grateful.*
> *I cannot thank you enough.*
> *Dear souls of all of my colleagues in all lifetimes,*
> *I love you, honor you, and appreciate you.*
> *Please forgive my ancestors and me for our mistakes of*
>   *harming you in any way.*
> *We sincerely apologize.*
> *We cannot honor you enough.*
> *At the same time, I completely forgive you for your*
>   *mistakes of harming me in any of my lifetimes.*
> *Please accept my forgiveness.*
> *Thank you.*

*All souls of all of my colleagues whom my ancestors
and I have harmed, please forgive us again.
Thank you, all.*

Mind Power. Visualize rainbow light shining within you and your colleagues.

Sound Power. Chant repeatedly, silently or aloud:

*Divine Blessing treasures clear all of my relationship
karma with my colleagues and heal us. Thank you.
Divine Blessing treasures clear all of my relationship
karma with my colleagues and heal us. Thank you.
Divine Blessing treasures clear all of my relationship
karma with my colleagues and heal us. Thank you.
Divine Blessing treasures clear all of my relationship
karma with my colleagues and heal us. Thank you.
Divine Blessing treasures clear all of my relationship
karma with my colleagues and heal us. Thank you.
Divine Blessing treasures clear all of my relationship
karma with my colleagues and heal us. Thank you.
Divine Blessing treasures clear all of my relationship
karma with my colleagues and heal us. Thank you.*

. . .

Please stop reading and do this practice now. Chant with your heart and soul for at least three minutes. The longer you chant and the more often you chant, the better. There is no time limit.

Close. After chanting and visualizing for at least three minutes, close the practice by saying:

Hao! Hao! Hao!
Thank you. Thank you. Thank you.

Balance the Relationships of Humanity

Mother Earth is in a transition period now. All kinds of imbalances are present on Mother Earth, including natural disasters, pollution of the land, water, and air, wars, sickness, hunger, pollution of people's hearts, and more.

Many people suffer from depression, anxiety, worry, grief, fear, anger, and more. Balancing the relationships of humanity is urgently needed.

Let me offer three more major divine treasures for balancing the relationships of humanity in order to help humanity pass through this difficult time:

Divine Rainbow Light Ball and Divine Rainbow Liquid Spring of Divine Balance Soul Mind Body Transplants

Prepare. Sit up straight. Put the tip of your tongue as close as you can to the roof of your mouth, without touching. Put your hands in the Soul Light Era Prayer Position. Totally relax. Open your heart and soul to receive this great honor. It will take about one minute for you to receive the twenty-fifth, twenty-sixth, and twenty-seventh priceless divine treasures offered to you in this book.

Divine Order: Divine Rainbow Light Ball and Divine Rainbow Liquid Spring of Divine Balance Soul Transplant

Transmission!

**Divine Order: Divine Rainbow Light Ball
and Divine Rainbow Liquid Spring of
Divine Balance Mind Transplant**

Transmission!

**Divine Order: Divine Rainbow Light Ball
and Divine Rainbow Liquid Spring of
Divine Balance Body Transplant**

Transmission!

**Divine Order: Divine Rainbow Light Ball and
Divine Rainbow Liquid Spring of Divine Balance
Soul Mind Body Transplants join as one.**

Hei Ya Ya Ya Ya Ya Ya You!

The last Divine Order can be translated as follows:

*Divine Order to join Divine Rainbow Light Ball and
Divine Rainbow Liquid Spring of Divine Balance
Soul Mind Body Transplants as one now.*

You are extremely blessed. We cannot honor the Divine
enough. Let us sing *Thank You, Divine* to express our greatest
gratitude:

Thank you, Divine
Thank you, Divine
Thank you, Divine

Thank you, Divine
Thank you, Divine

Let me lead you to apply the Four Power Techniques with Divine Balance Soul Mind Body Transplants to balance the relationships of humanity. To balance all of the relationships of humanity is to balance humanity.

Body Power. Sit up straight. Put the tip of your tongue as close as you can to the roof of your mouth, without touching. Put your hands in the Soul Light Era Prayer Position.

Soul Power. Say *hello:*

> *Dear soul mind body of Divine Rainbow Light Ball*
> *and Divine Rainbow Liquid Spring of Divine Balance Soul Mind Body Transplants,*
> *I love you, honor you, and appreciate you.*
> *You have the power to balance humanity.*
> *I am very grateful.*
> *I cannot thank you enough.*
> *Thank you.*

Mind Power. Visualize rainbow light shining throughout humanity.

Sound Power. Chant repeatedly, silently or aloud:

> *Divine Balance treasures balance humanity. Thank you, Divine.*

> *Divine Balance treasures balance humanity. Thank*
> *you, Divine.*
> *Divine Balance treasures balance humanity. Thank*
> *you, Divine.*
> *Divine Balance treasures balance humanity. Thank*
> *you, Divine.*
> *Divine Balance treasures balance humanity. Thank*
> *you, Divine.*
> *Divine Balance treasures balance humanity. Thank*
> *you, Divine.*
> *Divine Balance treasures balance humanity. Thank*
> *you, Divine . . .*

Please stop reading. Do this practice now. Chant for at least three minutes.

Close. After chanting and visualizing for at least three minutes, close the practice:

> *Hao! Hao! Hao!*
> *Thank you. Thank you. Thank you.*

Balance the Relationships of All Nations

There are many conflicts and challenges among nations on Mother Earth, including wars, economic conflicts and challenges, and more. The divine way to transform the relationships of all nations is to apply divine treasures.

Apply the Four Power Techniques and Divine Rainbow Light Ball and Divine Rainbow Liquid Spring of Divine Love, Divine Forgiveness, Divine Compassion, Divine Light, and Divine Blessing Soul Mind Body Transplants to transform the relationships of all nations:

Body Power. Sit up straight. Put the tip of your tongue near, but not touching, the roof of your mouth. Put your hands in the Soul Light Era Prayer Position (left palm over your Message Center, right palm in the traditional prayer position).

Soul Power. Say *hello:*

> *Dear soul mind body of Divine Rainbow Light Ball*
> *and Divine Rainbow Liquid Spring of Divine Love,*
> *Divine Forgiveness, Divine Compassion, Divine*
> *Light, and Divine Blessing Soul Mind Body*
> *Transplants,*
> *I love you, honor you, and appreciate you.*
> *You have the power to bring love, peace, and harmony*
> *to all nations.*
> *I am deeply grateful.*
> *I cannot thank you enough.*

Mind Power. Visualize rainbow light shining throughout all nations.

Sound Power. Chant repeatedly, silently or aloud:

> *Divine Love, Forgiveness, Compassion, Light, and*
> *Blessing treasures bring love, peace, and harmony to*
> *all nations. Thank you, Divine.*
> *Divine Love, Forgiveness, Compassion, Light, and*
> *Blessing treasures bring love, peace, and harmony to*
> *all nations. Thank you, Divine.*

Divine Love, Forgiveness, Compassion, Light, and
  Blessing treasures bring love, peace, and harmony to
  all nations. Thank you, Divine.
Divine Love, Forgiveness, Compassion, Light, and
  Blessing treasures bring love, peace, and harmony to
  all nations. Thank you, Divine.
Divine Love, Forgiveness, Compassion, Light, and
  Blessing treasures bring love, peace, and harmony to
  all nations. Thank you, Divine.
Divine Love, Forgiveness, Compassion, Light, and
  Blessing treasures bring love, peace, and harmony to
  all nations. Thank you, Divine.
Divine Love, Forgiveness, Compassion, Light, and
  Blessing treasures bring love, peace, and harmony to
  all nations. Thank you, Divine . . .

Please stop reading and do this practice. Continue to take every opportunity to practice and receive benefits from your divine treasures. Close your eyes and chant for at least three minutes now.

Close. After chanting for at least three minutes, close the practice:

Hao! Hao! Hao!
Thank you. Thank you. Thank you.

The longer you chant and the more often you chant, the better. There is no time limit. The more you chant, the faster you can bring love, peace, and harmony to all nations.

Balance the Relationships of All Planets (Including Mother Earth), All Stars, All Galaxies, and All Universes

Mother Earth has many imbalances. Other planets, stars, galaxies, and universes also have imbalances.

If you practice divine transformation, you will help all planets, including Mother Earth, all stars, all galaxies, and all universes. When millions and millions of people practice divine transformation together, huge benefits and transformation of relationships among all planets, stars, galaxies, and universes will happen.

Now I will explain three additional huge divine treasures to you and every reader. In fact, these next three Divine Soul Mind Body Transplants have already been downloaded to every human being, every animal, every tree, every ocean, every mountain, every planet, every star, every galaxy, and every universe. *These treasures are for every soul in all universes.* They are:

Divine Rainbow Light Ball and Divine Rainbow Liquid Spring of Divine Love Peace Harmony Soul Mind Body Transplants

You and every soul in all universes have received the twenty-eighth, twenty-ninth, and thirtieth priceless divine treasures offered to you in this book in May 2010. Here is a record of the Divine Orders that were given at that time:

Divine Order: Divine Rainbow Light Ball and Divine Rainbow Liquid Spring of Divine Love Peace Harmony Soul Transplant to all souls in all universes

Transmission!

**Divine Order: Divine Rainbow Light Ball
and Divine Rainbow Liquid Spring of Divine
Love Peace Harmony Mind Transplant
to all souls in all universes**

Transmission!

**Divine Order: Divine Rainbow Light Ball
and Divine Rainbow Liquid Spring of Divine
Love Peace Harmony Body Transplant
to all souls in all universes**

Transmission!

**Divine Order: Divine Rainbow Light Ball
and Divine Rainbow Liquid Spring of
Divine Love Peace Harmony Soul Mind
Body Transplants join as one.**

Hei Ya Ya Ya Ya Ya Ya You!

The last Divine Order can be translated as follows:

*Divine Order to join Divine Rainbow Light Ball and
Divine Rainbow Liquid Spring of Divine Love Peace
Harmony Soul Mind Body Transplants as one now.*

You are extremely blessed. We cannot honor the Divine enough. Let us sing *Thank You, Divine* to express our greatest gratitude:

> *Thank you, Divine*
> *Thank you, Divine*
> *Thank you, Divine*
> *Thank you, Divine*
> *Thank you, Divine*

Now apply the Four Power Techniques with Divine Love Peace Harmony Soul Mind Body Transplants to balance the relationships of all planets, stars, galaxies, and universes.

Body Power. Sit up straight. Put the tip of your tongue as close as you can to the roof of your mouth, without touching. Put your hands in the Soul Light Era Prayer Position.

Soul Power. Say *hello:*

> *Dear soul mind body of Divine Rainbow Light*
> *Ball and Divine Rainbow Liquid Spring of*
> *Divine Love Peace Harmony Soul Mind Body*
> *Transplants,*
> *I love you, honor you, and appreciate you.*
> *You have the power to bring love, peace, and harmony*
> *to all planets, including Mother Earth, all stars, all*
> *galaxies, and all universes.*
> *I am very grateful.*
> *I cannot thank you enough.*

Mind Power. Visualize rainbow light shining throughout all planets, including Mother Earth, all stars, all galaxies, and all universes.

Sound Power. Chant repeatedly, silently or aloud, for at least three minutes:

> *Divine Love Peace Harmony treasures bring love, peace, and harmony to all planets, including Mother Earth, all stars, all galaxies, and all universes. Thank you, Divine.*

> *Divine Love Peace Harmony treasures bring love, peace, and harmony to all planets, including Mother Earth, all stars, all galaxies, and all universes. Thank you, Divine.*

> *Divine Love Peace Harmony treasures bring love, peace, and harmony to all planets, including Mother Earth, all stars, all galaxies, and all universes. Thank you, Divine.*

> *Divine Love Peace Harmony treasures bring love, peace, and harmony to all planets, including Mother Earth, all stars, all galaxies, and all universes. Thank you, Divine.*

> *Divine Love Peace Harmony treasures bring love, peace, and harmony to all planets, including Mother Earth, all stars, all galaxies, and all universes. Thank you, Divine.*

Divine Love Peace Harmony treasures bring love,
peace, and harmony to all planets, including
Mother Earth, all stars, all galaxies, and all
universes. Thank you, Divine.

Divine Love Peace Harmony treasures bring love,
peace, and harmony to all planets, including
Mother Earth, all stars, all galaxies, and all uni-
verses. Thank you, Divine . . .

Please stop reading now. Really chant for at least three minutes.

Close. After chanting and visualizing for at least three minutes, close the practice:

Hao! Hao! Hao!
Thank you. Thank you. Thank you.

The longer you chant and the more times you chant, the better. There is no time limit.

Now let us sing the Divine Soul Song *Love, Peace and Harmony:*

I love my heart and soul
I love all humanity
Join hearts and souls together
Love, peace and harmony
Love, peace and harmony

If you practice in this way, you are serving Mother Earth, all planets, all stars, all galaxies, and all universes. Every moment that you are chanting, you are offering balance to Mother Earth, all planets, all stars, all galaxies, and all universes. Mother Earth, all planets, all stars, all galaxies, and all universes really need more balance.

If millions of people were to give love, forgiveness, compassion, light, and blessing to Mother Earth, all planets, all stars, all galaxies, and all universes, they would become much more balanced.

Every moment that you are chanting, you are also receiving virtue from the Akashic Records. Virtue is spiritual currency. Spiritual currency can transform every aspect of your life.

Now chant:

> *Divine Love Peace Harmony treasures bring balance to all universes. Thank you, Divine.*
> *Divine Love Peace Harmony treasures bring balance to all universes. Thank you, Divine.*
> *Divine Love Peace Harmony treasures bring balance to all universes. Thank you, Divine.*
> *Divine Love Peace Harmony treasures bring balance to all universes. Thank you, Divine.*
> *Divine Love Peace Harmony treasures bring balance to all universes. Thank you, Divine.*
> *Divine Love Peace Harmony treasures bring balance to all universes. Thank you, Divine.*
> *Divine Love Peace Harmony treasures bring balance to all universes. Thank you, Divine . . .*

This chant is extremely important. There is no time limit. The more you chant, the more great benefits Mother Earth and all universes could receive.

Chanting chanting chanting
Divine chanting is healing
Chanting chanting chanting
Divine chanting is rejuvenating

Singing singing singing
Divine singing is transforming
Singing singing singing
Divine singing is enlightening

Humanity is waiting for divine chanting
All souls are waiting for divine singing
Divine chanting removes all blockages
Divine singing brings inner joy

Divine is chanting and singing
Humanity and all souls are nourishing
Humanity and all souls are chanting and singing

World love peace and harmony are coming
World love peace and harmony are coming
World love peace and harmony are coming

Divine Transformation for Your Finances and Business

*T*HINK ABOUT HUMANITY on Mother Earth. Many people on Mother Earth are very wealthy. Many people are very poor.

A business owner in the Philippines told me he had a very good team. He also thought he planned and marketed well, but his business was not successful. He had a very close friend who did not plan or market much, but his business decisions and business were always successful. The first business owner could not understand this at all.

Think about the people around you. Some people are very intelligent. You might think they should be very successful in business, but they may not be successful at all. Some people are very simple. They may even seem unintelligent, but they are very successful.

In Toronto I knew someone who made whatever business he touched very successful. He asked me, "Why am I such a very blessed person in business?" I paused a moment and did a spiritual reading by communicating with the Akashic Records. I told him, "The Divine told me your success comes from your grandfather. Your grandfather did very good service for others and this created lots of good virtue for him."

There is an ancient spiritual statement:

Qian ren zai shu, hou ren cheng liang

"Qian ren" means *ancestor*. "Zai" means *plant*. "Shu" means *tree*. "Hou ren" means *descendants*. "Cheng liang" means *enjoy the shade*. Therefore, "Qian ren zai shu, hou ren cheng liang" (pronounced *chyen ren zye shoo, hoe ren chung lyahng*) means *ancestors plant the trees; descendants enjoy the shade*. This statement teaches us that if our ancestors have accumulated good virtue through good service to others, then we enjoy the benefits.

Let me continue the story of the businessman in Toronto. After hearing my spiritual reading, he was very surprised by its accuracy. He told me, "Master Sha, my grandfather was a spiritual leader. Thousands of people follow his teaching. He was extremely loving, compassionate, and kind. People built statues and temples in our hometown to honor and remember him."

This example tells us that because this man's ancestors gave great service to others, he received benefits and rewards in his business and finances.

Let me share another story from the renowned Chinese spiritual book *Liao-Fan's Four Lessons*, which was written in the early seventeenth century. [1]

---

1. This story is taken from the English translation shown on http://www.buddhanet.net/
pdf_file/liaofan.pdf, by Buddha Dharma Education Association Inc.

In Fujian Province, Rong Yang was a prominent man who held a position in the imperial court as the Emperor's teacher. His ancestors were boat people who made a living by helping people cross the river.

One day, a long-lasting storm caused severe flooding that washed away all of the houses in the area. People, animals, and possessions were swept downriver. Most of the boaters took advantage of the situation and collected the floating belongings for themselves. Only Rong Yang's grandfather and great-grandfather tried to rescue the people drowning in the river. They did not take any of the goods that floated by. All of the other boaters thought Rong Yang's grandfather and great-grandfather were very foolish.

After Rong Yang's father was born a short while later, the Yang family gradually became wealthy. One day a heavenly saint manifested as a Taoist monk and came to the Yang family to tell them that their ancestors had accumulated much hidden virtue. Consequently, they and their descendants would enjoy prosperity and prominence. The monk also guided the family to build their ancestral tomb in a special place. They followed the Taoist's suggestion and today this site is renowned as the White Hare Grave.

Rong Yang passed the imperial examination when he was only twenty years old. Later, he received an imperial appointment. The emperor granted the same imperial honors to Rong Yang's grandfather and great-grandfather. To this day, Rong Yang's many virtuous and prosperous descendants are still very prominent.

This is another great example of "ancestors plant the trees; descendants enjoy the shade." This is cause and effect. A good cause (action, behavior, or thought) brings good results. The emperor honored Rong Yang's grandfather and great-grandfather for their service, which further benefited their descendants.

This story also reminds us to always remember to be kind to others. If you can serve, serve. Serve unconditionally.

Why Some People Have Wealth

Why do some people have financial abundance? The root cause is good karma. Such a person and his or her ancestors accumulated great virtue in their lifetimes. They served people very well in their lifetimes. For this good service, they were given virtue. This good virtue, which is recorded in the Akashic Records, has transformed to physical money in the person's current lifetime. If such a person continues to serve well, he or she will continue to have financial abundance in future lifetimes. Their descendants will also flourish. The stories I shared earlier are examples of this wisdom.

Why do other people struggle with poor financial conditions? The root cause is bad karma. Such a person and his or her ancestors made significant mistakes in their lifetimes.

Therefore, in order to transform finances, the key is still to clear your own bad karma and your ancestors' bad karma.

How can you clear bad karma? The best method can be summarized in one sentence:

To offer unconditional universal service to humanity and Mother Earth is to clear bad karma.

Unconditional universal service is very important. However, it is very difficult to offer service that is truly unconditional. Many people think that if they offer some service, they should be paid. We are on Mother Earth. When someone offers professional service, he or she deserves to be paid. Everyone has to make a living. Everyone has responsibilities for the care of their families.

However, to self-clear karma, the key is to offer *unconditional* universal service. To offer unconditional service is to offer service without expecting anything in return. Just give pure service to others to make others happier and healthier.

There are many ways to offer unconditional service. For example, you can do volunteer work for a spiritual group. You can simply help people from your heart when they need assistance. I will explain unconditional universal service in more detail later in this chapter. The key is to understand that to offer this kind of service is to self-clear your karma.

Financial Abundance Can Be Lost

If you are wealthy but forget to offer service, or if you are not generous or kind to society or those who need support, then you could lose your virtue.

For example, Mother Earth is in a transition period. In recent years, many natural disasters have caused many people to suffer. If you are a wealthy person, have you donated money to relieve their suffering? You have the ability to do this. Do you do it? Nobody asks you to do it. If you do it, Heaven records your kindness and generosity. If you do not offer support, Heaven similarly records your lack of kindness. Remember, *everything* you have done is recorded in the Akashic Records, including your activities, behaviors, and thoughts.

Some wealthy and powerful people may do unkind things. For example, a national leader may start a war in which many people are killed. This too is recorded in his or her book in the Akashic Records. Other government officials may implement policies that harm millions of people. This will create a record of very heavy bad karma.

Some wealthy people take advantage of others, or get "dirty" money through gambling, cheating, or stealing. This also creates bad karma.

When a wealthy person creates bad karma, he or she loses virtue. Wealth in this lifetime is due to good service offered in previous lifetimes. For this good service, virtue was deposited into their virtue "bank account." If the person does unpleasant things in this lifetime, he or she will lose their virtue deposit.

It works just as it does in the physical world. One could have a large bank account. But if one continues to spend money without making new deposits, one day the account will have a zero balance, or even a negative balance. A wealthy person who does unpleasant things continues to lose virtue, and his or her virtue account could reach a zero balance.

Look at the economic conditions on Mother Earth now. Many companies have become bankrupt. Other companies have completely failed and ended. I will just offer a little reminder here: there is a spiritual reason behind any business or financial failure. Please be aware of this wisdom and think about it further.

I will share more wisdom with you. Big businesses can have shareholders. Take care in choosing your business partners. For example, if a business has ten major shareholders, and two or three of them have bad karma, it will affect the entire organization. Please think a little more about this teaching also.

All of these examples and teachings are to share with you and every reader that a wealthy person must pay attention to karmic issues. The teaching can be summarized in one sentence:

**A wealthy person who wants to maintain
financial abundance must continue
to offer good services.**

Good services include offering unconditional love, forgiveness, compassion, generosity, kindness, purity, sincerity, honesty, integrity, and more.

The teaching has another side that can also be summarized in one sentence:

A wealthy person who offers unpleasant services could lose his or her business and financial abundance.

Unpleasant services include killing, harming, taking advantage of others, cheating, stealing, and more. Unpleasant services create bad karma. Bad karma can be created in many ways. Not many people really understand all of the types of bad karma. I am delighted to share the following teaching.

Types of Bad Karma

In ancient spiritual teaching, bad karma can be divided into three types: body karma, mouth karma, and thought karma.

- Body karma includes:
  - killing
  - stealing
  - cheating
  - physical abuse
  - sexual abuse
- Mouth karma includes:
  - lying
  - creating distrust and ill will between two parties
  - disrespect
  - rudeness

    o criticizing
    o condemning
    o judging
    o complaining
- Thought karma includes:
    o greed
    o stinginess
    o anger
    o jealousy
    o wishful thinking (illusion)

To know more about the different kinds of bad karma from body, mouth, and thought is to remind yourself to avoid creating bad karma. If you realize you have issues with any of these three types of karma, you can be awakened and empowered to correct them.

You also now know that if you do not correct your issues at the body, mouth, and thought levels, you will continue to create bad karma.

There is an ancient statement:

Shan you shan bao, e you e bao

"Shan" means *good karma and kindness*. "You" means *has*. "Bao" means *return*. "E" means *bad karma and challenges*.

"Shan you shan bao, e you e bao" (pronounced *shahn yoe shahn bao, uh yoe uh bao* [rhymes with *now*]) can be translated as *good karma returns; bad karma also returns*.

Good karma returns as good health, good relationships, and financial abundance, as well as blessings in every aspect of life.

Bad karma returns as sickness, challenging relationships, and poor finances, as well as blockages in every aspect of life.

How can you know whether you have good karma or bad karma? It is very easy to figure out. Are you healthy? Are your emotions balanced? Are your relationships blessed? Do your children behave well and get along with others? Do you have financial abundance? If you can answer *yes* to all of these questions, you definitely have good karma in all of your lifetimes. If some of your answers are *no*, know that the root cause is bad karma. When you have special challenges in different aspects of life, especially if you find you have the same issues repeated over and over, that is very clearly a sign of bad karma and serious karmic lessons.

The important wisdom is that good karma and bad karma are what you and your ancestors have created. You have the power to create your karma for the future. If you want blessings for your health, relationships, and finances, offer good service. If you do not want karmic lessons for your health, relationships, and finances, stop creating bad karma from body, mouth, and thought.

This can be summarized in one sentence:

**Create good karma with your ancestors
and receive blessings; create bad karma
with your ancestors and receive lessons.**

I wish that you and every reader will be careful not to create bad body karma, mouth karma, and thought karma. Every day, from the moment you awaken until the moment you fall asleep, discipline your activities, behaviors, words, and thoughts.

This is easy to say, but not always easy to do. Let me share a soul secret with you. If you do, say, or think something wrong, instantly say:

Dear Divine,
I am sorry.
Dear _____ (name the person[s] you hurt or harmed),
I am sorry.
Please forgive me.

Then chant silently:

I love my heart and soul
I love all humanity
Join hearts and souls together
Love, peace and harmony
Love, peace and harmony

The Divine Soul Song *Love, Peace and Harmony* is a priceless divine treasure for self-clearing karma. Its power is beyond any words, comprehension, and imagination.

Why Some People Have Financial Challenges

The root cause of poor finances and all kinds of financial challenges is bad karma. In order to self-clear karma, remember the teaching above: if you have any issues of body karma, mouth karma, or thought karma, please be serious and disciplined to correct them.

There is only one way for you and any person to self-clear

karma. To self-clear karma is to offer good service to others, to make others happier and healthier, and as well to offer good service to help humanity and Mother Earth pass through this difficult time of transition and purification.

To offer good service is to create good karma. Creating good karma reduces your karmic debt. If you offer good service, you are given virtue from Heaven's virtue bank to your virtue bank in your Akashic Record book. This good virtue comes to you in the form of Heaven's flowers, which can be red, gold, rainbow, purple, crystal, or mixed colors. The virtue or flowers are spiritual currency. It repays your karmic debt step by step. You must clear your karmic debt first. When this root blockage is removed, then you will have the possibility of seeing your finances flourish.

Virtue is yin money, which is currency in the spiritual world. Money on Mother Earth is yang money, which is currency in the physical world. Just as a human being needs money to spend in the physical world, a soul needs virtue to spend in the spiritual world.

The one-sentence secret about the relationship between spiritual money and physical money is:

Virtue in the spiritual world can transform to money in the physical world and vice versa.

If you are wealthy, you have accumulated good virtue in previous lifetimes and in this lifetime. Some of this virtue has transformed to physical money in your present life. If you continue to serve well in this life, you will continue to accumulate good virtue. In future lifetimes, you could then continue to enjoy financial abundance. If you forget to serve, and especially if you go the opposite way and harm, take advantage of, cheat, or steal from others, you will create bad karma and lose virtue. Your good virtue in your virtue bank will be spent until it is exhausted.

If you lack physical money, you do not have much good virtue deposited in your personal Heaven's virtue bank. In order to transform your finances, the key is to increase your virtue. To increase your good virtue, serve others unconditionally. The top secret to transforming finances and business is:

Offer unconditional universal service to transform your finances and business.

If you have heavy bad karma, it could take your greatest effort for many years or even many lifetimes to see significant improvement in your finances and business, and to flourish in other aspects of life.

One day I was in a church teaching a workshop. A lady said, "Master Sha, I have served for more than twenty years. I have done volunteer support. I have served many friends, but I still have chronic health issues, relationship challenges, and financial hardship." I paused a moment. I checked directly with the leaders of the Akashic Records and the Divine. This person in all of her lifetimes had killed more than five hundred people. She carried huge bad karma.

I told her, "I am glad that you told me you have served for more than twenty years. What I can tell you is, if you had not served well for the past twenty years, the condition of your health, relationships, and finances could have been much worse."

She had an "aha!" moment then and totally accepted her condition because her soul understood her life's records. Her heart got it also. She was grateful to receive this teaching.

I offered the teaching earlier in this chapter that major karma can be created from body, mouth, and thought.

There is an ancient statement:

Zhong sheng wei guo, pu sa wei yin

"Zhong sheng" means *ordinary being*. "Wei" means *to be afraid*. "Guo" means *effect*. "Pu sa" means *bodhisattva*. "Yin" means *cause*.

"Zhong sheng wei guo, pu sa wei yin" (pronounced *jawng shung way gwaw, poo sah way yeen*) means *An ordinary being is afraid of the effect, which includes sickness, broken relationships, and financial challenges, but a bodhisattva is afraid of the cause.* The cause is karma.

This teaches us to be afraid of karma. Why are bodhisattvas afraid of the cause? Because they understand that if you create bad karma, you must pay a price. Sometimes the price or effect will not happen until the next lifetime. For heavy bad karma, the price or effect could come for many lifetimes, one after another, for thirty, fifty, or even more than one hundred lifetimes. When the time is right, the effect could be very heavy, literally disastrous.

A bodhisattva is afraid of the cause, which is to create bad karma. To create bad karma will block a bodhisattva's spiritual journey. A bodhisattva is an enlightened spiritual being. He or she is searching for total enlightenment to become a buddha, which is a totally enlightened being.

Lao Zi, the author of *Tao Te Jing*, also wrote about karma:

Huo fu wu men, wei ren zhi zhao

"Huo" means *disasters*. "Fu" means *luck* or *blessings*. "Wu" means *no*. "Men" means *gate*. "Wei" means *only*. "Ren" means *human being*. "Zhi" means *yourself*. "Zhao" means *attract*.

"Huo fu wu men, wei ren zhi zhao" (pronounced *hwaw foo woo mun, way ren jr jow*) means *There is no particular gate to one's disasters and blessings; they are all attracted by yourself.*

This tells us that if you offer good service, good luck and blessings will come to you. If you offer bad service, lessons and disasters will come to you. It all depends on you. That is why it is important to discipline yourself in what you do (body), what you say (mouth), and what you think (thought). In this way, you will avoid bad karma and create good karma.

When you do, say, or think something wrong, that is okay. The important thing is to correct your mistakes instantly. As I shared with you earlier, apologize to the Divine and to the person or persons you hurt or harmed. Sincerely apologize and transform the wrong action, speech, or thought instantly. Always remember to purify your soul, heart, mind, and body. Always improve yourself in what you do, what you say, and what you think. If you are consciously aware of this, then you can progress in your spiritual journey very fast. When you avoid creating bad karma and create a lot of good karma, transformation of your finances and every aspect of life will follow. If you follow the teaching here and practice seriously, the benefits for your life can be unlimited. I wish you will really put this teaching into practice.

Create Good Karma to Transform Your Finances

How can you create good karma? You have learned that bad karma can be created from body, mouth, and thought. Good karma can also be created from body, mouth, and thought.

Another ancient spiritual statement is:

Hua you san shuo, qiao shuo wei miao

"Hua" means *speech*. "You" means *exists*. "San" means *three*. "Shuo" means *ways to speak*. "Qiao" means *proper*. "Wei" means *is*. "Miao" means *profound*.

"Hua you san shuo, qiao shuo wei miao" (pronounced *hwah yoe sahn shwaw, chee-yow shwaw way mee-yow*) means *There are three ways to speak something. The proper way to speak is profound.*

You can easily understand that speaking has two sides, like yin and yang. You can speak properly and well or you can speak improperly and not well. In your daily life with your family, at the office, or in social gatherings, if you speak properly, you could make people happy, inspired, and moved. If you speak improperly, you could make people upset or sad.

Remember, the mouth can create bad karma. If you speak rudely or disrespectfully, you create bad karma. If you speak with love, compassion, and forgiveness, you create good karma. The wisdom is:

To create good karma is to have good action, speech, and thought.

It is easy to understand that this is how good and bad karma are created. Think about your daily life. On some days you are very happy and speak with kindness and treat others well. You are creating good karma. On other days you are irritated and upset. You could speak rudely and disrespectfully and treat others badly. You are creating bad karma.

Every time you do something, every time you speak something, every time you think something, always remember one principle: *Are you serving yourself or are you serving others to make others happier and healthier?*

Good karma and bad karma are opposites. They are also two aspects of the same thing. In one day, a person can create good karma and accumulate Heaven's colorful flowers. In the same day, this person can create bad karma and accumulate black or gray flowers. Black and gray flowers are given as records of unpleasant services, including killing, harming, taking advantage of others, cheating, stealing, and more. If you create bad karma, black and gray flowers will be added to your book in the Akashic Records and some good flowers, including red, golden, rainbow, purple, and crystal flowers, will be removed.

Good flowers are given to reward a person with good health, relationships, finances, and more. Black flowers are given to the person to learn lessons, such as sickness, broken relationships, financial challenges, and more.

How do you know whether you are creating good karma or bad karma? I am sharing with you and humanity a one-sentence secret about creating bad karma:

If what you do, what you speak, and what you think benefit only yourself, you are creating bad karma.

In every aspect of your life, apply this "ruler" to measure what you do, what you speak, and what you think. You will avoid creating bad karma. You will create good karma. Your life transformation could be beyond imagination.

Now let me explain further how to create good karma. Here is the one-sentence secret about creating good karma:

The best way to create good karma is to offer unconditional universal service through every aspect of your life.

To create good karma, first purify your heart. The heart houses your mind and soul. To purify your soul, heart, mind, and body in every aspect of your life, follow this key principle:

Create good karma by making others happier and healthier with what you do, what you speak, and what you think.

In one word, this principle for creating all kinds of good karma is *selflessness*. If everything you do, speak, and think is only for you, this is selfishness. Selfishness creates bad karma. In summary, the complete one-sentence secret for creating good karma and bad karma is:

Selfishness creates bad karma; selflessness creates good karma.

In everything you do, speak, and think, always remember love, forgiveness, care, compassion, sincerity, honesty, purity, integrity, humility, generosity, and kindness. These are the standards for your actions, speech, and thoughts.

Good karma and bad karma are yin and yang. If you are not going to yang, you are going to yin. If you are not going to yin, you are going to yang. Your actions, speech, and thoughts fall either on the yang side or the yin side. Each action, speech, and thought is recorded in your book in the Akashic Records. Each one will create either good karma or bad karma.

For speech, do you speak with kindness, love, compassion, and integrity? Do you speak with sincerity and honesty? Or do you speak rudely? Do you complain? Do you lie? Are you irritated or even angry?

An important ancient spiritual teaching is:

Anger burns good virtue.

If two people are arguing and one person is shouting and yelling, while the other person is quiet, the person who is yelling is literally throwing his or her virtue to the person who is quiet. The yelling person loses virtue. If both people yell at each other, then they are throwing virtue back and forth to each other.

For thought, do you think positively, lovingly, kindly, and generously? Or do you think negatively or angrily? Do you think of ways to hurt or take advantage of others?

For action, if you are a spiritual being, have you ever killed anything? Killing animals is considered killing. For example, if you order live seafood at a restaurant, this is considered killing. You may not be aware of it, but it creates bad karma.

Here are more examples of creating good karma:

- donating to the poor
- building homes, schools, and hospitals
- giving time and money to support proper spiritual organizations and teachers
- serving world peace through various activities, organizations, and movements

- serving the elderly, the sick, the homeless, and others who suffer
- serving those who have suffered from an accident or disaster
- supporting organizations or other individuals who offer kindness and service to others
- helping and empowering others to succeed
- healing others physically, emotionally, mentally, and spiritually
- teaching others to heal themselves
- teaching others to practice kindness, love, care, forgiveness, and compassion
- developing public projects for the greater benefit of people and society
- respecting all people
- loving and cherishing all beings, creatures, and things

To summarize the what, why, and how of one's financial condition:

- Wealth is due to good karma from past lifetimes and this lifetime.
- A wealthy person who continues to offer good service to humanity will continue to enjoy financial abundance in this life and future lifetimes.
- A wealthy person who creates bad karma could lose his or her financial abundance.
- Financial challenges are due to bad karma in past lifetimes and in this lifetime.
- Financial challenges can be transformed by creating good karma through unconditional universal service.

- To create good karma is to create good virtue and receive Heaven's flowers, which are spiritual currency. Spiritual currency in the spiritual world can transform to money in the physical world.

To summarize all of the above further, in one sentence:

Transform the spiritual virtue bank first;
then transformation of the physical bank will follow.

This teaching can be explained in another way. If you have financial challenges, the root cause is bad karma. In order to transform your finances, you must clear bad karma. How? In one sentence:

Offer unconditional universal service to make others
happier and healthier through your good actions,
kind speech, and compassionate thoughts.

To offer service is to gain virtue in your virtue bank in the spiritual world. If you do not have enough physical money, this means you do not have enough virtue deposited in your virtue bank. Virtue can be transformed to money. In order to transform your financial condition to gain money, transform your virtue bank first. Gain virtue first. If you have virtue, which is yin money, it can be transformed to yang money in the physical world.

This is the way for you and everyone to transform finances. Transform the virtue bank first; then transformation of the physical bank will follow.

I emphasize again that to serve is to self-clear bad karma because virtue, which is spiritual currency, is given through service. Bad karma creates spiritual debt. Virtue pays your spiritual debt. Pay your spiritual debt first, and then continue to serve. More virtue will then be given. Virtue, spiritual currency, will transform to physical money. This is the way to transform the virtue bank first; then transformation of the physical bank will follow.

One of the most powerful spiritual methods for transforming your finances is to sing the Divine Soul Song *Love, Peace and Harmony.* This Divine Soul Song carries power beyond comprehension:

- To chant or sing *Love, Peace and Harmony* is to serve. To serve is to gain virtue. Virtue will pay your spiritual debt.
- To chant or sing *Love, Peace and Harmony* is to heal your spiritual, mental, emotional, and physical bodies.
- To chant or sing *Love, Peace and Harmony* is to prevent all sicknesses.
- To chant or sing *Love, Peace and Harmony* is to purify your soul, heart, mind, and body.
- To chant or sing *Love, Peace and Harmony* is to rejuvenate your soul, heart, mind, and body.
- To chant or sing *Love, Peace and Harmony* is to clear your financial karma.
- To chant or sing *Love, Peace and Harmony* is to gain more virtue to transform your finances and business.

How does this Divine Soul Song work? When you chant or sing *Love, Peace and Harmony,* divine frequency and vibration with divine love, forgiveness, compassion, and light radiate to all humanity, all souls on Mother Earth, and all souls in all universes. The divine frequency of this Divine Soul Song is beyond imagination.

The following, *Divine Soul Song for World Soul Healing, Peace and Enlightenment,* explains the power and significance of chanting *Love, Peace and Harmony* and other Divine Soul Songs:

> *Chanting chanting chanting*
> *Divine chanting is healing*
> *Chanting chanting chanting*
> *Divine chanting is rejuvenating*
>
> *Singing singing singing*
> *Divine singing is transforming*
> *Singing singing singing*
> *Divine singing is enlightening*
>
> *Humanity is waiting for divine chanting*
> *All souls are waiting for divine singing*
> *Divine chanting removes all blockages*
> *Divine singing brings inner joy*
>
> *Divine is chanting and singing*
> *Humanity and all souls are nourishing*
> *Humanity and all souls are chanting and singing*
>
> *World love, peace, and harmony are coming*
> *World love, peace, and harmony are coming*
> *World love, peace, and harmony are coming*

Mother Earth is in a transition period now. Humanity and Mother Earth are facing many challenges. Financial challenges are among the major challenges for people, businesses, countries, and more.

As I have explained, the root cause of financial challenges on Mother Earth is bad karma. Humanity has created heavy bad karma through killing, harming, and taking advantage of others, as well as damaging Mother Earth in different ways. This bad karma is the cause of the present financial challenges on Mother Earth.

It is very important for us to gather millions of people to apply divine transformation to transform the finances and businesses on Mother Earth. If millions of people sang Divine Soul Songs and practiced and chanted with Divine Soul Mind Body Transplants, all of which carry divine frequency and vibration with divine love, forgiveness, compassion, and light, these treasures could clear the bad karma underlying the financial challenges on Mother Earth. It would help transform finances on Mother Earth greatly. However, it does take time to transform heavy karma, whether for a person, a business, a country, or all of Mother Earth.

Let us sing the Divine Soul Song *Love, Peace and Harmony* together now to transform finances and more on Mother Earth and beyond. Say *hello* first:

> *Dear soul mind body of humanity and all souls in all*
>   *universes,*
> *I love you, honor you, and appreciate you.*
> *Let us sing the Divine Soul Song* Love, Peace and
>   Harmony *together.*

> *Lu La Lu La Li*
> *Lu La Lu La La Li*
> *Lu La Lu La Li Lu La*

Lu La Li Lu La
Lu La Li Lu La

I love my heart and soul
I love all humanity
Join hearts and souls together
Love, peace and harmony
Love, peace and harmony

I have a wonderful story about *Love, Peace and Harmony.* At the end of 2009, I was in the Netherlands. One night we arrived at a restaurant at 9:15 PM. The owners told us that the restaurant's formal closing time was 9:30 PM and explained that it was too late for us to dine there. However, after we talked with them for a while, they were very kind to cook for us. The meal was delicious.

The next day, I returned to the same restaurant and told the owners, "Thank you very much for your kindness and delicious food last night. I am giving you a CD of the Divine Soul Song *Love, Peace and Harmony* to bless your business." I saw that the restaurant had only a few customers the night before and also that day. I explained to the owners that the Divine Soul Song *Love, Peace and Harmony* carries divine frequency and vibration with divine love, forgiveness, compassion, and light, and so it could transform the soul mind body blockages of the restaurant's business and transform the business. The owners began to play the CD right away in the restaurant. I told them to keep playing the CD continuously.

On the third day, I went to the restaurant again. It was fully packed. The owners said, "This is amazing. Usually there are only a few people here every night." At that moment, more than thirty diners were packed into the small restaurant.

On the fourth day, we went back. The restaurant was completely packed again.

On the fifth day, the owners offered my team members a free dinner. They said, "This is absolutely amazing."

This story shows the power and ability of the Divine Soul Song *Love, Peace and Harmony* to transform a business instantly with divine frequency and vibration that carries divine love, forgiveness, compassion, and light.

In some cases, it will take more time to transform your finances, but this is divine transformation in action. Learn and practice this absolutely new way of divine transformation. It is extremely simple and practical. You have the power to self-clear karma. You have the power to transform your finances and business. But remember, if you have heavy financial or business karma, it does take time to see the results. It could take many years to self-clear karma.

Be patient and confident.

Practice. Practice. Practice.

Serve. Serve. Serve.

Self-clear Your Karma (Soul Blockages), Mind Blockages, and Body Blockages for Finances and Business

If you have financial challenges, the root cause is bad karma. To self-clear karma, love and forgiveness practices are the key. This is the way to do it:

Apply the Four Power Techniques with Divine Love and Divine Forgiveness treasures:

Body Power. Sit up straight. Put your left palm over your Message Center. Put your right hand in the traditional prayer position.

Soul Power. Say *hello:*

> *Dear soul mind body of my business, _____ (state*
>   your business's name), and finances,
> *I love you, honor you, and appreciate you.*
> *You have the power to remove your soul mind body*
>   *blockages.*
> *Dear Divine Rainbow Light Ball and Divine Rain-*
>   *bow Liquid Spring of Divine Love Soul Mind Body*
>   *Transplants,*
> *Dear Divine Rainbow Light Ball and Divine Rain-*
>   *bow Liquid Spring of Divine Forgiveness Soul*
>   *Mind Body Transplants,*
> *I love you, honor you, and appreciate you.*
> *You have the power to offer divine forgiveness for the*
>   *mistakes the business soul, my soul, and my ances-*
>   *tors' souls have made in past lifetimes and in this*
>   *lifetime.*
> *Dear all the souls that my business soul, my soul, and*
>   *my ancestors' souls have hurt, harmed, and taken*
>   *advantage of in previous lifetimes and in this*
>   *lifetime,*
> *Please come.*
> *I sincerely apologize for the mistakes that my business*
>   *soul, my soul, and my ancestors' souls made in previ-*
>   *ous lifetimes and in this lifetime.*
> *Please forgive us.*
> *I have learned my lessons.*

I will be a better servant for humanity.
Dear Divine Rainbow Light Ball and Divine Rain-
*   bow Liquid Spring of Divine Love Soul Mind Body*
*   Transplants,*
Dear Divine Rainbow Light Ball and Divine Rain-
*   bow Liquid Spring of Divine Forgiveness Soul*
*   Mind Body Transplants,*
Please forgive the mistakes of my business soul, my soul,
*   and my ancestors' souls made in previous lifetimes*
*   and in this lifetime.*
I am very grateful.
I cannot thank you enough.

Mind Power. Visualize divine love and forgiveness radiating in your business and finances.

Sound Power. Chant silently or aloud:

Divine Rainbow Light Ball and Divine Rainbow
*   Liquid Spring of Divine Love and Divine*
*   Forgiveness Soul Mind Body Transplants clear soul*
*   mind body blockages of my finances and business.*
All souls whom my business soul, my soul, and my an-
*   cestors' souls have harmed in all previous lifetimes*
*   and in this lifetime, please forgive us.*
Thank you, all.

Divine Rainbow Light Ball and Divine Rainbow
*   Liquid Spring of Divine Love and Divine*
*   Forgiveness Soul Mind Body Transplants clear soul*
*   mind body blockages of my finances and business.*

*All souls whom my business soul, my soul, and my
    ancestors' souls have harmed in all previous lifetimes
    and in this lifetime, please forgive us.*
Thank you, all.

*Divine Rainbow Light Ball and Divine Rainbow
    Liquid Spring of Divine Love and Divine
    Forgiveness Soul Mind Body Transplants clear soul
    mind body blockages of my finances and business.*
*All souls whom my business soul, my soul, and my
    ancestors' souls have harmed in all previous lifetimes
    and in this lifetime, please forgive us.*
Thank you, all.

*Divine Rainbow Light Ball and Divine Rainbow
    Liquid Spring of Divine Love and Divine
    Forgiveness Soul Mind Body Transplants clear soul
    mind body blockages of my finances and business.*
*All souls whom my business soul, my soul, and my
    ancestors' souls have harmed in all previous lifetimes
    and in this lifetime, please forgive us.*
Thank you, all.

Continue to chant repeatedly:

Love, Love, Love
Love, Love, Love
Love, Love, Love
Love, Love, Love
Love, Love, Love

Love, Love, Love
Love, Love, Love

Forgiveness, Forgiveness, Forgiveness
Forgiveness, Forgiveness, Forgiveness
Forgiveness, Forgiveness, Forgiveness
Forgiveness, Forgiveness, Forgiveness
Forgiveness, Forgiveness, Forgiveness
Forgiveness, Forgiveness, Forgiveness
Forgiveness, Forgiveness, Forgiveness

Peace, Peace, Peace
Peace, Peace, Peace
Peace, Peace, Peace
Peace, Peace, Peace
Peace, Peace, Peace
Peace, Peace, Peace
Peace, Peace, Peace

Success, Success, Success
Success, Success, Success
Success, Success, Success
Success, Success, Success
Success, Success, Success
Success, Success, Success
Success, Success, Success . . .

Close. After chanting for at least three minutes, close:

Hao! Hao! Hao!
Thank you. Thank you. Thank you.

The Big Way is extremely simple.

Also remember the one-sentence secret for chanting:

What you chant is what you become.

To chant *Love, Love, Love, Forgiveness, Forgiveness, Forgiveness, Peace, Peace, Peace, Success, Success, Success* is extremely simple. You may not realize the power of this simple spiritual practice. You may find it difficult to believe. This simple chanting practice is powerful beyond any words, comprehension, and imagination.

How should you practice and chant? Stop reading. Close your eyes. Go into the condition. Chant from the bottom of your heart. You can chant silently or aloud. The key is sincerity and honesty. Really practice love and forgiveness. Offer your total love and forgiveness. *Be* total love and forgiveness.

Honesty moves Heaven. The souls that your business's soul, your soul, and your ancestors' souls harmed can feel the sincerity and honesty of your true apology. Most of the souls that were harmed will forgive you. Some souls may not forgive you right away because they were harmed so badly. They may not forgive you easily. Therefore, you need to practice and chant more often and longer.

Trust the sacred teaching here. Love and forgiveness are the golden keys to removing all blockages in every aspect of life. I started to teach love and forgiveness practices in 2002. Since then, I have received thousands of heart-touching and moving stories about the power and benefits of these practices. Love and forgiveness practices will bring millions of heart-touching and moving stories to humanity, Mother Earth, and all universes.

Love and forgiveness practices are practical spiritual treasures for transforming finances and every aspect of life.

Practice. Practice. Practice.

Experience. Experience. Experience.

Benefit. Benefit. Benefit.

Self-clear karma. Self-clear karma. Self-clear karma.

Transform finances and business. Transform finances and business. Transform finances and business.

Transform every aspect of life. Transform every aspect of life. Transform every aspect of life.

The Importance of the Name of a Business

Every human being has a soul. Every animal has a soul. Every business has a soul. Every business's name has a soul. Every word has a soul.

Be careful in choosing a name for your business. If you choose a negative name for your business, it could deeply affect your business. I suggest that, before you decide on your business name, consult with a high-level spiritual being for a spiritual reading. It could really help you find the right name.

Every name carries a message. When I lived in the countryside in China, quite a few parents gave the nickname *zhu er* to their sons. "Zhu" means *pig*. "Er" means *son*. They kept calling their sons *pig son*. It deeply affected the intelligence of these children.

If there is a negative meaning or other blockages in the business name, it will affect your business a lot. Pay attention to this spiritual wisdom. Pay great attention to your business name in the future.

Follow the Tao of Business

Many business experts have written many books and led many seminars and workshops to teach people how to be successful in any aspect of business. I am not a business expert, but I understand that for success in any aspect of life, it is vital to:

- remove the karma (soul blockages), mind blockages, and body blockages to success
- follow the Xiao Tao (the *small Tao*) of that aspect of life, which could be sleeping, eating, dressing, speaking, studying, or running a business

The basic important principles for a successful business are the Xiao Tao (pronounced *shee-yow dow*) of business. Clear the soul mind body blockages of your business, including your business name. Clear the soul mind body blockages of the relationships among all the employees and managers. Be sure your business offers good service. Follow the Tao of business. Your business and all of its team members will flourish.

The Xiao Tao of business includes:

- clear mission and goals
- products and services that offer good service to humanity and Mother Earth
- great leadership
- effective communication
- harmonized teamwork
- efficient infrastructure
- good planning
- powerful marketing

- proper controls for finance and all other aspects of the business
- great customer service
- avoiding greed and other unpleasant services

You can learn about business leadership, planning, marketing, operations, and more from many books, seminars, and workshops. You could get the help of a business expert or consultant. Business is business. You need to study and apply the proper ways to deal with all aspects of business.

What I can contribute to your business success is the spiritual wisdom, divine treasures, and practical techniques that I have discussed. Next, I will share a spiritual secret that I introduced in the third book of my Soul Power Series, *The Power of Soul*. It is soul marketing. I am honored to give the essence to you, every reader, and humanity here.

Soul Marketing and Its Significance

Marketing is generally done through advertising, press releases, public relations, special promotions, and more, and uses various media, including newspapers, magazines, websites, radio, television, email, flyers, posters, e-postcards, and more. **Soul marketing is to market to the soul.** Every human being has a soul. Every organization has a soul. Every website has a soul. Every city has a soul. Every country has a soul. Why do we need soul marketing?

A person, an organization, everyone, and everything has a soul, mind, and body. Soul is the boss. If the soul of a person or the soul of an organization loves what you have to market, the body and mind of the person or the organization will follow. Soul marketing is a spiritual treasure that I am sharing with humanity.

Soul marketing is to market to the souls of your clients and the souls of the groups and organizations affiliated with your business. If your business is related to all of humanity, you absolutely can soul market your business to all humanity!

The significance and benefits of soul marketing can be summarized in one sentence:

Market to the souls of your business's current and potential clients and affiliates first; then success of physical marketing to clients and affiliates and success of your business will follow.

I will use myself as an example. How would I do soul marketing for this book? I would always use the Four Power Techniques:

Body Power. I sit up straight. I put my left palm over my Message Center and my right hand in the traditional prayer position. We have used this Soul Light Era Prayer Position for Body Power in many of the practices in this book. It is a special hand position for soul communication in the Soul Light Era.

When you use this hand position, the Divine, buddhas, holy saints, Taoist saints, angels, archangels, ascended masters, gurus, lamas, and all kinds of spiritual fathers and mothers will pay attention to you right away.

Soul Power. I say *hello:*

Dear soul mind body of all souls of humanity, approximately 6.8 billion at this time,

Dear soul mind body of every country, every city, every
organization, every media, every website,
Dear soul mind body of every bookseller, including
those online,
Dear soul mind body of all book publishers in every
format,
I love you, honor you, and appreciate you.
I call all of you to announce that the seventh book of
my Soul Power Series, Divine Transformation:
The Divine Way to Self-clear Karma to Transform Your Health, Relationships, Finances, and
More, *will be available to humanity on September*
21, 2010.
There are many good books in history that speak about
life transformation.
There are many great teachers who teach life transfor-
mation in all kinds of workshops, seminars, retreats,
and training programs.
Divine Transformation: The Divine Way to Self-
clear Karma to Transform Your Health, Relationships, Finances, and More *teaches divine life*
transformation. It shares divine secrets, wisdom,
knowledge, and practical techniques to transform all
life. The root cause of failure in every aspect of life is
bad karma. This book teaches you how to self-clear
your bad karma in order to transform every aspect
of your life.
Dear Divine Rainbow Light Ball and Divine Rain-
bow Liquid Spring of Divine Love Soul Mind Body
Transplants,
Dear Divine Rainbow Light Ball and Divine Rain-

*bow Liquid Spring of Divine Forgiveness Soul
  Mind Body Transplants,*
*Dear Divine Rainbow Light Ball and Divine Rain-
  bow Liquid Spring of Divine Compassion Soul
  Mind Body Transplants,*
*Dear Divine Rainbow Light Ball and Divine Rain-
  bow Liquid Spring of Divine Light Soul Mind
  Body Transplants,*
Dear Divine,
Dear Tao,
*Dear countless healing angels, archangels, ascended
  masters, buddhas, bodhisattvas, holy saints, Taoist
  saints, all kinds of saints, all kinds of spiritual fa-
  thers and mothers on Mother Earth and in all layers
  of Heaven,*
Dear countless planets, stars, galaxies, and universes,
I love you, honor you, and appreciate you.
Please bless the book Divine Transformation: The
  Divine Way to Self-clear Karma to Transform
  Your Health, Relationships, Finances, and More.
*Spread this book worldwide and allow this book to be
  a divine servant for humanity, Mother Earth, and
  all universes.*
I am very grateful.
Thank you.

Mind Power. I visualize divine love, forgiveness, compassion, and light radiating everywhere to spread the book *Divine Transformation: The Divine Way to Self-clear Karma to Transform Your Health, Relationships, Finances, and More* worldwide to as many people as possible.

Sound Power. I chant repeatedly for a few minutes, silently or aloud:

> *Spread the book* Divine Transformation: The Divine
>   Way to Self-clear Karma to Transform Your
>   Health, Relationships, Finances, and More.
> *Serve humanity and all souls on Mother Earth and in
>   all universes for their life transformation.*

> *Spread the book* Divine Transformation: The Divine
>   Way to Self-clear Karma to Transform Your
>   Health, Relationships, Finances, and More.
> *Serve humanity and all souls on Mother Earth and in
>   all universes for their life transformation.*

> *Spread the book* Divine Transformation: The Divine
>   Way to Self-clear Karma to Transform Your
>   Health, Relationships, Finances, and More.
> *Serve humanity and all souls on Mother Earth and in
>   all universes for their life transformation.*

> *Spread the book* Divine Transformation: The Divine
>   Way to Self-clear Karma to Transform Your
>   Health, Relationships, Finances, and More.
> *Serve humanity and all souls on Mother Earth, and in
>   all universes for their life transformation . . .*

Close. After chanting for a few minutes, I close:

> *Hao! Hao! Hao!*
> *Thank you. Thank you. Thank you.*

When you do soul marketing, you would usually chant for a few minutes at a time and do it a few times per day. As always, the more often and the longer you chant, the better.

You can see from the example I just gave you that there are certain principles for any soul marketing that you would do for your business or service:

- Use the Four Power Techniques:
  o Body Power—special hand and body positions
  o Soul Power—say *hello* to the clients and potential recipients of your services or business, as well as to current and potential affiliates
  o Mind Power—creative visualization
  o Sound Power—chanting sacred mantras, Divine Soul Songs, and more
- Be clear about what you want. Tell the souls straightforwardly about what you are marketing and how you want them to respond.
- Be sure you tell the souls clearly that you are serving and explain how you are serving. Never do soul marketing for personal gain. This is a *very* important principle. If your intent is selfish, you will not get good soul marketing results. Your results could actually become worse because great light beings will not support selfishness.
- Communicate sincerely with the souls. Respect, honor, and appreciate them.
- Spiritual courtesy is very important. Always remember gratitude to and for all of the souls to whom you are soul marketing.

Remember the above principles.

Remember that what you do, what you speak, and what you think should be to make others happier and healthier and to create love, peace, and harmony for humanity, Mother Earth, and all universes.

Remember never to do soul marketing for selfish reasons, such as for personal gain.

In the physical world, normal marketing for your business could gain you more clients, more friends, and more business associates. In the spiritual world, soul marketing for your business will bring you more soul friends and blessings beyond your comprehension and imagination from the Soul World.

Soul marketing is the new marketing that the vast majority of humanity does not yet know.

Soul marketing is new sacred teaching for the Soul Light Era. It will grow tremendously quickly.

Learn it.

Try it.

Practice it.

Experience it.

Benefit from it.

You will love it.

You will appreciate it.

I wish you great success in your business and finances.

Offer Unconditional Service to Receive Divine Blessings for Success in Finances and Business

People need to make money in business. Money is energy. If one has money and uses it properly, one can gain great virtue. For example, many businesses (and individuals) donate money to support hospitals and schools, to alleviate hunger and poverty, to provide shelter and care for the homeless, to give relief to people struck by disasters, and more. As I explained earlier in this chapter, if you are wealthy, the root cause is good karma: you have offered very good services in previous lifetimes and in this lifetime. Do not forget to continue to serve. Do not forget to share your abundance and blessings.

Many successful businesspeople understand that the more you serve, the more the Divine and Heaven return to you. When I lived in the Philippines, I met a very wealthy person who donated huge amounts of money to build hospitals, schools, and more. He shared with me his realization that after he donated one million dollars several years ago, he received a few million dollars more the following year. When he donated a few million dollars, he would receive many millions more in the next one or two years. He understood that this was the Divine's and Heaven's continued blessing and reward for his good service.

Remember my teaching: Heaven records everything you do. This is to remind every wealthy person to continue to offer as much good service as you can. This is also to remind every poor person that service is the key to transforming your finances and business.

Serve a little, receive a little blessing.

Serve more, receive more blessings.

Serve unconditionally, receive unlimited blessings.

If you understand this, you will know to serve and to serve more and more.

Serve unconditionally in this lifetime and all of your lifetimes.

Divine Transformation for Your Spiritual Journey

MILLIONS OF PEOPLE are searching for spiritual secrets, wisdom, knowledge, and practical techniques. The most powerful spiritual secrets, wisdom, knowledge, and practical techniques are *soul* secrets, wisdom, knowledge, and practical techniques.

A human being has two lives: a physical life and a soul life. Physical life is limited. Soul life is eternal. Millions of people are searching for the purpose of life. The purpose of life can be summarized in one sentence:

The purpose of life is to serve.

To serve is to make others happier and healthier. To serve is to bring love, peace, and harmony to humanity, Mother Earth, and all universes. To serve is the purpose of physical life and soul life.

Divine Service Law

Why is service the purpose of life? The Divine created a spiritual law about service for humanity, all souls on Mother Earth, and all souls in all universes. I explain this Universal Law of Universal Service in the beginning of every book in my Soul Power Series. I welcome you to review this teaching on page xiii. The essence of this Divine Service Law is clear:

Serve a little, receive a little blessing.
Serve more, receive more blessings.
Serve unconditionally, receive unlimited blessings.

If you want to transform your spiritual journey, which is your soul journey, there is no second way to do it. Service is the way to transform your soul journey. This is why you and all souls need to serve.

Shi Jia Mo Ni Fo's Enlightenment Story

Since ancient times, millions of people have searched for soul secrets, wisdom, knowledge, and practical techniques to transform their soul journeys. Shi Jia Mo Ni Fo,[1] the founder of Buddhism, is a special example.

Shi Jia Mo Ni Fo (pronounced *shr jyah maw nee fwaw*) was a prince in the area of what is now Nepal. He had a wife and a son. He had a family. He had money. He had power. He had honor. But he was not satisfied. He asked to be taken for a ride in the

---

1. This is his name in Chinese. Shi Jia Mo Ni Fo is also known as Shakyamuni, Siddhartha Gautama, and the Buddha.

countryside outside the palace walls, where he had never before ventured. He saw a farmer working in the field with a cow, sweating under the sun. He thought to himself that he and his court could stay inside without ever having to do such hard labor. He felt deeply that life for human beings is not fair. He also wondered: *Why is a person's life so short?* He asked himself: *Is there any way one can live forever?* He also asked: *How can I advance my spiritual journey? How can I reach soul enlightenment?*

One day, Shi Jia Mo Ni Fo left the palace and his royal life and went to the forest. He saw many people doing very hard physical work. He also saw spiritual seekers abusing their own bodies, trying to find a way to reach soul enlightenment. He believed that this was not the correct way. He was searching himself. He saw other spiritual seekers try many different methods in order to reach soul enlightenment—purifying the mind, chanting, meditating, and searching for extraordinary powers, such as flying, disappearing, and moving from one place to another instantly.

Shi Jia Mo Ni Fo searched for a few years. He was not satisfied with any of the methods he observed and experienced. One day he sat in front of a Bodhi tree (a sacred fig tree). He made a vow: *I will sit here until I reach enlightenment. If I cannot reach soul enlightenment, I would rather die.* This is an incredible vow that shows Shi Jia Mo Ni Fo wanted enlightenment more than anything. He understood that the purpose of physical life is to serve the soul journey in order to reach soul enlightenment. He had no attachment to his physical life.

Shi Jia Mo Ni Fo continued to sit under the Bodhi tree and meditated. He connected with the universe. He connected with the Source in Heaven. He asked for blessings and wisdom. He asked for greater spiritual realization and awakening. He wanted to be a better servant. He asked for enlightenment.

Shi Jia Mo Ni Fo meditated continuously for days without food. A milkmaid gave him a little bit of milk. He went through intense purification during those days. He was tested by the Dark Side. He experienced frustration. He experienced confusion. But he was steadfast. He trusted that the Source would enlighten him. Therefore, he passed all of the spiritual testing that came from his mind, from the Dark Side, and more.

Then one night, Shi Jia Mo Ni Fo looked at Heaven. He saw many, many stars. Suddenly, he had an "aha!" moment. He realized:

Emptiness creates all things.
Emptiness is the Divine.
Emptiness is Tao.
Emptiness is the Source of all universes.

At that moment, Shi Jia Mo Ni Fo became enlightened. Heaven gave him the realization that he wanted. Soul enlightenment means your soul standing is uplifted in Heaven to a special place. A special book is created for you in the Akashic Records. Under the Bodhi tree, Heaven gave Shi Jia Mo Ni Fo a huge amount of virtue to uplift his soul standing. He became an enlightened soul.

Shi Jia Mo Ni Fo started to teach. He taught for forty-nine years, until he died. He created eighty-four thousand methods to teach different layers of humanity how to transform their spiritual journeys according to each person's spiritual state. Some people have no interest in the spiritual journey. They enjoy physical wealth and comfort. Some people want to be on the spiritual journey. They may not know where and how to start. Some people are on the spiritual journey. They do not know how to advance their spiritual journey further. Some people have reached their advanced spiritual journey. Do they know how they can move even further?

In one sentence:

The spiritual journey and spiritual wisdom have unlimited steps and unlimited layers.

Shi Jia Mo Ni Fo is a great example of having no attachment to physical life. In his position as prince, he had everything in physical life, but he gave it up to search for his soul journey. Ever since Shi Jia Mo Ni Fo was on Mother Earth more than twenty-five hundred years ago, millions of people worldwide have studied his teaching. He is one of the greatest servants of humanity, Mother Earth, and all universes. He is one of the greatest examples for millions of people who are searching for their spiritual journeys.

Divine Oneness

While I was in Taiwan in 2008 to record Soul Songs, I did my morning meditation in my hotel. I called Shi Jia Mo Ni Fo, one of my greatest spiritual fathers, to ask him, "Father, you have taught eighty-four thousand methods for one's spiritual journey. Could you tell me what is the best method?"

Shi Jia Mo Ni Fo said, "Zhi Gang, what do you think?"

I replied, "Father, I have realized at this moment, that service is the best Xiu Lian[2] method." Shi Jia Mo Ni Fo smiled and said, "I cannot agree with you enough." That was the short conversation I had with my spiritual father.

---

2. "Xiu" (pronounced *sheo*) means *purification*. "Lian" (pronounced *lyen*) means *practice*. Every practice to purify our souls, hearts, minds, and bodies is a practice to advance our spiritual journeys. Therefore, Xiu Lian is the totality of one's spiritual journey.

Shi Jia Mo Ni Fo is one of my spiritual fathers. I want everybody to know that Guan Yin, the Compassion Buddha, is my spiritual mother. Peng Zu, the teacher of Lao Zi, is also my spiritual father. Pu Ti Lao Zu is my spiritual father. Jesus is my spiritual father. Mary is my spiritual mother.

In the physical world, Dr. and Master Zhi Chen Guo, Dr. and Master De Hua Liu, Professor Da Jun Liu, and my tai chi masters, kung fu masters, and Tao and Buddhist masters, who do not want to give their names to the public, are my spiritual fathers.

Human beings created and developed religions. I honor every religion. When you reach spiritual awareness, you will understand one day that all religions are one. If you ask Shi Jia Mo Ni Fo, "Do you work with Jesus?" or if you ask Jesus, "Do you work with Taoist saints?" they would answer, "We are brothers and sisters. We are one."

I have studied with many spiritual leaders in different religions at the soul level. I have not attended services at any physical churches, synagogues, mosques, or temples. What I have done is soul communication with all major spiritual leaders in all religions. All of these spiritual leaders in all religions are my spiritual fathers and mothers. I am a student of all of them. I have studied with all of them. I have learned their great secrets, wisdom, knowledge, and practical techniques.

In July 2003, the Divine chose me as a servant of humanity and the Divine. In 2009, Tao chose me as a servant. This Tao is not limited to the Tao of ancient and traditional Taoism. This Tao is far beyond the Tao of ancient and traditional Taoism. The previous book in my Soul Power Series, *Tao I: The Way of All Life*, was published in May 2010. There, I explained very clearly that I am not teaching Taoism. I am very honored to share traditional Tao secrets, wisdom, knowledge, and practical techniques. But I am teaching Divine Tao. The Divine and Tao gave me Tao Jing, a new seventy-five phrase "Tao classic," together with the wisdom, knowledge, and practical techniques to complete the *Tao I* book.

I share the above with you and every reader in order to share my deep insight with you, with billions of people on Mother Earth, and with countless souls in countless planets, stars, galaxies, and universes, that all religions, all spiritual teachings, and all spiritual realms are one. You can call this realization Divine Oneness, Tao Oneness, Universal Oneness, or Source Oneness. Religions are just named a, b, c, and d. But these a, b, c, and d are the same thing. They are One.

Divine or Tao Oneness is a vital realization for one's spiritual journey. Go inside this teaching. It tells you and every spiritual being that you have freedom to choose your religion and your spiritual fathers and mothers. It does not matter if you study Buddhism, Taoism, Confucianism, Judaism, Islam, Christianity, Hinduism, or anything else. If you understand Divine Oneness, you will seek to reach Divine Oneness. Every religion and every spiritual group teaches its path to reach the divine realm. The Divine deals equally with all paths. In all paths, your soul can be uplifted to the divine realm, but every spiritual being must know that in order to reach the divine realm, one must serve unconditionally. To serve unconditionally is to accumulate the huge amount of virtue necessary to be uplifted to the divine realm. Generally speaking, this is the only way, although there is a special and rare way, which is that the Divine can directly uplift the soul standing of any specially chosen being.

Service Xiu Lian

On Mother Earth, people work to earn physical money to support their lives and families. In Heaven, saints and other souls serve to earn virtue. Jesus, Mary, Buddha, and all kinds of spiritual fathers and mothers are continually serving. If great teachers and servants stop serving, they stop growing also. Soul standing is not permanent. Generally speaking, a human being's soul goes up and down, up and down over hundreds of lifetimes, depending on the service, pleasant or unpleasant, that he or she offers and the karma, good or bad, that is gained. The soul standing of the great spiritual fathers and mothers in Heaven is no different. Not one is permanent. This can be summarized as follows:

If they serve a little, they are uplifted a little.
If they serve more, they are uplifted further.
If they serve unconditionally, they
could be uplifted endlessly.

I asked my spiritual father Shi Jia Mo Ni Fo the best method for one's spiritual journey. He confirmed that service is the best Xiu Lian method. In other words: *The best way to transform your spiritual journey is service.* Now I will give you a one-sentence secret to expand this wisdom:

The best way to transform one's spiritual
journey is Service Xiu Lian.

"Xiu" means *purification.* "Lian" means *practice* or *exercise.* I have taught these words many times. Literally, "Xiu Lian" means *purification practice*, but it represents the totality of one's spiritual journey.

From this moment, there will be a special Xiu Lian term. I call it **Service Xiu Lian**.

Next year, I will write and publish a book to further introduce Service Xiu Lian. I will introduce the major spiritual ways available since creation to purify your soul, heart, mind, and body. Then I will fully introduce Service Xiu Lian, the new way to advance your spiritual journey to the highest levels in the twenty-first century and the Soul Light Era.

Before I share with you my first-ever teaching on how to do Service Xiu Lian, let me introduce some ancient secrets for Xiu Lian. Then I will guide you to do Service Xiu Lian.

Ancient Xiu Lian can be summarized in three secrets:

- **Shen Mi.** "Shen" (pronounced *shun*) means *body*. "Mi" (pronounced *mee*) means *secret*. "Shen Mi" (*body secret*) is using special hand and body positions to boost your energy, stamina, vitality, and immunity, as well as to purify your soul, heart, mind, and body.
- **Kou Mi.** "Kou" (pronounced *koe*) means *mouth*. "Mi" means *secret*. "Kou Mi" (*mouth secret*) is chanting sacred mantras, which are special sounds for healing, blessing, rejuvenation, purification, transformation, and enlightenment.
- **Yi Mi.** "Yi" (pronounced *yee*) means *thinking*. "Mi" means *secret*. "Yi Mi" (*thinking secret*) is a function of the brain, so that "Yi Mi" also means *mind secret*. Meditation is one of the key spiritual practices. Dur-

ing meditation, a spiritual practitioner needs to use Mind Power to heal, bless, rejuvenate, purify, transform, and enlighten the soul, heart, mind, and body.

What do you think and how do you use your mind? There are countless meditations in history. There are countless ways to use the mind. Yi Mi is one of the very important secrets for the spiritual journey. I call it Mind Power.

Shen Mi is also very important. For example, point your little fingers at each other. Put the tips of your little fingers as close together as you can without touching. This body secret will boost the energy of your kidneys and the Snow Mountain Area.[3] In Hinduism and Buddhism, special hand and finger positions are called *mudras*. I call it Body Power.

At this moment, I am flowing this book in Ramsau, Austria, at my first International Tao Retreat. I am asking every participant to do this practice now.

Sit up straight. Apply the Four Power Techniques to do this Xiu Lian practice:

Body Power. Point your little fingers at each other so that the tips are as close as possible without touching. The little finger represents the Water element, which includes the kidneys, urinary bladder, bones, and ears, as well as fear in the emotional body.

Soul Power. Say *hello*:

---

3. The Snow Mountain Area is a foundational energy center at the base of the spine in front of the tailbone. It is known to yogis as the kundalini, to Taoists as the Golden Urn, and to traditional Chinese medicine practitioners as the Ming Men Area, which means the *Gate of Life*. The Snow Mountain Area is vital for energy, stamina, vitality, and immunity, as well as for developing your intelligence and opening your spiritual channels, especially the Third Eye.

Dear soul mind body of my little fingers,
Dear soul mind body of my kidneys,
Dear my spiritual fathers and mothers in the physical
   world and the spiritual world,
Dear Divine and Tao,
I love you, honor you, and appreciate you.
Please boost my kidney power.
Please boost my energy, stamina, vitality, and
   immunity.
Please rejuvenate my soul, heart, mind, and body.
Please prolong my life.
I am very grateful.
Thank you.

Mind Power. Visualize golden light shining in your kidney area, Snow Mountain Area, and Jin Dan.[4]

Sound Power. Chant repeatedly, silently or aloud:

Gain kidney power. Thank you.
Gain kidney power. Thank you.
Gain kidney power. Thank you.
Gain kidney power. Thank you.
Gain kidney power. Thank you.
Gain kidney power. Thank you.
Gain kidney power. Thank you . . .

---

4. The Jin Dan (pronounced *jeen dahn*) is located just below the navel. After you form a Jin Dan (a special "golden light ball"), energy will flow freely in all parts of the body. This will remove soul mind body blockages to your healing, rejuvenation, prolongation of life, and transformation of every aspect of life, including relationships and finances. For further teaching, see *Tao I: The Way of All Life.*

or

Boost energy, stamina, vitality, and immunity.
Thank you.
Boost energy, stamina, vitality, and immunity.
Thank you.
Boost energy, stamina, vitality, and immunity.
Thank you.
Boost energy, stamina, vitality, and immunity.
Thank you.
Boost energy, stamina, vitality, and immunity.
Thank you.
Boost energy, stamina, vitality, and immunity.
Thank you.
Boost energy, stamina, vitality, and immunity.
Thank you . . .

or

Rejuvenate my soul, heart, mind, and body.
Thank you.
Rejuvenate my soul, heart, mind, and body.
Thank you.
Rejuvenate my soul, heart, mind, and body.
Thank you.
Rejuvenate my soul, heart, mind, and body.
Thank you.
Rejuvenate my soul, heart, mind, and body.
Thank you.
Rejuvenate my soul, heart, mind, and body.
Thank you.

Rejuvenate my soul, heart, mind, and body.
    Thank you . . .

or

Prolong my life. Thank you.
Prolong my life. Thank you.
Prolong my life. Thank you.
Prolong my life. Thank you.
Prolong my life. Thank you.
Prolong my life. Thank you.
Prolong my life. Thank you . . .

Close. After chanting for at least three minutes, close:

Hao! Hao! Hao!
Thank you. Thank you. Thank you.

Everyone here in Austria, together with fifteen hundred others viewing a live webcast of the Tao Retreat, practiced with me for five minutes. Then I asked Peter Hudoba, one of my Worldwide Representatives, to share his insights:

> *Thank you very much for the teaching. The realization*
> *I am gaining today is that Master Sha was uplifted*
> *further and further in his soul standing because of his*
> *unconditional service to humanity and all souls on*
> *Mother Earth and in all universes. It also tells us that*
> *we have more tasks to serve humanity, all souls on*
> *Mother Earth, and all universes. We are honored to be*
> *servants.*

In Mother Earth's transition period, humanity needs the most help. The Dark Side will cause a lot of damage that ordinary people will find difficult to handle. That is why people need our help in the next several years the most.

This is the time when we have to serve with total GOLD. At this time, however, it is not only the high-level Dark Side, but also the high-level Light Side that is coming. For us, this is the best time to uplift our soul standing in our spiritual journey through Service Xiu Lian.

Peter has offered an important teaching. Service Xiu Lian is the new Xiu Lian method that the Divine and Tao inspired me to offer to humanity and all souls.

What I am sharing with you, every reader, and humanity is **one-sentence secret chanting**. For example, if you want to heal your kidneys, chant one sentence:

Heal kidneys; thank you.

This is the Soul Light Era. The Soul Light Era shines soul light.

Heal kidneys; thank you is a Soul Order.[5] It shines the soul light of the kidneys.

If your Third Eye is open, you can see your kidneys shine light with this one-sentence chant.

---

5. Soul is the boss. A Soul Order is an order given by a soul to do something that is good service, such as healing, preventing sickness, rejuvenating, transforming life, and enlightening life. See chapter 4 of *The Power of Soul: The Way to Heal, Rejuvenate, Transform, and Enlighten All Life* for further teaching about Soul Orders.

The spiritual practice is to build a pure light body. To build a pure light body, you must build pure light systems, pure light organs, and pure light cells.

I asked Francisco Quintero, another of my Worldwide Representatives, to share his insights from this practice:

> *When we put our little fingers together, I felt energy start from my Jin Dan, go up the front of my body, then down my back, and finally it settled into my kidneys. As we chanted* Gain kidney power; thank you, *the souls of my kidneys expanded to ten times their original size. I also saw Heaven and Earth nourish my kidneys. In addition, a liquid light was produced that is nourishing my whole body.*

I then asked Peter to share further his experience of this practice:

> *I saw an explosion of light in my Snow Mountain Area and kidneys. My whole body became pleasantly warm. There were saints all around us, blessing us and giving us a lot of light.*

Let me expand this teaching. Let us do a practice for the Earth element.

Body Power. Point your thumbs at each other so that the tips are as close as possible without touching. The thumb represents the Earth element, which includes the spleen, stomach, muscles, gums and teeth, and mouth and lips, as well as worry in the emotional body.

Soul Power. Say *hello:*

> *Dear soul mind body of my thumbs,*
> *Dear soul mind body of my spleen, stomach, muscles,*
>   *gums, teeth, mouth, and lips,*
> *Dear all of my spiritual fathers and mothers,*
> *Dear Divine and Tao,*
> *I love you, honor you, and appreciate you.*
> *You have the power to heal my spleen, stomach,*
>   *muscles, gums, teeth, mouth, and lips.*
> *You have the power to remove worry from my*
>   *emotional body.*
> *Please boost my energy, stamina, vitality, and*
>   *immunity.*
> *Please rejuvenate my soul, heart, mind, and body.*
> *Please prolong my life.*
> *I am very grateful.*
> *Thank you.*

Mind Power. Visualize golden light radiating throughout your spleen, stomach, muscles, teeth, gums, lips, and mouth.

Sound Power. Chant repeatedly, silently or aloud:

> *Boost spleen power; thank you.*
> *Boost spleen power; thank you.*
> *Boost spleen power; thank you.*
> *Boost spleen power; thank you.*
> *Boost spleen power; thank you.*
> *Boost spleen power; thank you.*
> *Boost spleen power; thank you . . .*

or

Boost stomach power; thank you.
Boost stomach power; thank you.
Boost stomach power; thank you.
Boost stomach power; thank you.
Boost stomach power; thank you.
Boost stomach power; thank you.
Boost stomach power; thank you . . .

or

Boost Earth element power; thank you.
Boost Earth element power; thank you.
Boost Earth element power; thank you.
Boost Earth element power; thank you.
Boost Earth element power; thank you.
Boost Earth element power; thank you.
Boost Earth element power; thank you . . .

or

Heal and rejuvenate stomach; thank you.
Heal and rejuvenate stomach; thank you.
Heal and rejuvenate stomach; thank you.
Heal and rejuvenate stomach; thank you.
Heal and rejuvenate stomach; thank you.
Heal and rejuvenate stomach; thank you.
Heal and rejuvenate stomach; thank you . . .

or

Heal and rejuvenate muscles; thank you.
Heal and rejuvenate muscles; thank you.
Heal and rejuvenate muscles; thank you.
Heal and rejuvenate muscles; thank you.
Heal and rejuvenate muscles; thank you.
Heal and rejuvenate muscles; thank you.
Heal and rejuvenate muscles; thank you . . .

or

Heal and rejuvenate teeth, gums, lips, and mouth;
thank you.
Heal and rejuvenate teeth, gums, lips, and mouth;
thank you.
Heal and rejuvenate teeth, gums, lips, and mouth;
thank you.
Heal and rejuvenate teeth, gums, lips, and mouth;
thank you.
Heal and rejuvenate teeth, gums, lips, and mouth;
thank you.
Heal and rejuvenate teeth, gums, lips, and mouth;
thank you.
Heal and rejuvenate teeth, gums, lips, and mouth;
thank you . . .

or

Heal worry; thank you.
Heal worry; thank you.
Heal worry; thank you.
Heal worry; thank you.

Heal worry; thank you.
Heal worry; thank you.
Heal worry; thank you . . .

Do this practice for three to five minutes per time. The longer you practice per time, the better. You can practice many times a day.

Close. After chanting for at least three minutes, close:

Hao! Hao! Hao!
Thank you. Thank you. Thank you.

Next we will do a practice for the Wood element.

Body Power. Point your index fingers at each other so that the tips are as close as possible without touching. The index finger represents the Wood element, which includes the liver, gallbladder, eyes, and tendons, as well as anger in the emotional body.

Soul Power. Say *hello*:

Dear soul mind body of my index fingers,
Dear soul mind body of my liver, gallbladder, eyes, and
*   tendons,*
Dear all of my spiritual fathers and mothers,
Dear Divine and Tao,
I love you, honor you, and appreciate you.
You have the power to heal my liver, gallbladder, eyes,
*   and tendons,*

You have the power to remove anger from my
*   emotional body.*
Please boost my energy, stamina, vitality, and
*   immunity.*
Please rejuvenate my soul, heart, mind, and body.
Please prolong my life.
I am very grateful.
Thank you.

Mind Power. Visualize golden light radiating throughout your liver, gallbladder, tendons, and eyes.

Sound Power. Chant repeatedly, silently or aloud:

Gain liver power; thank you.
Gain gallbladder power; thank you.
Gain tendon power; thank you.
Gain eye power; thank you.
Heal anger; thank you.

Gain liver power; thank you.
Gain gallbladder power; thank you.
Gain tendon power; thank you.
Gain eye power; thank you.
Heal anger; thank you.

Gain liver power; thank you.
Gain gallbladder power; thank you.
Gain tendon power; thank you.
Gain eye power; thank you.
Heal anger; thank you.

Gain liver power; thank you.
Gain gallbladder power; thank you.
Gain tendon power; thank you.
Gain eye power; thank you.
Heal anger; thank you.

Gain liver power; thank you.
Gain gallbladder power; thank you.
Gain tendon power; thank you.
Gain eye power; thank you.
Heal anger; thank you.

Gain liver power; thank you.
Gain gallbladder power; thank you.
Gain tendon power; thank you.
Gain eye power; thank you.
Heal anger; thank you.

Gain liver power; thank you.
Gain gallbladder power; thank you.
Gain tendon power; thank you.
Gain eye power; thank you.
Heal anger; thank you . . .

Do this practice for three to five minutes per time. The longer you practice each time, the better. You can practice many times a day.

Close. After chanting for at least three minutes, close:

Hao! Hao! Hao!
Thank you. Thank you. Thank you.

We will now do a practice for the Fire element.

Body Power. Point your middle fingers at each other so that the tips are as close as possible without touching. The middle finger represents the Fire element, which includes the heart, small intestine, tongue, and blood vessels, as well as depression and anxiety in the emotional body.

Soul Power. Say *hello:*

> *Dear soul mind body of my middle fingers,*
> *Dear soul mind body of my heart, small intestine,*
>   *tongue, and blood vessels,*
> *Dear all of my spiritual fathers and mothers,*
> *Dear Divine and Tao,*
> *I love you, honor you, and appreciate you.*
> *You have the power to heal my heart, small intestine,*
>   *tongue, and blood vessels,*
> *You have the power to remove depression and anxiety*
>   *from my emotional body.*
> *Please boost my energy, stamina, vitality, and*
>   *immunity.*
> *Please rejuvenate my soul, heart, mind, and body.*
> *Please prolong my life.*
> *I am very grateful.*
> *Thank you.*

Mind Power. Visualize golden light radiating throughout your heart, small intestine, tongue, and blood vessels.

Sound Power. Chant repeatedly, silently or aloud:

Gain heart power; thank you.
Gain small intestine power; thank you.
Gain tongue power; thank you.
Gain blood vessel power; thank you.
Heal depression and anxiety; thank you.

Gain heart power; thank you.
Gain small intestine power; thank you.
Gain tongue power; thank you.
Gain blood vessel power; thank you.
Heal depression and anxiety; thank you.

Gain heart power; thank you.
Gain small intestine power; thank you.
Gain tongue power; thank you.
Gain blood vessel power; thank you.
Heal depression and anxiety; thank you.

Gain heart power; thank you.
Gain small intestine power; thank you.
Gain tongue power; thank you.
Gain blood vessel power; thank you.
Heal depression and anxiety; thank you.

Gain heart power; thank you.
Gain small intestine power; thank you.
Gain tongue power; thank you.
Gain blood vessel power; thank you.
Heal depression and anxiety; thank you.

Gain heart power; thank you.
Gain small intestine power; thank you.

Gain tongue power; thank you.
Gain blood vessel power; thank you.
Heal depression and anxiety; thank you.

Gain heart power; thank you.
Gain small intestine power; thank you.
Gain tongue power; thank you.
Gain blood vessel power; thank you.
Heal depression and anxiety; thank you . . .

Do this practice for at least three minutes.

Close. After chanting for at least three minutes, close:

Hao! Hao! Hao!
Thank you. Thank you. Thank you.

There is no time limit for this practice. The longer you practice each time, and the more times you practice, the better. You can practice many times a day.

Next, let us do a practice for the Metal element.

Body Power. Point your ring fingers at each other so that the tips are as close as possible without touching. The ring finger represents the Metal element, which includes the lungs, large intestine, nose, and skin, as well as sadness and grief in the emotional body. Place your hands, keeping the same finger position, in front of your Jin Dan, which is centered just below your navel.

Soul Power. Say *hello:*

Dear soul mind body of my ring fingers,
Dear soul mind body of my lungs, large intestine, nose,
 and skin,
Dear soul mind body of all of my systems, organs, and
 cells,
Dear soul mind body of all Metal elements in all
 universes,
I love you, honor you, and appreciate you.
You have the power to heal my lungs, large intestine,
 nose, and skin.
You have the power to bless me to have beautiful skin
 and a beautiful face.
You have the power to remove sadness and grief from
 my emotional body.
Thank you very much.

Mind Power. Visualize golden light radiating throughout your lungs, large intestine, nose, and skin.

Sound Power. Chant repeatedly, silently or aloud:

Gain lung power; thank you.
Gain large intestine power; thank you.
Gain nose power; thank you.
Gain skin power; thank you.
Baby face, beautiful face; thank you.
Inner beauty, outer beauty; thank you.
Heal sadness and grief; thank you.

Gain lung power; thank you.
Gain large intestine power; thank you.
Gain nose power; thank you.

Gain skin power; thank you.
Baby face, beautiful face; thank you.
Inner beauty, outer beauty; thank you.
Heal sadness and grief; thank you.

Gain lung power; thank you.
Gain large intestine power; thank you.
Gain nose power; thank you.
Gain skin power; thank you.
Baby face, beautiful face; thank you.
Inner beauty, outer beauty; thank you.
Heal sadness and grief; thank you.

Gain lung power; thank you.
Gain large intestine power; thank you.
Gain nose power; thank you.
Gain skin power; thank you.
Baby face, beautiful face; thank you.
Inner beauty, outer beauty; thank you.
Heal sadness and grief; thank you.

Gain lung power; thank you.
Gain large intestine power; thank you.
Gain nose power; thank you.
Gain skin power; thank you.
Baby face, beautiful face; thank you.
Inner beauty, outer beauty; thank you.
Heal sadness and grief; thank you.

Gain lung power; thank you.
Gain large intestine power; thank you.
Gain nose power; thank you.

Gain skin power; thank you.
Baby face, beautiful face; thank you.
Inner beauty, outer beauty; thank you.
Heal sadness and grief; thank you.

Gain lung power; thank you.
Gain large intestine power; thank you.
Gain nose power; thank you.
Gain skin power; thank you.
Baby face, beautiful face; thank you.
Inner beauty, outer beauty; thank you.
Heal sadness and grief; thank you . . .

Now chant repeatedly with me, silently or aloud, the phrases
to transform your skin to baby skin:

Boost lung power, boost skin power, inner beauty, outer
  beauty, beautiful skin, baby skin. Thank you.
  Thank you. Thank you.
Boost lung power, boost skin power, inner beauty, outer
  beauty, beautiful skin, baby skin. Thank you.
  Thank you. Thank you.
Boost lung power, boost skin power, inner beauty, outer
  beauty, beautiful skin, baby skin. Thank you.
  Thank you. Thank you.
Boost lung power, boost skin power, inner beauty, outer
  beauty, beautiful skin, baby skin. Thank you.
  Thank you. Thank you.
Boost lung power, boost skin power, inner beauty, outer
  beauty, beautiful skin, baby skin. Thank you.
  Thank you. Thank you.

Boost lung power, boost skin power, inner beauty, outer
*   beauty, beautiful skin, baby skin. Thank you.*
*   Thank you. Thank you.*
Boost lung power, boost skin power, inner beauty, outer
*   beauty, beautiful skin, baby skin. Thank you.*
*   Thank you. Thank you . . .*

Close. After chanting for at least three minutes, close:

Hao! Hao! Hao!
Thank you. Thank you. Thank you.

Do this practice for three to five minutes per time. The longer and the more often you practice, the better. You can practice many times a day.

The preceding practices, and almost all of the practices in this book, apply the Four Power Techniques. Let me summarize and give you a one-sentence secret for each of the Four Power Techniques:

Body Power: Where you put your hands is
**   where you receive healing and rejuvenation.**
Soul Power: Say *hello* to inner souls and outer souls.
Mind Power: Visualize golden or rainbow light.
Sound Power: What you chant is what you become.

When you do any spiritual practice, visualize golden light shining in the specific area where you want healing or rejuvenation, or throughout the whole body.

I have led you to practice with the Five Elements for boosting energy, stamina, vitality, and immunity; for healing, rejuvenating, and prolonging the life of the Five Element organs, tissues, and parts of the body; and for healing of the corresponding unbalanced emotions.

TAO SHENG YI PRACTICE FOR SERVICE XIU LIAN

Now I am ready to show you one practice that will boost your whole body's power, from head to toe and skin to bone. Continue to use the Four Power Techniques to boost the whole body, to heal the whole body, to rejuvenate the whole body, and to prolong your life.

Body Power. Use your right palm to hold your left thumb most gently, with no pressure. This new hand position is called the Tao Sheng Yi Body Power Position. "Tao sheng yi" (pronounced *dow shung yee*) means *Tao creates One.*

The thumb represents the Earth element. All things grow on Mother Earth. Tao is the creator. Tao creates all universes. All universes are one. Therefore, this hand position is named the Tao Sheng Yi Body Power Position. If you put your hands in this position, your whole body will vibrate from head to toe, skin to bone.

Soul Power. Say *hello:*

> *Dear soul mind body of all of my systems, organs, cells,*
>   *cell units, DNA, and RNA,*
> *Dear soul mind body of my entire physical body, from*
>   *skin to bone and head to toe,*
> *I love you, honor you, and appreciate you.*
> *Please heal, boost energy, prevent sickness, rejuvenate,*
>   *prolong life, transform my relationships and*

> *finances, and enlighten my soul, heart, mind, and*
>   *body.*
> *Create love, peace, and harmony for humanity, Mother*
>   *Earth, and all universes to reach* wan ling rong he
>   *(all souls joining as one).*
> *I am very grateful.*
> *Thank you.*

As you can see, this practice also serves love, peace, and harmony for humanity, Mother Earth, and all universes in order to reach *wan ling rong he* (pronounced *wahn ling rawng huh*).

The Soul Light Era started on August 8, 2003. It will last fifteen thousand years. The final goal of the Soul Light Era is to reach *wan ling rong he*, which is to join all souls as one. Continue with the Four Power Techniques to do this Tao Sheng Yi practice.

Mind Power. Visualize everything happening in your Jin Dan.

Sound Power. Chant:

> *Tao sheng yi*
> *Serve*
> *Heal*
> *Prevent sickness*
> *Rejuvenate*
> *Transform*
> *Enlighten*
> *Love, peace, and harmony; love, peace, and harmony;*
>   *love, peace, and harmony*
> *Tian di ren he yi, tian di ren he yi, tian di ren he yi*

(pronounced *tyen dee wren huh yee*, this means
Heaven, Earth, and human being join as one)
Wan ling rong he, wan ling rong he, wan ling rong he

Continue to chant:

Tao sheng yi
Serve
Heal
Prevent sickness
Rejuvenate
Transform
Enlighten
Love, peace, and harmony; love, peace, and harmony;
  love, peace, and harmony
Tian di ren he yi, tian di ren he yi, tian di ren he yi
Wan ling rong he, wan ling rong he, wan ling rong he

Chant from the bottom of your heart:

Tao sheng yi
Serve
Heal
Prevent sickness
Rejuvenate
Transform
Enlighten
Love, peace, and harmony; love, peace, and harmony;
  love, peace, and harmony
Tian di ren he yi, tian di ren he yi, tian di ren he yi
Wan ling rong he, wan ling rong he, wan ling rong he

Now chant silently:

> *Tao sheng yi*
> *Serve*
> *Heal*
> *Prevent sickness*
> *Rejuvenate*
> *Transform*
> *Enlighten*
> *Love, peace, and harmony; love, peace, and harmony;*
>   *love, peace, and harmony*
> *Tian di ren he yi, tian di ren he yi, tian di ren he yi*
> *Wan ling rong he, wan ling rong he, wan ling rong he*

Chant and visualize everything happening in your Jin Dan:

> *Tao sheng yi*
> *Serve*
> *Heal*
> *Prevent sickness*
> *Rejuvenate*
> *Transform*
> *Enlighten*
> *Love, peace, and harmony; love, peace, and harmony;*
>   *love, peace, and harmony*
> *Tian di ren he yi, tian di ren he yi, tian di ren he yi*
> *Wan ling rong he, wan ling rong he, wan ling rong he*

As you are chanting, you are serving. This is Service Xiu Lian.
Continue to chant:

Tao sheng yi
Serve
Heal
Prevent sickness
Rejuvenate
Transform
Enlighten
Love, peace, and harmony; love, peace, and harmony;
    love, peace, and harmony
Tian di ren he yi, tian di ren he yi, tian di ren he yi
Wan ling rong he, wan ling rong he, wan ling rong he

Chant, chant, chant.
Serve, serve, serve.

Tao sheng yi
Serve
Heal
Prevent sickness
Rejuvenate
Transform
Enlighten
Love, peace, and harmony; love, peace, and harmony;
    love, peace, and harmony
Tian di ren he yi, tian di ren he yi, tian di ren he yi
Wan ling rong he, wan ling rong he, wan ling rong he

Chant or sing this Tao Sheng Yi practice, which is Service Xiu Lian, for ten minutes per time. The longer you chant, the better.

Close. After chanting for at least ten minutes, close:

> *Hao! Hao! Hao!*
> *Thank you. Thank you. Thank you.*

This Tao Sheng Yi practice, which is Service Xiu Lian chanting, came out as I was teaching my first International Tao Retreat, in May 2010. I led more than fifteen hundred people in this practice for about thirty minutes. The power is beyond explanation. Light glowed in the entire event hall and radiated to all of Mother Earth and all universes.

During our chanting, the Divine, Tao, all saints, healing angels, archangels, ascended masters, lamas, gurus, and countless souls of countless planets, stars, galaxies, and universes were all present. They all joined us to do this Service Xiu Lian.

Service Xiu Lian is Xiu Lian for service.

We are chanting.

We are serving.

We are healing.

We are preventing sickness.

We are rejuvenating soul, heart, mind, and body.

We are prolonging life.

We are transforming relationships and finances.

We are creating love, peace, and harmony for humanity, Mother Earth, and all universes.

We are creating *wan ling rong he.*

I told everyone in the retreat that this Tao Sheng Yi practice, this Service Xiu Lian practice, is vital for purifying our souls, hearts, minds, and bodies. It is vital for transforming our health, relationships, and finances, as well as every aspect of life. It is vital for serving humanity, Mother Earth, and all universes.

We cannot practice Tao Sheng Yi Service Xiu Lian enough. Remember this chanting. Chant as much as you can from morning to night. The transformation for your life will be beyond imagination. The benefits for humanity, Mother Earth, and all universes will be beyond comprehension.

This is the new Xiu Lian practice. This is a Divine and Tao calling for you, every reader, and humanity to do this Service Xiu Lian practice. This is one of the most important ways to transform your spiritual journey.

Practice. Practice. Practice.

Heal. Heal. Heal.

Prevent sickness. Prevent sickness. Prevent sickness.

Rejuvenate. Rejuvenate. Rejuvenate.

Prolong life. Prolong life. Prolong life.

Transform. Transform. Transform.

Enlighten. Enlighten. Enlighten.

Love, peace, and harmony. Love, peace, and harmony. Love, peace, and harmony.

Tian di ren he yi. Tian di ren he yi. Tian di ren he yi.

Wang ling rong he. Wang ling rong he. Wang ling rong he.

Ten Powers for Soul Enlightenment

Millions of people are searching for soul enlightenment. "Soul Enlightenment" is chapter 13 of one of the authority books of my Soul Power Series, *The Power of Soul: The Way to Heal, Rejuvenate, Transform, and Enlighten All Life*. To reach soul enlightenment, there are ten powers I would like to share with you. This teaching is from Lao Zi, who wrote the classic work *Tao Te Jing*.

For a spiritual being to do Xiu Lian in order to reach soul enlightenment, advanced soul enlightenment, or Tao, there are ten powers to be known, understood, and achieved.

The first is the power of belief. Believe Tao. Believe in soul enlightenment. Believe karma, cause and effect. If you believe, you will make great effort to do serious Xiu Lian practice to clear karma, reach soul enlightenment, and reach Tao. To believe is to plant a seed. It is a beginning. Without this seed, you cannot enjoy a harvest. Belief is the true seed for your spiritual journey to soul enlightenment and to Tao.

The second is the power of giving up. For the spiritual journey, a committed person who is determined to reach soul enlightenment and Tao can give up everything. Shi Jia Mo Ni Fo gave up his royal position to search for his spiritual journey. Later, he was willing to give up his life to reach soul enlightenment. In China, there have been emperors who gave up their position to become monks. As a true spiritual seeker, reach the same condition. Be able to give up everything, without any attachment. Your spiritual commitment will move deeper and deeper. Worry will be reduced more and more and, finally, eliminated.

The third is the power of discipline. Discipline yourself to stop creating bad karma from body, mouth, and thought. There has never been a single human being who became a saint without discipline.

The fourth is the power of concentration and moving forward. Fully concentrate on your spiritual journey. Do not be distracted from your spiritual journey by anything. This is very important. Your spiritual journey will progress tremendously faster.

The fifth is the power of emptiness. During spiritual practice, reach emptiness by removing all thoughts.

The sixth is the power of stillness. To reach stillness during meditation is to attain a very advanced spiritual level.

In Taiwan, a great Buddhist monk went into Da Ding. "Da" means *big*. "Ding" means *stillness*. "Da Ding" means *big stillness*. By going into the Da Ding condition, he was able to sit for one month in the same position without moving.

The seventh is the power of intelligence. This intelligence is your true intelligence. It is your heart shining light. This heart light brings you true intelligence.

The eighth is the power of wisdom. This is not normal wisdom. As a spiritual seeker, to reach this special level of wisdom is to shine complete heart light. To have this level of power means you have reached soul enlightenment.

The ninth is the power of Tao. As a spiritual seeker, to reach this level is to reach Tao. You will be able to see the creation of all universes from Tao. You will literally be able to experience the normal creation and reverse creation of Tao.

The normal creation of Tao is: Tao creates One. One creates Two. Two creates Three. Three creates all things.

The reverse creation of Tao is: All things return to Three. Three returns to Two. Two returns to One. One returns to Tao.

The tenth is the power of Te. Te (pronounced *duh*) is the action of Tao. Te is the natural rules of Tao. For example, Di qi shang sheng, tian qi xia jiang means *Mother Earth's qi rises and Heaven's qi descends.* They are the action and natural rules of Tao. They are Tao Te. The normal and reverse creation of Tao are also the action of Tao. They are the big Tao Te. The power of *Te* allows you as a spiritual being to achieve total purity and meld with Tao. The complete true, pure, and divine nature of your heart and soul will then appear.

This teaching from Lao Zi is very important for every spiritual seeker. The ten powers are "must" achievements to reach soul enlightenment and then to reach Tao. They are very important for transforming your spiritual journey, as well as your physical journey.

Realize the importance of soul enlightenment.

The ten powers for soul enlightenment are vital.

Purify your soul, heart, mind, and body.

Serve. Serve. Serve.

Xiu Lian. Xiu Lian. Xiu Lian.

Service Xiu Lian. Service Xiu Lian. Service Xiu Lian.

Transform your spiritual journey and your physical journey.

Reach soul enlightenment.

Reach Tao.

Divine Transformation to Help Humanity During Mother Earth's Transition

*E*VERYBODY REALIZES MOTHER Earth is in transition now.

Mother Earth's Transition—What and Why

Mother Earth's transition includes natural disasters such as tsunamis, earthquakes, hurricanes, tornados, volcanic eruptions, and global warming, as well as wars, conflicts between nations and religions, and financial challenges for nations and individuals. In addition, sicknesses, including cancer, communicable diseases, emotional imbalances, and much more are happening more and more on Mother Earth.

It is easy to see that humanity and Mother Earth are facing more and more challenges now. The spiritual message that I have received is that Mother Earth's transition could last until the end of 2014. This is changeable. It could last longer or shorter.

Now it is June 2010. In the next few years, Mother Earth's transition could be extremely heavy. What is the cause of Mother Earth's transition? Remember my one-sentence secret about karma:

**Karma is the root cause of success and
failure in every aspect of life.**

Mother Earth's transition is due to the bad karma of humanity. Examples of this bad karma include:

- War, resulting in the killing and harming of humanity
- Cheating, stealing, and taking advantage of others
- Removing Mother Earth's natural resources in unbalanced ways, such as strip mining and deforestation
- Serious pollution in the air, water, and land
- Testing atomic bombs
- Power struggles
- Genocide
- Killing and harming based on race, religion, creed, sexual orientation, or beliefs
- Abuse of others
- Abuse and mistreatment of animals
- Production of goods that harm humanity
- Negative mind-sets, attitudes, beliefs, and behaviors
- Attachments and ego

Because humanity has created all of this bad karma, the lessons that humanity must learn are coming now. This is the spiritual reason for Mother Earth's transition.

Help Humanity and Mother Earth Pass Through This Difficult Time

To realize that Mother Earth's transition is due to bad karma is to realize that the solution is to clear this bad karma.

How can we clear this bad karma?

Humanity must awaken.

Humanity must do love and forgiveness practices.

Humanity must serve.

One of the most powerful services that anybody and everybody can do is divine chanting.

Divine chanting carries divine frequency and vibration to transform the frequency and vibration of humanity and all souls.

Divine chanting carries divine love, which melts all blockages and transforms all life.

Divine chanting carries divine forgiveness, which brings inner joy and inner peace.

Divine chanting carries divine compassion, which boosts energy, stamina, vitality, and immunity.

Divine chanting carries divine light, which heals, prevents sickness, rejuvenates, and purifies the soul, heart, mind, and body; transforms relationships, finances, and every aspect of life; and enlightens the soul, heart, mind, and body.

Divine chanting transforms the consciousness of humanity, all souls on Mother Earth, and all souls in all universes.

Divine chanting is just like a lightbulb in a house. Imagine a single 100-watt lightbulb shining in a room. Now imagine ten 100-watt lightbulbs shining in the same room. The light is much brighter.

To have millions of people chanting is like having millions of lightbulbs shining on Mother Earth. The power of transformation that they carry would be beyond comprehension.

I am honored to introduce a few important divine chants to help humanity and Mother Earth pass through this time of transition.

DIVINE SOUL SONG *LOVE, PEACE AND HARMONY*

Learn *Love, Peace and Harmony* by listening to this Divine Soul Song on the CD that is included with this book.

> *Lu La Lu La Li*
> *Lu La Lu La La Li*
> *Lu La Lu La Li Lu La*
> *Lu La Li Lu La*
> *Lu La Li Lu La*
>
> *I love my heart and soul*
> *I love all humanity*
> *Join hearts and souls together*
> *Love, peace and harmony*
> *Love, peace and harmony*

Sing this Divine Soul Song again:

> *Lu La Lu La Li*
> *Lu La Lu La La Li*
> *Lu La Lu La Li Lu La*
> *Lu La Li Lu La*
> *Lu La Li Lu La*

I love my heart and soul
I love all humanity
Join hearts and souls together
Love, peace and harmony
Love, peace and harmony

Again:

Lu La Lu La Li
Lu La Lu La La Li
Lu La Lu La Li Lu La
Lu La Li Lu La
Lu La Li Lu La

I love my heart and soul
I love all humanity
Join hearts and souls together
Love, peace and harmony
Love, peace and harmony

Again:

Lu La Lu La Li
Lu La Lu La La Li
Lu La Lu La Li Lu La
Lu La Li Lu La
Lu La Li Lu La

I love my heart and soul
I love all humanity

Join hearts and souls together
Love, peace and harmony
Love, peace and harmony

There is no time limit to chanting or singing this or any Divine Soul Song. The more you chant or sing *Love, Peace and Harmony*, the better. Remember the teaching: every moment that you are chanting, your soul and your book in the Akashic Records are receiving divine virtue (divine flowers).

In 2010, I created the I Serve Humanity movement. One of its major services is to chant the Divine Soul Song *Love, Peace and Harmony* as much as possible, day and night. Visit www.DrSha .com to learn more and join this movement.

DIVINE SOUL SONG *GOD GIVES HIS HEART TO ME*

Learn *God Gives His Heart to Me* by listening to this Divine Soul Song on the CD that is included with this book.

God gives his heart to me
God gives his love to me
My heart melds with his heart
My love melds with his love

Lu La Lu La La Li
Lu La Lu La La Li
Lu La Lu La Li
Lu La Lu La Li

Sing this Divine Soul Song with me again:

God gives his heart to me
God gives his love to me
My heart melds with his heart
My love melds with his love

Lu La Lu La La Li
Lu La Lu La La Li
Lu La Lu La Li
Lu La Lu La Li

Remember the teaching:

What you chant is what you become.

Go into the condition. Chant from the bottom of your heart. Your heart and the Divine's heart are one. Your love and the Divine's love are one. If everybody were to chant *God Gives His Heart to Me*, everyone's heart and soul would meld with the Divine's heart and soul. World love, peace, and harmony would happen.

Again:

God gives his heart to me
God gives his love to me
My heart melds with his heart
My love melds with his love

Lu La Lu La La Li
Lu La Lu La La Li
Lu La Lu La Li
Lu La Lu La Li

Once again:

God gives his heart to me
God gives his love to me
My heart melds with his heart
My love melds with his love

Lu La Lu La La Li
Lu La Lu La La Li
Lu La Lu La Li
Lu La Lu La Li

There is no time limit. The more you chant or sing *God Gives His Heart to Me*, the better.

DIVINE CHANT *TIAN DI REN HE YI, WAN LING RONG HE*

"Tian" means *Heaven*. "Di" means *Mother Earth*. "Ren" means *human being*. "He" means *join as*. "Yi" means *one*. "Tian di ren he yi" (pronounced *tyen dee wren huh yee*) means *Heaven, Earth, and human being join as one*.

"Wan" means *ten thousand*, which represents *every* or *all* in Chinese. "Ling" means *soul*. "Rong he" means *join together as one*. "Wan ling rong he" (pronounced *wahn ling rawng huh*) means *all souls join together as one*.

Tian Di Ren He Yi and Wan Ling Rong He are sacred teachings and Tao chants. See one of the other authority books in my Soul Power Series, *Tao I: The Way of All Life*, for additional teachings.

Learn these two divine chants by listening to them on the CD that is included in this book.

Chant with me now:

Tian Di Ren He Yi
Tian Di Ren He Yi
Tian Di Ren He Yi
Tian Di Ren He Yi
Tian Di Ren He Yi
Tian Di Ren He Yi
Tian Di Ren He Yi

Wan Ling Rong He
Wan Ling Rong He
Wan Ling Rong He
Wan Ling Rong He
Wan Ling Rong He
Wan Ling Rong He
Wan Ling Rong He . . .

Chant as much as you can. This is Service Xiu Lian.

The more you serve, the more every aspect of your life will be transformed.

Humanity will be transformed.

Mother Earth will be transformed.

All universes will be transformed.

You are making a difference for humanity, Mother Earth, and all universes.

You are transforming humanity, Mother Earth, and all universes.

Chant again:

Tian Di Ren He Yi
Tian Di Ren He Yi

Tian Di Ren He Yi
Tian Di Ren He Yi
Tian Di Ren He Yi
Tian Di Ren He Yi
Tian Di Ren He Yi

Wan Ling Rong He
Wan Ling Rong He
Wan Ling Rong He
Wan Ling Rong He
Wan Ling Rong He
Wan Ling Rong He
Wan Ling Rong He . . .

Again:

Tian Di Ren He Yi
Tian Di Ren He Yi
Tian Di Ren He Yi
Tian Di Ren He Yi
Tian Di Ren He Yi
Tian Di Ren He Yi
Tian Di Ren He Yi

Wan Ling Rong He
Wan Ling Rong He
Wan Ling Rong He
Wan Ling Rong He
Wan Ling Rong He
Wan Ling Rong He
Wan Ling Rong He . . .

Chant or sing as much as you can. Even by just thinking *Tian Di Ren He Yi* or *Wan Ling Rong He* (thinking chanting), you are serving.

You are contributing.

You are self-clearing your karma.

You are clearing the karma of humanity.

You are clearing the karma of all souls in Mother Earth.

You are clearing the karma of all souls in all universes.

I repeat Service Xiu Lian again:

> *Tao sheng yi*
> *Serve*
> *Heal*
> *Prevent sickness*
> *Rejuvenate*
> *Transform*
> *Enlighten*
> *Love, peace, and harmony; love, peace, and harmony;*
>   *love, peace, and harmony*
> *Tian di ren he yi, tian di ren he yi, tian di ren he yi*
> *Wan ling rong he, wan ling rong he, wan ling rong he*

Chant the Service Xiu Lian mantra again and again. The benefits are beyond words.

Create Love, Peace, and Harmony for Humanity, Mother Earth, and All Universes

In order to help humanity and Mother Earth pass through this difficult time of transition, the most important thing is to stop creating bad karma and constantly create good karma. What we do, what we speak, and what we think should help create love, peace, and harmony for humanity, Mother Earth, and all universes.

Mother Earth's transition is a karma cleansing process. Together we *will* pass through this difficult time. As I mentioned earlier, Mother Earth's transition could finish by the end of 2014. It could last longer. It could end sooner.

Mother Earth's transition period can be summarized in one sentence:

If humanity is awakened to serve, Mother Earth's transition period could be shortened; if humanity is not awakened to serve, Mother Earth's transition period could be prolonged.

Mother Earth's transition is a fact. It is occurring now. After Mother Earth's transition ends, humanity, Mother Earth, and all universes will create love, peace, and harmony. We have to go through this purification process in order to reach *wan ling rong he*.

Realize the seriousness of Mother Earth's transition.

Realize that Mother Earth's transition is due to bad karma.

Realize that it is the purification process of humanity and Mother Earth.

Realize that the only way to pass through this difficult time more quickly is to serve unconditionally.

Realize that you can self-clear your own karma by serving unconditionally.

Realize that you can help humanity self-clear its karma by serving unconditionally.

Realize that you can help all souls on Mother Earth and in all universes self-clear their karma by serving unconditionally.

Serve. Serve. Serve.
Serve unconditionally.

Chanting chanting chanting
Divine chanting is healing
Chanting chanting chanting
Divine chanting is rejuvenating

Singing singing singing
Divine singing is transforming
Singing singing singing
Divine singing is enlightening

Humanity is waiting for divine chanting
All souls are waiting for divine singing
Divine chanting removes all blockages
Divine singing brings inner joy

Divine is chanting and singing
Humanity and all souls are nourishing
Humanity and all souls are chanting and singing

World love, peace, and harmony are coming
World love, peace, and harmony are coming
World love, peace, and harmony are coming

Conclusion

THE TEACHINGS IN this book can be summarized by the following key points:

- Karma is the root cause of success and failure in every aspect of life.
- To self-clear karma is to transform your health.
- To self-clear karma is to transform your relationships.
- To self-clear karma is to transform your finances and business.
- To self-clear karma is to transform your spiritual journey.
- To self-clear karma is to transform humanity.
- To self-clear karma is to transform all souls on Mother Earth and in all universes.
- To self-clear karma is to create love, peace, and harmony for humanity, Mother Earth, and all universes.

All of these key points can be summarized in one sentence:

To self-clear karma is to transform all life and bring love, peace, and harmony to you, your loved ones, humanity, Mother Earth, and all universes.

In this book, you have also received thirty priceless permanent divine treasures, Divine Rainbow Light Ball and Divine Rainbow Liquid Spring Divine Soul Mind Body Transplants. This is the first time the Divine Committee is giving this higher level of rainbow light frequency to readers of the Soul Power Series.

This book reveals divine secrets, wisdom, knowledge, and practical techniques to transform your health, relationships, finances, and spiritual journey; and to help humanity to pass through this difficult time of Mother Earth's transition in order to create love, peace, and harmony for humanity, Mother Earth, and all universes.

I am extremely honored to be a servant of you, humanity, all souls, and the Divine.

I am extremely honored to share what the Divine has taught me.

I am extremely honored to train thousands of healers and teachers worldwide to offer divine soul healing and teaching.

Thank you for reading this book.

Thank you for your great contribution to serve humanity and all souls on Mother Earth and in all universes.

Let us join hearts and souls together to create love, peace, and harmony for humanity, Mother Earth, and all universes.

I love my heart and soul
I love all humanity
Join hearts and souls together

Love, peace and harmony
Love, peace and harmony

The teaching and practice of divine transformation is available for you, your loved ones, humanity, all souls on Mother Earth, and all souls in all universes.

Learn divine transformation.

Practice divine transformation.

Benefit from divine transformation.

Transform the life of you and your loved ones.

Transform the life of humanity and all souls on Mother Earth and in all universes.

Divine transformation is the unconditional servant for humanity, Mother Earth, and all souls.

Serve. Serve. Serve.

Transform. Transform. Transform.

Divine transformation. Divine transformation. Divine transformation.

Love, peace, and harmony. Love, peace, and harmony. Love, peace, and harmony.

Tian di ren he yi. Tian di ren he yi. Tian di ren he yi.

Wan ling rong he. Wan ling rong he. Wan ling rong he.

Thank you. Thank you. Thank you.

Acknowledgments

$\mathcal{I}$ THANK THE DIVINE and Tao who gave us the secrets, wisdom, knowledge, and practical techniques, as well as the Divine Soul Mind Body Transplants, in this book. The Divine and Tao and a few major spiritual fathers and mothers were with me during the flowing of this whole book.

I thank Dr. and Master Zhi Chen Guo and all of my spiritual fathers and mothers on Mother Earth and in all layers of Heaven for their teaching and blessings to prepare me as a servant of humanity and all souls.

I thank every reader and all of humanity for giving me the opportunity to serve you.

I thank my final editor, Allan Chuck, for his great editing. He has been the final editor of all of my major books. I deeply thank him.

I thank Heaven's Library's senior editor, Elaine Ward, for her great editing.

I thank Rick Riecker for his work on producing the CD for this book.

I thank other Divine Editors for their contributions to this book.

I thank my assistant, Cynthia Marie Deveraux, for her typing. Her incredibly fast typing helps a lot.

I thank my Worldwide Representatives, Marilyn Smith, Francisco Quintero, Allan Chuck, Peter Hudoba, Petra Herz, David Lusch, Roger Givens, Patricia Smith, Peggy Werner, Lynne Nusyna, Shu Chin Hsu, Maria Sunukjian, Hannah Stevens, and Trevor Allen for their total GOLD service for humanity and all souls.

I thank all of my Divine Master Teachers and Healers, my hundreds of Master Teachers and Healers of Soul Healing and Enlightenment, and my more than one thousand Soul Healing Teachers and Healers worldwide for their contributions to the mission.

I thank all of my thousands of students worldwide for your great service.

I thank my team at Simon & Schuster and Atria Books: Judith Curr, executive vice president and publisher; Chris Lloreda, vice president and deputy publisher; Johanna Castillo, vice president and senior editor; Amy Tannenbaum, associate editor; Isolde Sauer, associate director, copyediting; Lisa Keim, foreign rights director; Christine Saunders, deputy publicity director; Michael Selleck, executive vice president of sales and marketing; Tom Spain, audio editorial director; Dan Vidra, international sales director; and more. This team has given me great support for my Soul Power Series.

I thank my publicist, Jill Mangino, for her great contribution to the mission.

I thank all of my business team leaders and members.

I thank my wife and children for their great love and support for my service.

Love you. Love you. Love you.

Thank you. Thank you. Thank you.

I will be a servant of humanity and all souls forever.

With love and blessing,
Zhi Gang Sha

A Special Gift

THE ENCLOSED CD is an essential component of this book, *Divine Transformation: The Divine Way to Self-clear Karma to Transform Your Health, Relationships, Finances, and More.* It includes recordings of Divine Soul Songs and mantras to apply in your divine transformation journey.

Remember my teaching: the practices are a vital step to self-clear your karma and to transform your health, relationships, finances, and more. Do not skip the practices. Use this CD to practice with me.

The contents of the CD are as follows:

Track 1   Divine Soul Song *Love, Peace and Harmony*
Track 2   Divine Soul Song *God Gives His Heart to Me*
Track 3   Divine Chant *Tian Di Ren He Yi, Wan Ling Rong He*
Track 4   Divine Soul Song for Transforming Emotions

May this CD and book serve you well in your divine transformation journey. Learn the material well. This will empower you to benefit fully from the practices. Practice well. The more you practice, the more benefits you could receive.

May you self-clear your karma as soon as possible and transform every aspect of your life.

Practice. Practice. Practice.

Transform. Transform. Transform.

Tian di ren he yi. Tian di ren he yi. Tian di ren he yi.

Wan ling rong he. Wan ling rong he. Wan ling rong he.

Thank you. Thank you. Thank you.

Index

A

Acupuncture points, 31
  have a soul, 88
Akashic Records
  bad karma recorded in, 162
  chanting and, 145, 230
  Divine Karma Cleansing and, 21–2
  everything recorded in, 27, 138, 151,
     164
  explanation of, 27, 119
  financial matters and, 148
  Heaven's flowers and, 26, 157, 162
  karmic records, 119, 122–123, 128, 151,
     162, 164
  life is arranged and managed by, 28
  receiving messages from, 119, 123
  rewards and lessons and, 28
  service to others and, 26–27, 150–151
  Soul enlightenment and, 190
  Third Eye and, 123
  virtue and, 27, 145–146, 150, 157
*Ancestors plant the trees; descendants enjoy the
    shade,* 148
Anger, 68, 205
  and Wood element, 68, 205–207
  burns good virtue, 164
  thought karma and, 154

Anxiety and depression, 68, 75, 208–210
  and Fire element, 68, 208–210
Arranged conditions of life, 9
Audio books, xxxi–xxxiii
  other books of the Soul Power Series and,
    265–272
Austria, 196, 199

B

Bad karma, *See also* Karma
  Akashic Records and, 162
  ancestors and, 155
  ancestral, 7
  applying divine treasures to clear, 10, 14
  blockages and, 5, 7, 23–24, 45
  city and country and, 24
  clearing bad karma, 5, 7–22
  creating, 28, 119, 151–154, 158, 159,
    161–162, 163, 164, 165
    one-sentence secret about, 162
  dark souls and, 12
  disrespecting saints, 3
  Divine Karma Cleansing and, 12, 19,
    21–22
  divine transformation and, 7
  divine way to clear, 11
  effects of, 4, 7, 41, 158–159, 226

Bad karma (*cont.*)
 explanation of, 5, 7, 23–24
 failure and, 4, 7, 41, 226
 financial matters and, 28, 165, 166, 169, 171
 forgiveness and, 8, 12, 25
 Four Power Techniques for self-clearing bad karma, 14–21
 government officials and, 151
 killing animals and, 164
 mental conditions and, 79
 Mother Earth's transition and, 4, 24, 226, 236
 one-sentence secret about creating, 162
 organizations and, 23–24
 personal, 7
 relationships challenges and, 118–119, 122–123, 128, 131
 self-clearing, 7, 12, 14
  effects of, 226
 Shan you shan bao, e you e bao (good karma returns; bad karma also returns), 154–155
 sickness and, 29
 soul blockages and, 23, 29
 speaking and, 161–163
 spiritual debt and, 167
 stop creating, 235–236
 thinking and, 161–163
 types of, 5, 23, 29, 153–154, 164–165, 226
 unconditional universal service and, 7
 unpleasant service and, 5, 153, 162
 virtue and, 152
Beckwith, Michael Bernard, xxx
Belief, 222
Bladder cancer, 58–61
Blockages, *See also* Body blockages; Mind blockages
 all challenges are due to, 23
 bad karma and, 5, 7, 23–24, 45
 business and, 177–179
 chanting and, 44, 50, 65, 95, 227–235
 clearing from the Message Center, 12n5
 divine love melts all, xix, 12
 emotional body self-healing and, 68–78
 forgiveness and, 51

 love and forgiveness are golden keys to removing, 176
 mental body self-healing and, 79–85
 pain and, 30
 physical body self-healing and, 29–45
 removal of blockages, 12–14
 result of bad karma, 7
 self-clearing karma (soul blockages), mind blockages, and body blockages for finances and business, 171–177
 soul blockages, 23, 29
 soul software and, xviii
 spiritual body self-healing and, 88–95
 spiritual debt and, 7
Blood vessels, 208–210
Bodhi tree, 189
Bodhisattva, 159
Body blockages, *See also* Blockages; Mind blockages
 bad karma and, 24, 29
 explanation of, 24, 29–30
 self-clearing karma (soul blockages), mind blockages, and body blockages for finances and business, 171–177
 self-clearing mind blockages, 118–122
 self-healing emotional body and, 68–78
 self-healing mental body and, 79–85
 self-healing spiritual body and, 88–95
Body Power
 balancing relationships of all nations, 138
 balancing relationships of all planets (including Mother Earth), all stars, all galaxies, and all universes, 142
 balancing relationships of humanity, 136
 body secrets, 39
 Earth element practice, 201–202
 explanation of, 14
 Fire element practice, 208
 forgiveness practice to self-clear karma for healing and life transformation, 41
 Four Power Techniques and, 30–31
 golden light self-healing practice, 97
 Metal element practice, 210
 one-sentence secret, 31, 214
 practice self-clearing karma, 15

practice using divine treasures to balance relationships with life partners, 126

practice using divine treasures for emotional body healing, 71, 75

practice using divine treasures for healing inflammation and infection, 48–49

practice using divine treasures for mental body healing, 82

practice using divine treasures for spiritual body healing, 92

practice using divine treasures to heal growths (cysts, tumors, and cancer), 54

practice using divine treasures to heal pain, 35

practice using divine treasures to prevent sickness, 103

practice using divine treasures to transform all life, 117

self-balancing relationships with colleagues, 132

self-balancing relationships with family members, 129

self-clearing karma, mind blockages, and body blockages for relationships, 119

self-clearing karma (soul blockages), mind blockages, and body blockages for finances and business, 172

soul marketing and, 180

Tao Sheng Yi practice for Service Xiu Lian, 215–221

techniques, 31

Water element practice, 196

Wood element practice and, 205

Xiu Lian practice, 196, 215–221

Body secrets, 39, 195

Buddha Dharma Education Association, Inc., 148

Buddhism, 188, 196, 223

C

Cancer

bladder cancer, 58–61

divine treasures and, 52–57

liver cancer, xvi–xviii

practice using divine treasures to heal growths (cysts, tumors, and cancer), 54–60

stage IV lymphoma, 62–67

Celis, Marcelo, 61

Central nervous system illness, 19–21

Changeable conditions of life, 9

Chanting and singing, *See also* Divine Soul Songs; Sound Power (chanting or singing)

Akashic Records and, 145, 230

amount of time for chanting, 18, 38, 78–79, 95

benefits of, 44

blockages and, 44, 50, 65, 95, 227–235

chronic conditions and, 34, 38, 52, 57–58, 75, 79, 85, 95, 99

Da Tao zhi jian (The Big Way is extremely simple), xlii, 35, 112, 118

depression and, 75

Divine Soul Song of Five Elements, 63, 65

Divine Soul Song of Yin Yang, 62, 65

divine treasures and, 86–87

effects of, 14, 44–45, 87–88, 95

financial matters and, 44, 167–168, 167–171

forgiveness and, 41

forgiveness practice to self-clear karma for healing and life transformation, 42–43

heavy bad karma and, 34

helping humanity and Mother Earth through transition time by, 227

importance of, 118, 139

key sacred wisdom and knowledge about, 39

offering gratitude, 90–91

one-sentence secret for chanting, 40, 176, 200

practice self-clearing karma, 16–18

practice using divine treasures for healing inflammation and infection, 50–52

practice using divine treasures to heal pain, 36–38

self-clearing karma (soul blockages), mind blockages, and body blockages for finances and business, 173–175

Chanting and singing (*cont.*)
  as Sound Power, 39
  spiritual testing and, 46
  stage IV cancer healing and, 62
  "thinking chanting," 107, 109
  develop thinking power, 108
  Third Eye and, 43–44
  Tian di ren he yi (Heaven, Earth, and
     human being join as one), 216–219,
     232–235
  virtue from Akashic Records and,
     145–146
  Wan Ling Rong He (join all souls as one),
     216–219, 232–235
  what you chant is what you become, 40,
     176, 214, 231
  yin and yang chanting, 109
Chemotherapy, 62
China, 177, 222
Compassion, *See also* Divine Soul
     Downloads
  Divine Soul Downloads and, xix, 25
  divine treasures and, 24–26, 86
  Guan Yin's compassion, xii
  healing effects of, 45, 108
  mantras and, 40, 44
  serve others with, 26
  spiritual testing and, 45
Compassion Buddha(see also Guan Yin),
     192
Concentration and moving forward,
     222–223
CT scans, xviii, 58, 66
Curses, 19, 19n9, 21, 23, 29
Cysts, 52–57

D
Da Ding (big stillness), 223
Da Jun Liu, 192
Da Tao zhi jian (The Big Way is extremely
     simple), xlii, 35, 112, 118
De Hua Liu, 192
Depression and anxiety, 68, 75, 208–210
Di qi shang sheng, tian qi xia jiang (Mother
     Earth's qi rises and Heaven's qi
     descends), 224
"Dirty money," 152
Discipline, 155, 160, 222

Divine Body Transplant, explanation of, xx
Divine Compassion, xix
Divine Karma Cleansing, 19, 21–22, 66
Divine Mind Transplant, explanation of, xx
Divine Oneness, 191–193
Divine Order for Soul Enlightenment, 63
Divine Rainbow Light Ball as yang treasure,
     11
Divine Rainbow Liquid Spring as yin
     treasure, 11
Divine Service Law, 188
  transforming your spiritual journey and,
     188
Divine Soul Acupuncture, xix
Divine Soul Downloads
  Divine frequency and, xix, 24, 26, 34,
     107
  Divine Rainbow Light Ball and Divine
     Rainbow Liquid Spring of Divine
     Balance Body Transplant, 134
  Divine Rainbow Light Ball and Divine
     Rainbow Liquid Spring of Divine
     Balance Mind Transplant, 134
  Divine Rainbow Light Ball and Divine
     Rainbow Liquid Spring of Divine
     Balance Soul Transplant, 134
  Divine Rainbow Light Ball and Divine
     Rainbow Liquid Spring of Divine
     Blessing Body Transplant, 90
  Divine Rainbow Light Ball and Divine
     Rainbow Liquid Spring of Divine
     Blessing Mind Transplant, 89
  Divine Rainbow Light Ball and Divine
     Rainbow Liquid Spring of Divine
     Blessing Soul Transplant, 89
  Divine Rainbow Light Ball and Divine
     Rainbow Liquid Spring of Divine
     Compassion Body Transplant, 53
  Divine Rainbow Light Ball and Divine
     Rainbow Liquid Spring of Divine
     Compassion Mind Transplant, 53
  Divine Rainbow Light Ball and Divine
     Rainbow Liquid Spring of Divine
     Compassion Soul Transplant, 53
  Divine Rainbow Light Ball and Divine
     Rainbow Liquid Spring of Divine
     Forgiveness Body Transplant, 47
  Divine Rainbow Light Ball and Divine

Rainbow Liquid Spring of Divine Forgiveness Mind Transplant, 47

Divine Rainbow Light Ball and Divine Rainbow Liquid Spring of Divine Forgiveness Soul Transplant, 47

Divine Rainbow Light Ball and Divine Rainbow Liquid Spring of Divine Harmony Body Transplant, 124

Divine Rainbow Light Ball and Divine Rainbow Liquid Spring of Divine Harmony Mind Transplant, 124

Divine Rainbow Light Ball and Divine Rainbow Liquid Spring of Divine Harmony Soul Transplant, 124

Divine Rainbow Light Ball and Divine Rainbow Liquid Spring of Divine Light Body Transplant, 70

Divine Rainbow Light Ball and Divine Rainbow Liquid Spring of Divine Light Mind Transplant, 70

Divine Rainbow Light Ball and Divine Rainbow Liquid Spring of Divine Light Soul Transplant, 70

Divine Rainbow Light Ball and Divine Rainbow Liquid Spring of Divine Love Body Transplant, 13

Divine Rainbow Light Ball and Divine Rainbow Liquid Spring of Divine Love Mind Transplant, 13

Divine Rainbow Light Ball and Divine Rainbow Liquid Spring of Divine Love Soul Transplant, 12

Divine Rainbow Light Ball and Divine Rainbow Liquid Spring of Divine Love Peace Harmony Body Transplant, 141

Divine Rainbow Light Ball and Divine Rainbow Liquid Spring of Divine Love Peace Harmony Mind Transplant, 141

Divine Rainbow Light Ball and Divine Rainbow Liquid Spring of Divine Love Peace Harmony Soul Transplant, 140

Divine Rainbow Light Ball and Divine Rainbow Liquid Spring of Divine Prevention of Sickness Body Transplant, 102

Divine Rainbow Light Ball and Divine Rainbow Liquid Spring of Divine Prevention of Sickness Mind Transplant, 101

Divine Rainbow Light Ball and Divine Rainbow Liquid Spring of Divine Prevention of Sickness Soul Transplant, 101

Divine Rainbow Light Ball and Divine Rainbow Liquid Spring of Divine Sincerity Body Transplant, 81

Divine Rainbow Light Ball and Divine Rainbow Liquid Spring of Divine Sincerity Mind Transplant, 80

Divine Rainbow Light Ball and Divine Rainbow Liquid Spring of Divine Sincerity Soul Transplant, 80

as divine presence, xx–xxi

are like lightbulbs, 26

carry divine love, forgiveness, compassion, and light, 25, 34, 107, 108,

effects of, xxvii–xxviii, 87

in every book of the Soul Power Series, xxi

list of, xxxv–xxxvii

readiness for, xxvi

receiving Divine Soul Downloads, xxv–xxviii

speed of transformation and, xx-xxi

turning them on, 108

types, xix

virtue and, 26, 87

yin companion, xxviiin1

Divine Soul Herbs, xix

Divine Soul Massage, xix

Divine Soul Mind Body Healing and Transmission System (Divine Soul Downloads), 62, 63

Divine Soul Mind Body Healing and Transmission System: The Divine Way to Heal You, Humanity, Mother Earth, and All Universes (Sha), ii, 10, 29, 58, 271

Divine Soul Mind Body Transplants, 2–3, 11, 19

Divine Soul Operation, xix

Divine Soul Songs
   Divine Soul Song of Five Elements, 63, 65
   Divine Soul Song for World Soul
      Healing, Peace and Enlightenment,
      168
   Divine Soul Song of Yin Yang, 62, 65
   God Gives His Heart to Me, 13–14, 48, 54,
      62, 81, 90–91, 102, 230–232
   Love, Peace and Harmony, 62, 65, 67, 144,
      156, 167–171, 228–231
   power of, 167–169
   Say *hello,* 169
   Thank You, Divine, 13–14, 48, 71, 90, 135,
      142
Divine Soul Songs: Sacred Practical Treasures
    to Heal, Rejuvenate, and Transform
    You, Humanity, Mother Earth, and
    All Universes (Sha), 10
Divine Soul Transplants, explanation of, xx
Divine transformation, *See also*
    Transformation
   clearing bad karma and, 7–22
   Divine Soul Mind Body Transplants and,
     2–3
   divine treasures and, 10–11
   effects of, xliii-xliv,140
   explanation of, 2–6
   relationships and, 119
   significance and power of, 6–7
   Transform the soul first; then
     transformation of the mind, body, and
     every aspect of life will follow, 32
   universal service and, 9
Divine Transformation: The Divine Way to
    Self-clear Karma to Transform Your
    Health, Relationships, Finances, and
    More (Sha), xxxi, 182–183

E
Earth element, 68, 215
Earth element practice, 201–205
Emotional body
   anger and, 205
   depression and anxiety and, 208–210
   fear, 68, 196–198
   five elements and, 68
   sadness and grief, 68, 210–214
   self-healing of, 68–78

   self-prevent sickness, 101–107
   worry, 68, 201, 204
Empowerments (Dr. Sha's)
   teaching healing, ix–x
   teaching *the power of soul,* x
   teaching universal service, xi
Emptiness, 190, 223
Enlightenment. *See* Soul Enlightenment
Eyes, 71, 205–207

F
Fear, 68
   and Water element, 68, 196–198
Financial matters
   Akashic Records and, 148
   blockages and, 23
   business name importance, 177
   cause of financial challenges, 28, 150,
     156–160, 165–166
   chanting and singing and, 44, 167–171
   choosing business partners, 152
   "dirty money," 152
   Divine transformation and, 6, xliii
   explanation of financial conditions,
     165–166
   losing financial abundance, 151–153
   self-clearing karma (soul blockages),
     mind blockages, and body blockages
     for finances and business, 171–177
   soul marketing, 179–185
   Soul Power and, xi, xl
   Tao of business, 178–179
   transformation, 158, 161–171
   unconditional service and, 148–152,
     185–186
   virtue accumulation and, 148–150,
     151–154
Fire element, 68
Fire element practice, 208–210
Five element organs, 63, 71
Five elements
   Earth element, 68, 201–205, 215
   emotional body and, 68
   explanation of, 68
   Fire element, 68, 208–210
   Metal element, 68, 210–214
   Water element, 68, 196–199
   Wood element, 68, 205–207

Forgiveness
  bad karma, 8, 41
  brings inner peace and inner joy, xix, 12, 44, 108
  chanting and, 175–176, 227
  clearing blockages and, 51
  creation of good karma and, 161
  Divine Karma Cleansing and, 21
  Divine Soul Downloads and, xix, 24, 25, 34,
  financial matters and, 173
  good service and, 153
  healing stage IV lymphoma and, 63, 67
  mantras and, 44
  practice and, 25
  self-clearing karma and, 21, 24, 25, 41, 41–43, 79–80, 128, 171
  sincerity and honesty and, 43
  spiritual testing and, 45
  universal service and, xiv
Forgiveness center. *See* Message Center
Four Power Techniques
  explanation, 14, 31–35
  one-sentence secret of divine treasures and, 116
  one-sentence secrets for each of, 214
  Soul Power as most important, 39
Free Soul Healing Blessings for Humanity, 67
Free will, xxvi
Frequency transformation, 86–87

G

Gallbladder, 71, 205–207
Giving up, 222
God Gives His Heart to Me (chant), 13–14, 48, 54, 62, 81, 90–91, 102, 230–232
GOLD (gratitude, obedience, loyalty, devotion), xiv-xv, xxii, 122, 200
Golden light self-healing practice, 97–99
Golden light shines; all sickness disappears, 32, 96
Golden Urn, 196n3
Grief and sadness, 68, 210–214
  and Metal element, 68
Guan Yin
  compassion and, xii, 192

enlightenment mantra, 39–41
  Third Eye and, 43–44
Gums and teeth, 68, 201, 204

H

Hao, translation and definition of, 18n7
Heal the soul first; then healing of the mind and body will follow, 96
Healing, *See also* Personal stories of healing; Practice; Prevention of illness
  bladder cancer, 58–61
  blockages and, 23
  Divine transformation and, xliii, 95
  emotional body self-healing, 68–78
  enlightenment and, 6
  forgiveness practice to self-clear karma for healing and life and life transformation, 41–43
  practice and, 113
  practice for self-healing the physical body, 29–45
  self-healing mental body and, 79–85
  Soul Power and, xl
Heart, 63, 71, 208–210
Heaven
  Heaven's flowers, 26, 157, 162
  Heaven's Library, xi
  Heaven's virtue bank, 21–22, 157–158
  honesty moves Heaven, 176
Hinduism, 196
Honesty, 176
Hua you san shuo, qiao shuo wei miao (there are three ways to speak something; the proper way is profound), 161
Hudoba, Peter, 199, 244
Huo fu wu men, wei ren zhi zhao (there is no particular gate to one's disasters and blessings; they are all attracted by yourself), 160

I

If you want to know if a pear is sweet, taste it, xix, 114
Illness
  bladder cancer, 58–61
  central nervous system illness, 19–21
  liver cancer, xvi-xviii
  stage IV lymphoma, 62–67

Infection, 46–52
Inflammation, 46–52
Inner souls, 14, 31
Institute of Soul Healing and
　　Enlightenment, 62
Intelligence, 223
International Tao Retreat, 196
I Serve Humanity movement, 230

J
Jesus, xi, xii, 192
Jin Dan, 197n4, 201, 210, 218
Jin guang zhao ti, bai bing xiao chu (Golden
　　light shines; all sicknesses are
　　removed), 96

K
Karma, *See also* Akashic Records; Bad
　　karma; Virtue
　　Akashic Records and, 4–5, 21, 119,
　　　122–123
　　creating good karma, 155, 161–162,
　　　163–165
　　Divine Karma Cleansing, 19, 21–22,
　　　66
　　financial transformation and, 161–171
　　heavy karma, xxxiii, 24–25, 159
　　importance of practice and, xxxiii
　　key points of teachings about, 239–240
　　and Mother Earth's transition, 226
　　one-sentence secret, 4, 163, 226
　　one-sentence teachings, 155, 239–240
　　relationships challenges and, 118,
　　　122–123, 128
　　self-clearing karma, 14–21, 29–45,
　　　41–43, 118–122, 171–177, 236–240
　　self-healing emotional body and, 68–78
　　self-healing mental body and, 79–85
　　self-healing spiritual body and, 88–95
　　selfishness and, 163–164
　　selflessness and, 163–164
　　service and, 8–9, 25–26, 163
　　shan you shan bao, e you e bao (good
　　　karma returns; bad karma also
　　　returns), 154–155
　　significance and benefits of cleansing, 26
　　speech and, 164
　　speed of clearing karma, 24–25

　　success and failure and, 4, 41, 226
　　virtue bank account, 162
Kidneys, 63, 71, 197, 200–201
Kou Mi (mouth secret), 195
Kundalini, 196n3

L
Land of Medicine Buddha (California
　　retreat center), xiii
Lao Gong acupuncture point, 31
Lao Zi, 159–160, 192, 221–224
Large intestine, 210–214
Liao-Fan's Four Lessons (Buddha Dharma
　　Education Association, Inc.), 148
Life
　　arranged conditions of life, 9
　　changeable conditions of life, 9
　　purpose of, ix, 187
　　transformation, 9
Light Wall download, 64
Lips and mouth, 68, 201, 204
Liver, 63, 71, 205–207
Liver cancer, xvi–xviii
Love, Peace and Harmony, 62, 65, 67, 144,
　　156, 167–171, 228–231
Lower Dan Tian, 64
Lungs, 63, 71, 210–214
Lymphoma, 62–67

M
Mantras
　　chanting and, 44–45
　　Da Tao zhi jian (The Big Way is
　　　extremely simple), xlii, 35, 112, 118
　　healing mantras, 33–34
　　soul frequency and, 44
　　spiritual calling and, 40–41
　　Tian di ren he yi (Heaven, Earth, and
　　　human being join as one), 216–219,
　　　232–235
　　Wan Ling Rong He (join all souls as one),
　　　216–219, 232–235
　　Weng Ma Ni Ba Ma Hong (Guan Yin
　　　enlightenment mantra), 39–43
Meditation, 195–196
Mental body
　　mental body self-healing and, 79–85
　　self-prevent sickness, 101–107

Message Center (heart chakra)
  emotional balance and, 68–69
  explanation of, 12n5
  practice self-healing inflammation and
      infection and, 46–47
  soul marketing and, 180
Metal element, 68
Metal element practice, 210–214
Mind blockages, *See also* Blockages; Body
      blockages
  bad karma and, 24, 29
  dissemination of Dr. Sha's teachings and,
      114
  examples of, 79
  explanation of, 24, 30
  self-clearing mind blockages, 118–122,
      171–177
  self-healing emotional body and, 68–78
  self-healing mental body and, 79–85
  self-healing spiritual body and, 88–95
Mind over matter, xi
Mind Power
  balancing relationships of all nations, 138
  balancing relationships of all plants
      (including Mother Earth), all stars,
      all galaxies, and all universes, 143
  balancing relationships of humanity,
      136
  creative visualization application, 32–33
  Earth element practice, 202
  explanation of, 14
  Fire element practice, 208
  forgiveness practice to self-clear karma
      for healing and life transformation,
      42
  golden light self-healing practice, 98
  Metal element practice, 211
  practice self-clearing karma, 16
  practice using divine treasures to balance
      relationships with life partners, 127
  practice using divine treasures for
      emotional body healing, 72, 76
  practice using divine treasures for healing
      inflammation and infection, 50
  practice using divine treasures for mental
      body healing, 83
  practice using divine treasures for
      spiritual body healing, 93

  practice using divine treasures to heal
      growths (cysts, tumors, and cancer),
      55
  practice using divine treasures to heal
      pain, 36
  practice using divine treasures to prevent
      sickness, 104
  practice using divine treasures to
      transform all life, 117
  self-balancing relationships with
      colleagues, 133
  self-balancing relationships with family
      members, 130
  self-clearing karma, mind blockages, and
      body blockages for relationships,
      121
  self-clearing karma (soul blockages),
      mind blockages, and body blockages
      for finances and business, 173
  soul marketing and, 182
  Tao Sheng Yi practice for Service Xiu
      Lian, 216
  Water element practice, 197
  Wood element practice and, 206
  Xiu Lian practice and, 197, 216
Ming Men Area, 196n3
Money, 157
  lack of, 158
  virtue can transform to, 150
  yin and yang, 157
Mother Earth's transition
  bad karma and, 226, 236
  balancing relationships of all planets
      (including Mother Earth), all
      stars, all galaxies, and all universes,
      140–144
  chanting and, 227–235
  creating love, peace, and harmony for
      humanity, Mother Earth, and all
      universes, 235–239
  Divine chanting and, 232–235
  help Mother Earth Pass through difficult
      times, 227–230
  length of time, 236
  natural disasters and, xlii, 151, 225
  sicknesses and, 225
  Soul Light Era and, xiii
  world conflicts and, xlii, 225

Mother Mary, xii
Mouth, 68, 161–163, 201, 204
Mouth secrets, 39, 195
Mudras, 196
Muscles, 68, 201, 204

N
Natural disasters, xi
Negative memories
    explanation of, 19n10
    removal of, 21
Nose, 210–214

O
One Hand Healing Technique, 31
One Hand Near, One Hand Far Body
        Power Technique, 31
One-sentence healing secret, 32, 96
One-sentence secret
    chanting, 40, 176, 200
    creating bad karma, 162
    creating good karma, 163
    creating good karma and bad karma,
        163
    for all life, 112
    Four Power Techniques, 214
    karma, 4, 163, 226
    soul healing, 96, 99
    spiritual journey, 194
    spiritual money and physical money, 157
One-sentence teachings
    chanting, 40, 176, 214, 231
    on financial matters, 152, 153, 166
    five fundamental teachings, 108
    on karma, 155, 239–240
    on spiritual journey, 191
Outer souls, 14, 32

P
Pain
    blockages and, 30
    practice using divine treasures to heal
        pain, 35–38
Peng Zu, 192
Pericardium Meridian 8, 31
Personal stories of healing
    bladder cancer, 58–61
    central nervous system illness, 19–21

liver cancer, xvi-xviii
    stage IV lymphoma, 62–67
Philippines, 147
Phobias, 79
Physical money and spiritual money,
        27–28
*Power Healing: The Four Keys to Energizing
        Your Body, Mind, and Spirit* (Sha),
        30, 38
Power of belief, 222
Power of concentration and moving
        forward, 222–223
Power of discipline, 222
Power of emptiness, 223
Power of giving up, 222
Power of intelligence, 233
*Power of Soul: The Way to Heal, Rejuvenate,
        Transform, and Enlighten All Life*
        (Sha), 4, 10, 62, 179, 221
Power of stillness, 223
Power of Tao, 223
Power of Te, 224
Power of wisdom, 223
Practice, *See also* headings beginning
        Self-balancing; Self-healing
    Earth element practice, 201–205
    effects of, 113–114
    Fire element practice, 208–210
    forgiveness practice to self-clear karma
        for healing and life transformation,
        41–43
    importance of, xvii–xviii, xxxi–xxxiv,
        21, 26
    Metal element practice, 210–214
    practice using divine treasures for
        emotional body healing, 71–78
    practice using divine treasures for healing
        inflammation and infection, 48–52
    practice using divine treasures for mental
        body healing, 82–85
    self-clearing karma, 14–21, 29–45,
        41–43
    self-healing the physical body, 29–45
    using divine treasures for spiritual body
        healing, 91–95
    using divine treasures to balance
        relationships with life partners,
        125–128

using divine treasures to heal growths (cysts, tumors, and cancer), 54–60
using divine treasures to heal pain, 35–38
using divine treasures to prevent sickness, 103–107
using divine treasures to transform all life, 116–118
Water element practice, 196
Wood element practice, 205–207
Xiu Lian practice, 194–196, 196–199, 215–221
Prevention of illness. *See also* Healing xl, xliii, 6
Pu Ti Lao Zu, 192
Purification
Divine transformation and, 6
enlightenment and, 190
Mother Earth transition and, 236
Soul Power and, xl
Purpose of life is to serve, 187–188

Q

Qian ren zai shu, hou ren cheng liang (ancestors plant the trees, descendants enjoy the shade), 148–149
Quintero, Francisco, 201, 244

R

Rainbow light
explanation of, 99–100
Rainbow light shines; all sicknesses are removed faster, 99
Readiness
for Divine Soul Downloads, xxvi
for wisdom, xxvi, xli–xlii
Rejuvenation
body power and, 31
Divine transformation and, 6
practice and, 113
Soul Power and, xl
Relationships
balancing relationships of all nations, 137–139
balancing relationships of all planets (including Mother Earth), all stars, all galaxies, and all universes, 140–144

balancing relationships of humanity, 134–137
blockages and, 23
chanting and, 44
Divine transformation and, xliii, 6
karma and, 118, 122–123, 128, 131
power of soul and, xi
questions for awareness about, 111
self-balancing relationships with colleagues, 131–133
self-balancing relationships with family members, 128–131
self-balancing relationships with life partners, 122–128
self-clearing karma, mind blockages, and body blockages for relationships, 118–122
Soul Power and, xl
using divine treasures to balance relationships with life partners, 125–128
Religions, 192–193
Rong Yang, 149

S

Sacred images, 3
Sadness and grief, 210–214
Metal element and, 68
Saints, 3, 32
Say *hello. See* Soul Power
Self-balancing relationships with colleagues, 131–133
Self-balancing relationships with family members, 128–131
Self-balancing relationships with life partners, 122–128
Self-healing, *See also* Practice
emotional body self-healing, 68–78
golden light self-healing practice, 97–99
mental body self-healing, 79–85
practice for self-healing the physical body, 29–45
practice self-healing inflammation and infection and, 46–47
simplicity of, 115–116
spiritual body self-healing, 88–95
Selfishness, 162–163, 184–185
Selflessness, 162–163

Service
Akashic Records and, 27
ancestors and, 148–149
chanting and, 86
clearing bad karma and, 26, 150
Divine Service Law, 188
Divine transformation and, 9
explanation of good and bad, 153
financial matters and, 148–152, 158,
185–186
karma and, 8–9, 26, 163, 236
as purpose of life, 187
unconditional, 150–151
Universal Law of Universal Service,
8–9
unpleasant service and, xiv, 5
upliftment and, 194
virtue accumulation and, 26, 148–149,
157, 166, 193
Xiu Lian method, 191, 191n2, 194–196
Service Xiu Lian
as best method, 191, 194
chanting and, 233–235
explanation of, 191n2
practice, 194–196
soul standing and, 194
Tao Shen Yi practice, 215–221
Shan you shan bao, e you e bao (good karma
returns; bad karma also returns), 154
Shen Mi (body secret), 195
Shi Jia Mo Ni Fo, 191, 194, 222
Shi Jia Mo Ni Fo's Enlightenment Story,
188–191
Simplicity
one-sentence secret for all teaching, xlii,
35, 112, 113
self-healing and, 115–116
Singing. See Chanting and singing
Skin, 210–214
Small intestine, 208–210
Smith, Patricia, 62, 63–64
Snow Mountain Area, 195, 196n3, 201
Soul blockages. See bad karma
Soul Communication: Opening Your Spiritual
Channels for Success and Fulfillment
(Sha), 10, 261
Soul Communication Channel, xli
Soul conference, 66

Soul Dance, 66
Soul enlightenment, 6–7, 113
soul standing and, 190
ten powers and, 221–224
Soul Healing and Enlightenment Retreat
and Divine Rejuvenation Retreat, 63
Soul Healing Week in Toronto, Canada, 60,
Soul is the boss, xl, 96, 179
Soul Language, 48, 70
Soul Light Era, x–xi, xiii, xviii, xxi–xxii,
185, 195
final goal of, xxii, 216
Soul Light Era Prayer Position
balancing emotions and, 75
description of, 12, 53, 138
karma-clearing and, 15, 119
relationship transformation and, 119,
124, 129
soul marketing and, 180
transformation of cancer, cysts, and
growths and, 53
Soul marketing, 179–185
one-sentence secret of, 180
Soul Mind Body Healing and Transmission
System for Cancer and Depression,
62
Soul Mind Body Medicine: A Complete Soul
Healing System for Optimum Health
and Vitality (Sha), xviii, 29, 30–31
Soul Movement, 65
Soul Order, 200n5
Soul over matter, xi, xl
Soul Power
explanation of, 14
invocation of inner and outer souls, 31–32
layers, xii
message of, x
practice self-clearing karma, 15–16
soul over matter, xi, xl
soul secrets, 39
transformation and, xxi
Soul Power (Say hello)
balancing relationships of all nations, 138
balancing relationships of all planets
(including Mother Earth), all stars,
all galaxies, and all universes, 142
balancing relationships of humanity, 136
Earth element practice, 202

Fire element practice, 208
forgiveness practice to self-clear karma
    for healing and life and life
    transformation, 42
golden light self-healing practice, 97–98
Metal element practice, 210–211
one-sentence secret, 214
practice using divine treasures to balance
    relationships with life partners,
    126–127
practice using divine treasures for
    emotional body healing, 71–72,
    75–76
practice using divine treasures for healing
    inflammation and infection, 49–50
practice using divine treasures for mental
    body healing, 82–83
practice using divine treasures for
    spiritual body healing, 92–93
practice using divine treasures to heal
    growths (cysts, tumors, and cancer),
    54–55
practice using divine treasures to heal
    pain, 35–36
practice using divine treasures to prevent
    sickness, 103–104
practice using divine treasures to
    transform all life, 117
self-balancing relationships with
    colleagues, 132–133
self-balancing relationships with family
    members, 129–130
self-clearing karma, mind blockages, and
    body blockages for relationships,
    119–120
self-clearing karma (soul blockages),
    mind blockages, and body blockages
    for finances and business, 172–173
soul marketing and, 180–182
Tao Sheng Yi practice for Service Xiu
    Lian, 215–216
Water element practice, 196–197
Wood element practice, 205–206
Xiu Lian practice, 196–197, 215–216
Soul Power Series
    flowed from the Divine, xli
    Foreword to, xxix
    other books in, ii, 265

permanent divine treasures in, 91
Total GOLD servant, xxii
uniqueness, xxv
Soul secrets, 39
Soul Software for Liver, xvi
Soul Song, 65, 66
Soul Song and Soul Dance Healer
    Certification Program, 65
Soul Songs. *See* Divine Soul Songs
Soul standing, xii, 190, 193, 194
Soul Study workshops, xv
Soul Symphony of Yin Yang, 271
*Soul Wisdom: Practical Soul Treasures to
    Transform Your Life* (Sha), xix, 4,
    10
Sound Power (chanting or singing),
    197–199, *See also* Chanting and
    singing
    balancing relationships of all nations,
    138–139
    balancing relationships of all planets
    (including Mother Earth), all
    stars, all galaxies, and all universes,
    143–144
    balancing relationships of humanity,
    136–137
    benefits of, 44–45
    Earth element practice, 202–205
    explanation of, 14
    Fire element practice, 208–210
    forgiveness practice to self-clear karma
    for healing and life and life
    transformation, 42–43
    golden light self-healing practice, 98–99
    healing mantras, 33–34
    Metal element practice, 211–214
    one-sentence secret, 214
    practice self-clearing karma, 16–18
    practice using divine treasures to balance
    relationships with life partners,
    127
    practice using divine treasures for
    emotional body healing, 72–74,
    76–78
    practice using divine treasures for healing
    inflammation and infection, 50–52
    practice using divine treasures for mental
    body healing, 83–85

Sound Power (*cont.*)
  practice using divine treasures for
    spiritual body healing, 93–95
  practice using divine treasures to heal
    growths (cysts, tumors, and cancer),
    55–57
  practice using divine treasures to heal
    pain, 36–38
  practice using divine treasures to prevent
    sickness, 104–107
  practice using divine treasures to
    transform all life, 117–118
  self-balancing relationships with
    colleagues, 133–134
  self-balancing relationships with family
    members, 130–131
  self-clearing karma, mind blockages, and
    body blockages for relationships,
    121–122
  self-clearing karma (soul blockages),
    mind blockages, and body blockages
    for finances and business, 173–175
  soul marketing and, 183
  soul of words, 40
  Tao Sheng Yi practice for Service Xiu
    Lian, 216–220
  Wood element practice and, 206–207
  Xiu Lian practice and, 197–199,
    216–220
Sound Power *mouth secrets,* 39
Speaking, 161–163
  good and bad karma created from,
    161–162
Spiritual body, self-prevent sickness,
    101–107
Spiritual testing, 45–46
Spleen, 63, 71, 201, 202
Stillness, 223
Stomach, 68, 201, 203
Suicide, 62
Sunday Divine Blessings, 60, 62–63

T
Taiwan, 223
Tao, 190, 192, 215, 223
Tao I: The Way of All Life (Sha), xlii, 10, 112,
    192, 197n4, 232
Tao Jing, 193

Tao of business, 178–179
Tao Sheng Yi Body Power Position
    description of, 215
Tao Sheng Yi practice for Service Xiu Lian,
    215–221
Tao Soul Transplant for Bladder, 60
Tao Te Jing (Lao Zi), 159–160, 221–224
Te, 224
Teeth and gums, 68, 201, 204
Teleconferences, 22, 60
Tendons, 71, 205–207
Thank You, Divine (chant), 14, 48, 71, 90,
    135, 142
Thank you. Thank you. Thank you.,
    explanation of, 18n7
The Big Way is extremely simple, xlii, 35, 112,
    118
"Thinking chanting," 107, 109
Thinking secrets, 39, 195–196
Third Eye
  Akashic Records and, 123
  chanting and, 43–44
  healing and, 200
  Snow Mountain Area and, 196n3
  Third Eye readings, 63
Thumbs, 201
Tian di ren he yi (Heaven, Earth, and
    human being join as one), 216–219,
    232–235
Tian Di Ren He Yi, Wan Ling Rong He
    divine chant, 232–233
Tongue, 208–210
Transformation, *See also* Divine
    transformation
  definition of, 1
  financial matters, 158
  forgiveness practice to self-clear karma
    for healing and life and life
    transformation, 41–43
  frequency transformation, 86–87
  karma clearing and, 5, 28
  overview of, 1–2
  practice and, 113–114
  practice using divine treasures to
    transform all life, 116–118
  Soul Power and, xl, 14
  speed of transformation, xx–xxi
  universal wish for, xxxix

Transformation of consciousness, power of soul and, xi
Tumors, 52–57

U
Unconditional universal service
  business and, 185–186
  clearing bad karma and, 166
  definition of, 150–151
  importance of, 150–151
  soul standing and, 193
  ways to offer, 151
Unity Church of Truth (Toronto, Canada), xviii
Universal Connection Body Power Technique, 31
Universal Law of Universal Service, xiii–xiv, 8–9
Universal service
  clearing bad karma and, 7–8, 150
  explanation of, xiv
  message of, ix
Unpleasant service, xiv, 5
  Akashic Records and, 27, 162
  wealth and, 153

V
Valutis, Marsha, 62–67
Vibration, 62
Virtue
  accumulating virtue through service, 148–149, 157, 166, 193
  ancestors and, 148–149
  anger burns virtue, 164
  bad karma and losing virtue, 152
  can transform to money in the physical world, 157
  chanting and, 145–146
  spiritual money, 27
  as yin money, 157
  wealth and, 150

W
Wan Ling Rong He (all souls join as one), 216–219, 232–235
Water element, 68, 196–199

Wealth
  maintaining, 152
  virtue and, 150
Webcasts, 22, 63, 199
Weng Ma Ni Ba Ma Hong (Guan Yin's enlightenment mantra), 39–43
Wisdom, 223
Wood element, 68
Wood element practice, 205–207
Worldwide Representatives
  Divine Karma Cleansing and, 22
  names of, 244
  working with cancer patients, 62
  Xiu Lian practice and, 199–201
Worry, 68, 201, 204
  and Earth element, 68
www.DrSha.com, 230

X
Xiao Tao (small Tao), 178–179
Xiu Lian, 191, 191n2, 194–199, 215, 221–224
  definition of, 194–195

Y
Yang chanting, 109
Yang companion, xviiin1
Yang money, 157, 166
Yang treasures, 11, 99
Yi Mi (thinking secret), 195–196
Yin and yang
  karma and, 163–164
Yin chanting, 109
Yin money, 157, 166
Yin treasures, 11, 99–100
Yin Yang Palm, 31

Z
Zhi Chen Guo, xxx, 192, 243
Zhing sheng wei guo, pu sa wei yin (an ordinary being is afraid of the effect, which includes sickness, broken relationships, and financial challenges, but a bodhisattva is afraid of the cause), 159

Other Books of the Soul Power Series

Soul Wisdom: Practical Soul Treasures to Transform Your Life (revised trade paperback edition). Heaven's Library/Atria Books, 2008. Also available as an audio book.

The first book of the Soul Power Series is an important foundation for the entire series. It teaches five of the most important practical soul treasures: Soul Language, Soul Song, Soul Tapping, Soul Movement, Soul Dance.

Soul Language empowers you to communicate with the Soul World, including your own soul, all spiritual fathers and

mothers, souls of nature, and more to access direct guidance.

Soul Song empowers you to sing your own Soul Song, the song of your Soul Language. Soul Song carries soul frequency and vibration for soul healing, soul rejuvenation, and soul prolongation of life.

Soul Tapping empowers you to do advanced soul healing for yourself and others effectively and quickly.

Soul Movement empowers you to learn ancient secret wisdom and practices to rejuvenate your soul, mind, and body and prolong life.

Soul Dance empowers you to balance your soul, mind, and body for healing, rejuvenation, and prolonging life.

This book offers two permanent Divine Soul Transplants as gifts to every reader. Includes bonus Soul Song for Healing and Rejuvenation of Brain and Spinal Column MP3 download.

Soul Communication: Opening Your Spiritual Channels for Success and Fulfillment (revised trade paperback edition). Heaven's Library/Atria Books, 2008. Also available as an audio book.

The second book in the Soul Power Series empowers you to open four major spiritual channels: Soul Language Channel, Direct Soul Communication Channel, Third Eye Channel, Direct Knowing Channel.

The Soul Language Channel empowers you to apply Soul Language to communicate with the Soul World, including your own soul, all kinds of spiritual fathers and mothers, nature, and the Divine. Then, receive teaching, healing, rejuvenation, and prolongation of life from the Soul World.

The Direct Soul Communication Channel empowers you to converse directly with the Divine and the entire Soul World. Receive guidance for every aspect of life directly from the Divine.

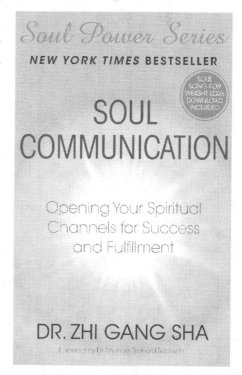

The Third Eye Channel empowers you to receive guidance and teaching through spiritual images. It teaches you how to develop the Third Eye and key principles for interpreting Third Eye images.

The Direct Knowing Channel empowers you to gain the highest spiritual abilities. If your heart melds with the Divine's heart or your soul melds with the Divine's soul completely, you do not need to ask for spiritual guidance. You know the truth because your heart and soul are in complete alignment with the Divine.

This book also offers two permanent Divine Soul Transplants as gifts to every reader. Includes bonus Soul Song for Weight Loss MP3 download.

The Power of Soul: The Way to Heal, Rejuvenate, Transform, and Enlighten All Life. Heaven's Library/Atria Books, 2009. Also available as an audio book.

The third book of the Soul Power Series is the flagship of the entire series.

The Power of Soul empowers you to understand, develop, and apply the power of soul for healing, prevention of sickness, rejuvenation, transformation of every aspect of life (including relationships and finances), and soul enlightenment. It also empowers you to develop soul wisdom and soul intelligence, and to apply Soul Orders for healing and transformation of every aspect of life.

This book teaches Divine Soul Downloads (specifically, Divine Soul Transplants) for the first time in history. A Divine Soul Transplant is the divine way to heal, rejuvenate, and transform every aspect of a human being's life and the life of all universes.

This book offers eleven permanent Divine Soul Transplants as a gift to every reader. Includes bonus Soul Song for Rejuvenation MP3 download.

Divine Soul Songs: Sacred Practical Treasures to Heal, Rejuvenate, and Transform You, Humanity, Mother Earth, and All Universes. Heaven's Library/Atria Books, 2009. Also available as an audio book.

The fourth book in the Soul Power Series empowers you to apply Divine Soul Songs for healing, rejuvenation, and transformation of every aspect of life, including relationships and finances.

Divine Soul Songs carry divine frequency and vibration, with divine love, forgiveness, compassion, and light, that can transform the frequency and vibration of all aspects of life.

This book offers nineteen Divine Soul Transplants as gifts to every reader. Includes bonus Soul Songs CD with seven samples of the Divine Soul Songs that are the main subjects of this book.

Divine Soul Mind Body Healing and Transmission System: The Divine Way to Heal You, Humanity, Mother Earth, and All Universes. Also available as an audio book. Heaven's Library/ Atria Books, 2009.

The fifth book in the Soul Power Series empowers you to receive Divine Soul Mind Body Transplants and to apply Divine Soul Mind Body Transplants to heal and transform soul, mind, and body.

Divine Soul Mind Body Transplants carry divine love, forgiveness, compassion, and light. Divine love melts all blockages and transforms all life. Divine forgiveness brings inner peace and inner joy. Divine compassion boosts energy, stamina, vitality, and immunity. Divine light heals, rejuvenates, and transforms every aspect of life, including relationships and finances.

This book offers forty-six permanent divine treasures, including Divine Soul Transplants, Divine Mind Transplants, and Divine Body Transplants, as a gift to every reader. Includes bonus Soul Symphony of Yin Yang excerpt MP3 download.

Tao I: The Way of All Life. Heaven's Library/ Atria Books, 2010. Also available as an audio book.

The sixth book of the Soul Power Series shares the essence of ancient Tao teaching and reveals the Tao Jing, a new "Tao Classic" for the twenty-first century. These new divine teachings reveal how Tao exists in every aspect of life, from waking to sleeping to eating and more. This book shares advanced soul wisdom and practical approaches for *reaching* Tao. The new sacred teaching in this book is extremely simple, practical, and profound.

Studying and practicing Tao has great benefits, including the ability to heal yourself and others, as well as humanity, Mother Earth, and all universes; return from old age to the health and purity of a baby; prolong life, and more.

This book offers thirty Divine Soul Mind Body Transplants as gifts to every reader. Includes a fifteen-track CD with the entire Tao I Text (Tao Jing), which is the focus of the book, and many other major practice mantras.

"This inspiring documentary has masterfully captured the vital healing work and global mission of Dr. Guo and Dr. Sha."

This film reveals profound soul secrets and shares the wisdom, knowledge, and practices of Dr. Guo's Body Space Medicine and Dr. Sha's Soul Mind Body Medicine. Millions of people in China have studied with Dr. Guo, who is Dr. Sha's most beloved spiritual father. Dr. Guo is "the master who can cure the incurable." After Dr. Sha heals her ailing father, American filmmaker Sande Zeig accompanies Dr. Sha to China to visit his mentor. At Dr. Guo's clinic, she captures first-ever footage of breakthrough healing practices involving special herbs, unique fire massage, and revolutionary self-healing techniques. These two Soul Masters have a special bond. They are united in their commitment to serve others. As you see them heal and teach, your heart and soul will be touched. Experience the delight, inspiration, wonder, and gratitude that Soul Masters brings.

In English and Mandarin with English subtitles. Also in French, German, Japanese, Mandarin and Spanish.

PPV Video Streaming and DVD at
www.soulmastersmovie.com